MASS MEDIA AND AMERICAN FOREIGN POLICY

Insider Perspectives on Global Journalism and the Foreign Policy Process

COMMUNICATION AND INFORMATION SCIENCE

Edited by
BRENDA DERVIN
The Ohio State University

Recent Titles

Mass Media and American Foreign Policy

Insider Perspectives on Global Journalism and the Foreign Policy Process

Patrick O'Heffernan

 ABLEX PUBLISHING CORPORATION
NORWOOD, NEW JERSEY

Library of Congress Cataloging-in-Publication Data

O'Heffernan, Patrick.
    Mass media and American foreign policy : insider perspectives on global journalism and the foreign policy process / by Patrick O'Heffernan.
        p.   cm.—(Communication and information science)
    Includes bibliographical references and index.
    ISBN 0-89391-728-1.—ISBN 0-89391-729-X (pbk.)
        1. United States—Foreign relations—1977–1981.   2. United States—
Foreign relations—1981–1989.   3. Mass media—Political aspects—
United States.   I. Title.   II. Series.
    E872.037   1991   90-25017
    327.73—dc20   CIP

Ablex Publishing Corporation
355 Chestnut St.
Norwood, NJ 07648

For Lynn Ellen and Megan Eileen

Table of Contents

Acknowledgments

In preparing this book I have been fortunate to have had assistance from many people and institutions. Thanks go to Professors Lincoln Bloomfield and Russell Neuman of MIT for their guidance and inspiration, and to Martin Linsky at the Shorenstein Center for Press, Politics, and Public Policy at Harvard University. Professor Linsky especially deserves special thanks for providing me with the raw data from his 1982 research. I also am indebted to Wendy Ballinger of the Ford Hall Forum for providing the "Rosetta Stone" of computer codes that enabled me to decipher the Harvard data after it had undergone the changes necessary to move it from PC to mainframe.

Another among those who helped make this research possible is my friend Robert Beckel, whose generosity with his time and influence opened many doors for the interviews. I also want to thank former CBS Moscow Bureau Chief Robert Evans for his early wisdom, and former White House Counsel Robert Lipshutz for his continuing assistance. Marvin Kalb of the Shorenstein Center was also very encouraging early in the conceptualization of the research.

The access to the unpublished summaries of American television news programming from the Vanderbilt Television News Archive at Vanderbilt University was invaluable. Vanderbilt Archive staff acted beyond the call of duty to provide me with the prepublication working drafts of summaries of news broadcasts of the *Intifada*, which saved months of waiting and many days of work. I am also grateful to the staff of the Carter Presidential Library for their patience and assistance.

I must also thank Dr. Kenneth Stein of the Carter Center at Emory University for his suggestions, guidance, and practical help with information and interviews regarding the *Intifada* and other events in the Middle East.

I must also thank Dr. Brenda Dervin, Barbara Bernstein, and Carol Davidson at Ablex for their help and encouragement, and Ablex's reviewers whose time and thoroughness made this a better book than I had seen in it. Of course, all errors, omissions, gaps in, and leaps of logic are purely my responsibility.

Finally, I must thank my wife Lynn Gutstadt for her patience and support as well as her help, and that of her colleagues at Turner Broadcasting and CNN, for the invaluable background and insights they provided about "the world's most important network." Especially helpful were TBS Chairman and CEO Ted Turner, TBS Vice President for Research Bob Seiber, and Headline (now CNN) anchor Bobbie Batista.

Introduction

The last major empirical exploration of the relationship between the media and U.S. foreign policy was undertaken by Bernard Cohen in 1962.[1] Cohen found at that time that the media worked closely with the foreign policy apparatus of the U.S. government and almost routinely supported American policy goals, not surprising given the Cold War and President Kennedy's skillful personal cultivation of reporters. Today, however, a look at a daily newspaper or a half-hour of any prime time network news broadcast tells a different story. It is obvious that the mass media—especially the U.S. mass media—have become a significant force shaping our cultural and political future and that of much of the world, and that they do so independent of the government.

But at the same time, it is also obvious that the government has developed and skillfully uses a vast apparatus for stimulating and influencing the outputs of the global media. The White House, the State Department, the Pentagon, and all other U.S. government agencies that deal in international issues use the tools of the media—from film production and press releases to the marshaling of "spin doctors" to insure that American and foreign readers, viewers, and listeners hear the government's official story in the way the government wants it told.

Occasionally, especially during crises, the government finds it must turn to the media for critical information—messages from terrorists, interviews with hostages, images from cities under siege, or speeches by enemies. On a daily basis, the various levels of foreign policy makers in the U.S. government read, watch, and listen to the media for news of what is going on around the world before the cables and reports come in. What they see and hear and read is often a broader and more diverse worldview than what they receive officially. How does this affect their judgment and the decisions they make? This may be one of the most critical foreign policy puzzles of the 21st century.

How do the mass media shape the political dimension of the world?

What is the relationship between the new global media and U.S. foreign policy outputs? What, if any, are the linkages between the mass media and the process of creating American foreign policy? How are the media used by the U.S. government to further its policy objectives around the world? What has the emergence of a multidimensional, independent global mass communications industry done to the nature and operation of U.S. foreign policy? The very questions reveal a complexity far beyond the source-reporter unit of analysis employed by Cohen.

The answers to these questions cannot easily be found in existing models of the U.S. foreign policy process, which classify the mass media as an external force separate from the policy makers and their decisions. This follows the classic "two-step theory" of media impact on policy making which was developed in Cohen's era when print media was the dominant news outlet and wire services were the international information transmission belt.[2] This theory—still the prevalent paradigm for incorporating media into policy-making analysis—postulates that the media influence "opinion makers" or "interested audiences" who subsequently influence government. Little empirical research has been published that examines direct media influence on U.S. foreign policy outputs or direct government use of media to further its foreign policy agenda, although any journalist or policy maker can tell stories exemplifying both. As a result, there are many anecdotes but no models of the U.S. foreign policy-media relationship as it exists in today's world of international mass media and worldwide television. With the advent of global news services by Turner Broadcasting, the international programming of Rupert Murdoch and Silvio Berlusconi, and the expansion of television and cable systems in Europe, Asia, and Africa, the question of the mass media's influence on foreign policy and international relations is now critical to understanding and guiding the policy process.[3]

This book is the product of a three-year study at MIT to attempt to begin to fill this gap through both empirical research and model building—in a sense, an update of Cohen's 1962 research. The study sought to test the general hypothesis that the U.S. foreign policy makers perceive that the policy process is profoundly affected by the mass media in a number of important and identifiable ways. Its conclusions offer a model of media-influenced U.S. foreign policy making from the policy officials viewpoint that can hopefully shed some light on this profound interaction.

The study examined the period of U.S. foreign policy roughly from November 1977 through March 1988, through case studies, and explored both past and present interactions between the mass media and the foreign policy process with former and active senior policy makers, including a former U.S. President. The study asked three basic questions:

1. *Did the mass media, and particularly television, influence U.S. policy officials' perceptions of the character of events during the research period?* This was approached through historical and attitudinal questions in personal interviews designed to probe the sources of information policy officials used and the inputs that shape their attitudes.
2. *Did the mass media, and particularly television, influence the outputs of U.S. policy officials regarding the Middle East?* This was examined by construction and analysis of case studies and anecdotal evidence from the interviews.
3. *Has a change occurred in policy makers' perception of the influence and utility of the mass media since the Carter Administration?* If so, how can these perceptions be characterized today? This was explored through a survey of senior foreign policy officials and attitudinal questions in personal interviews.

The study looked for evidence of *active media roles, and specific media influences* in the foreign policy process. These were detailed in the form of four research questions that could be answered with perceptual, anecdotal, and historical evidence indicating the existence and significance of specific media roles and influences in given foreign policy situations. They were:

1. Do mass media play active roles in foreign policy? What are they?
2. Do mass media influence the shaping and execution of American foreign policy through specific mechanisms? What are they?
3. Does television play any active roles separate from those of other media in the shaping of American foreign policy?
4. Does television exert particular influences separate from those of other media in the shaping of American foreign policy?

Each of these research questions was refined into detailed testable sub-propositions.

Five data sources were used to measure evidence supporting or rejecting the propositions:

1. Responses of senior foreign policy officials within a government-wide survey conducted by Martin Linsky et al. from October 1983 to January 1985 at the John F. Kennedy School of Government at Harvard University. The raw data from the study were graciously provided by Dr. Linsky on computer disks for analysis.
2. In-depth interviews conducted with policy officials involved with the Carter and Reagan Administrations and the Middle East from 1976 through 1982.
3. Transcripts of interviews of policy officials and journalists con-

ducted by Linsky et al., including Secretaries of States Vance and Kissinger, and National Security Advisor Brzezinski.

4. Documents from the Carter Presidential Library.
5. Case studies assembled using summaries of network news broadcasts from the Vanderbilt Television News Archives, and file copies of the *New York Times* and *Washington Post*.

The book is not meant to be a complete update of Cohen's landmark research. He interviewed reporters and sources in the foreign policy community—this research has only probed the policy community; a second phase of the study will involve the media.

The reason for this division was logistical—the world and U.S. policy within it is far more complex today than it was in Cohen's time, demanding a far more complex research endeavor. No longer does the press only influence the government through a few powerful columnists whispering in a Secretary's ear, or Reston-like, through the Congress, or through a steady broadside of advice in the *New York Times* or *Washington Post*. Today, the media (not the press!) create a reality—a paradigm—of the world, within which policy makers, nongovernmental organizations (NGOs) Members of Congress, the public, terrorists, corporations, other governments, and the rest of the multitude of actors on the world stage use as their map of the world they want to change. Duplicating Cohen's research today would have been unmanageable and would have forgone the insight of statistical and case-study tools. For practical as well as methodological reasons, I chose to break the research into two steps, the policy makers, and the media makers.

My first step was to describe the map the media drew for the policy makers as the policy makers saw it. Knowing that political psychologists have learned much since Cohen about the importance of cognitive factors such as mass media in policy makers' decisions—essentially, that policy is shaped by the reality policy officials think they are working within, this seemed a logical starting point. This study describes the media-policy reality officials think they are working within. The next step will be to conduct the same depth of research among practitioners of the media to detail their vision of the same reality. My suspicion from the anecdotal evidence gathered herein is that reporters and producers and editors will perceive that the policy makers manipulate reality as much as policy makers perceive the media do. Then we must ask, in a world of global mass media and global policy making, what is real and does it matter? But first, what is real in the White House, the State Department, and the Congress?

The propositions were tested quantitatively when possible to provide a standard acceptance or rejection of each proposition. The categorical responses from the interviews provided critical dimensions to each finding in the form of qualifications and circumstances. The result, hopefully, is an overview of some of the complex day-to-day symbiotic interactions between the mass media and the foreign policy establishment of the United States, and how this interaction has shaped not only the American agenda, but that of the world as a whole.

Chapter 1 describes the global media industry as it exists at the time of this writing. Given the speed of its expansion and global mergers and expansions now underway, it may have as much as doubled in size and influence by publication date. The first chapter also raises the questions that the global media raise for policy that will be explored in later chapters.

Chapters 2 through 4 detail the three case studies use to paint a concrete picture of how nations and NGOs use the media, how the media uses them, and what the effect on U.S. foreign policy outputs can be.

Chapters 5 and 6 detail media's foreign policy roles and influences as they emerged from the research. These two chapters combine the results from the survey analysis and statistics from the interviews with quotes from policy makers to paint both a quantitative and anecdotal picture.

Chapter 7 explores the special role of television in the U.S. foreign policy process. Chapter 8 highlights the findings from the specific interview questions that probed policy makers' perceptions of separate and discrete television effects on the foreign policy process.

Chapter 8 presents an Insider's Model of Media-Influenced Foreign Policy, which both uses the media and is influenced by it. The proposed "inside-outside" model utilizes Graham Allison's classic paradigms of foreign policy making derived from his 1971 study of the Cuban Missile Crisis.[4] It modifies Allison's models at specific points to incorporate the precise roles foreign policy makers perceive to be played by the media at various stages of the policy process.

Chapter 8 also examines the impact of the mass media on the global international system, and enumerates specific effects of the media on the U.S. role in the international system. This chapter is intended to stimulate thought, rather than define a completed theory. Hopefully, the analytic framework presented here will help organize further questions on the global media and relations between nations.

A great deal of research is needed in both communications and political theory to gain a clearer understanding of the effect the media has had and continues to have on the international system and the U.S. foreign policy process. This book is a very early guidepost to what may have to emerge as a distinct field of study if we are to understand and function in the information-driven world of the 21st century.

NOTES

[1] Cohen, Bernard. *The Press and Foreign Policy* (Princeton, NJ: Princeton University Press, 1963).

[2] Paul Lazarsfeld, Bernard Berelson, and Hazel Gaudet, *The People's Choice* (New York: Columbia University Press, 1948).

[3] L. Eric Elie, "Opportunity for TV Knocking in Europe," *Atlanta Constitution* Nov. 22, 1988, p. C1.

[4] Graham Allison, *The Essence of Decision* (Boston: Little Brown & Co., 1971).

1
Mass Media's Global Reach: The Impact On Foreign Policy

The use of satellites to broadcast to . . . other nations is a fact of diplomacy today. Reagan and Gorbachev are playing in each others backyards every day. It is a fundamental fact that international relations theory has not caught up with yet— that international relations today is a continual process . . . and television is a significant part of that interaction . . ." (U.S. Assistant Secretary of State Harold Saunders)[1]

Plain old American TV is more powerful than any military weapon. In fact, it should become our avowed way of making war. Call it the thermo-media battlefield: hard news, hard rock, tough talk and Coca-Cola commercials. No bullets, no bloodshed—no way we can lose (Dave Marash, *TV GUIDE*) [2]

In 1985 a small group of young Swedes launched a news network that sells satellite photographs to television news services worldwide. Called the Space Media Network, or SMN, it is geared to provide television networks and news organizations with recent photographs of troop and ship movements, nuclear and environmental disasters, chemical and nuclear weapons facilities under construction, and other items govern-

1

ments try to keep hidden from their own people and those in other countries.

Space Media Network's initial scoop was the distribution of the first photographs of the Chernobyl nuclear reactor disaster. Since then it has spotted secret preparations for a Soviet space shuttle, a powerful Russian laser installation, resumed Soviet nuclear tests, Chinese missile sites in Saudi Arabia, and new cocaine plantations in South America, among other discoveries. Each of these revealed by news networks who bought the pictures from SMN and broadcast them publicly, frequently to the distress of national governments.[3] SMN is not alone in this growing field. Other satellite photography distributors sell pictures from French, Canadian, and even Chinese satellites to news organizations.

SMN and similar suppliers are a symbol of a larger phenomenon, the global explosion of the mass media, especially television. Thanks to the introduction over the past 15–20 years of three television technologies—the minicam, cable systems, and communications satellites—the mass media industry today moves news, information, and entertainment across national borders and around the world in staggering volumes with lightning speed.[4]

The minicam has become ubiquitous in the hands of the thousands of independent news producers, freelance "shooters" (camera operators), and news crews selling program features and news packages on a bustling international news market. Down to 14 pounds with batteries, the Sony minicam is light enough for one person to operate easily. It quickly and unobtrusively goes anywhere from inside courtrooms and meetings to battlefields and disasters around the world. Combined with a portable microwave and a portable uplinks, the minicam can send information and images from virtually any part of the world to any other part of the world in seconds.[5] So versatile is the minicam that both Russian and Americans used it in a war of words and images during the Afghan war, equipping soldiers and rebels with mincams to produce footage that was later redited and provided to broadcast outlets to "prove" who was winning and which side was more humane.[6]

Cable television systems have created a new market for the prodigious output of the global minicam army. From an average of 6–10 stations per U.S. market 20 years ago and 1 or 2 in most other countries, cable has brought most U.S. markets up to over 30 channel options and doubled or tripled the choices in foreign markets.[7] Today there are growing cable systems serving over 10 million households in eight European countries, plus smaller systems in Australia, Saudi Arabia, Japan, Israel, and other countries. These cable systems often complete the link from satellite to home by bringing down and distributing foreign programming.[8] With the European Community's drive to lower media barriers among its members, Pan-European programming and advertising is expected to reach 340 million viewers in 1990.

In addition to cable, broadcast stations have multiplied as the technology of television broadcasting has spread and its price has fallen. The availability of thousands of hours of pretaped and prepackaged programming has made delivering international shows on a small television station far less expensive today than 10 or 20 years ago. As a result, broadcast television has undergone a revolution in the past decade, especially in Europe: West Germany expanded to three public channels and two private broadcasters; Britain expanded to four conventional channels and the new Sky Television, France evolved from a single government channel in 1980 to its six channels; and Italy added three private channels and 20 regional cable networks to its three public networks. Japan has added 5 private channels to its traditional public broadcasting system. Bootleg station TLN operates in Panama in defiance of government crackdowns, keeping mobile transmitters hidden and relying on tapes bought or bartered from independents for international programming.[9] Even the Soviet Union has expanded its television system to two national channels and dozens of local and regional channels. Television has become almost as omnipresent in Soviet life as it is in the United States: 93 percent of the population are viewers.[10]

This programming does not stop at national borders. CNN is received in almost every country, either legally or on bootleg dishes, and in many embassies and consulates around the world.[11] European stations constantly overspill into other countries, part of the pressure behind the drive to drop national barriers separating the European TV systems and adopt a Pan European standard.[12] The BBC is negotiating with British, French, and Australian media companies to launch a new satellite for joint broadcasting. Israelis and Jordanians routinely watch each other's news, as do East and West Germans and many Asians and South Americans. And MTV today has more viewers outside of the United States than within it.

The third element of the media revolution is satellite distribution. INTELSAT has grown to global coverage with footprints and downlinks in 170 countries, and has increased its global programming from 1000 hours per year in 1970 to 20,000–30,000 hours in just the trans-Atlantic market. Regional satellite networks have sprung up, including: AUSSAT in Australia, and CANCOM in Canada which send signals nationwide; ARABSAT which serves 22 Middle East and North African nations; NORDSAT which serves five Scandinavian nations; and ESA which serves eight nations in Western Europe, with EUROSAT soon to link all of Europe simultaneously. At present, these systems broadcast to stations or cable networks with the dishes and equipment necessary to receive and use the signals. Direct Broadcast Satellites, or DBS, which can transmit to a small home dish, entered the market in Europe with the launch of West Germany's TVSAT and France's TDF-1, followed by Murdoch's BDS service in the United Kingdom, as well as other emerging players on the global TV horizon.

Through satellites, cable systems, broadcast stations, and VCRs, every nation in the world now generates or receives television programming, much of it from abroad. The availability of satellite-delivered programs from other countries is not always welcome, because it provides the citizens with domestic and international news and perspectives sometimes deemed undesirable by their leaders. Governments in the Eastern Bloc, India, Singapore, and South Africa have attempted to control this transmission of news by banning private ownership of satellite dishes, without much success.[13]

Television is not the only news medium that has undergone a global revolution as a result of the satellite. Newsmagazines and newspapers now receive typeset copy and digitized photographs by satellite from around the world, enabling them to print same-day editions with current news. The explosion of niche market magazines with a global cast in the U.S., Europe, and Asia has increased the demand for international stories beyond the usual fashion and gossip. International wire services maintain bureaus in most world capitals and are often involved in joint ventures with television and radio networks to provide live feeds and to distribute their material.

While this global media explosion involves many nations' media industries, it is particularly American. Driven by economics, not politics, American broadcast and cable networks have led the creation of audiences in almost every country that ranges from the poorest villagers to the world's elite. The U.S. is by far the world's largest supplier of television programming, in both news and entertainment. During the 1970s, the U.S. exported approximately 150,000 hours of programming per year—more than three times the combined exports of the next three countries combined.[14] Today, the U.S. exports almost that much programming each week. U.S. TV exports are projected to reach $1.4 billion in 1990, four times the exports from Europe, its closest competitor.[15] The U.S. was the source of 75 percent of the programming in Latin America, 44 percent in Western Europe, and, along with the United Kingdom, was the major supplier of programming to Asia, South Africa, and the Middle East.[16]

Despite the rise of regional markets in television programming and the emergence of national television production industries in many countries, the dominance of the U.S. has not significantly changed since 1973, especially in news programming.[17] U.S. news broadcasts are watched worldwide, partially due to the global reach of CNN. An example of the power and reach of Turner Broadcasting occurred when CNN aired a Middle East briefing with Secretary of State George Schultz in February of 1988. Jordan's King Hussein, watching in Paris, immediately called the network's headquarters in Atlanta to respond on the next newscast.

American news networks are watched routinely by the Houses of Parliament in Sweden and Norway, the Kremlin, President Francisco Cossiga of Italy, the President and the Diet in Japan, the government and the leadership of Solidarity in Poland, virtually all the senior officials of the Israeli, Egyptian, Saudi, Iranian, and Iraqi governments, the leadership of the Contadora countries, and many more.[18]

Paralleling the increased complexity of the global media and growth in the reach of U.S. news media has been the increased size and complexity of the U.S. foreign policy agenda and the international system it responds to. The United State's agenda two decades ago was focused largely on the Vietnam War and its diplomatic effects, U.S.–Soviet relations, NATO and bilateral relations with our major allies and trading partners, plus the day-to-day diplomatic routines with the rest of the world. Few, if any, global issues were high on the priority list, or even on the government's agenda. Large-scale domestic involvement in foreign policy was becoming visible in the form of the antiwar movement but did not become politically effective for several years.

Today, the number of nations in the world has jumped to over 170. The world's population has grown close to 5 billion, with a coincident increase in governments, institutions, and competition for resources and power. The foreign policy agenda of the United States still focuses on U.S.–Soviet relations, followed by NATO and allies and trading partners, bilateral and multilateral relations with Central American nations.

But there is a new category of issue now demanding a growing amount of time and energy in the U.S. foreign establishment, *global* issues that transcend sovereignty and national borders.[19] These include the ozone layer, drugs, global warming, AIDS, the proliferation of chemical weapons, endangered species, regional ecological, and resource crises that may lead to conflict, exports of toxic wastes, and many others. The importance of these issues was signaled directly by President Bush in his National Security Review 12, in which he specifically asked for inclusion of global issues outside normal relations with the Soviet Union and defense policy.[20]

The new issues are joined by a new class of player in the international system, the nonstate player. Nonstate players range from terrorists to long-recognized nongovernmental organizations (NGO) and multilateral organizations, to new single-interest transnational organizations lobbying for their causes at both the domestic and international levels.

At home, U.S. foreign policy politics has also acquired a new category of player, home-grown foreign policy-interest groups.[21] Generally grass-roots-based organizations which have appeared largely in last ten years, these groups work to get global issues placed on the U.S. foreign policy agenda and to influence the government to adopt their solutions. Skilled in the use of the media, organizations ranging from Greenpeace to Pat Robertson's *700 Club* use television, mass mail, and print media to advance their causes on the foreign policy agenda, in some cases with surprising effectiveness.

Is there a connection between these developments? Ecologists analyzing the media and the international political system together as biological organisms would likely say they "co-evolved"—that is, grew together, interacting with one another and reinforcing and shaping each other's growth. The expansion of press, polling, and communication staffs in the White House, the State Department and the other agencies strongly suggest that the U.S. government sees and uses the global mass media as part of its repertoire of policy tools, both domestically and internationally. Several incidents also suggest that the global media cannot be divorced from the U.S. policy process or its outputs. These range from the takeover of the U.S. Embassy in Tehran and the skillful manipulation of U.S. television by the Iranian students holding American hostages, to U.N. Ambassador Kirkpatrick's use of videotape during a General Assembly session to obtain admission of responsibility from the Soviets for the KAL 007 airline disaster.[22]

The question of mass media's influence arises from changes that have taken place in the technology of the media and their worldwide diffusion. Information on events and people from around the world is available to policymakers more quickly, in greater amounts, and with greater immediacy than ever before as a result of the growth of the mass media.[23] The impact of this on foreign policy is twofold:

First, the mass media play *active roles* in U.S. foreign policy development and execution. The theory derived from this research proposes that, in specific situations, the mass media are *active players* in the policy process, directly effecting specific policy outputs and events. It also recognizes that government plays a role in media coverage and actually uses the media as policy tools. For lack of a better term this theory has been labeled *interdependent mutual exploitation* by the author.

Second, mass media exert *pervasive influences* on the foreign policy process, shaping the tone, style, and emphasis of U.S. foreign policy in various ways and to varying degrees, both in specific situations and across the board. This influence stems from policy makers' perception of the media's importance and utility, especially of the importance of the broadcast media, and from the media's injection of certain biases[24] into the policy-making process. The combination of these two media forces results in a new foreign policy that is media-influenced. It both uses media as an output, and it is itself profoundly effected by the media. One consequence of this is that models of foreign policy making must now account for and include the media acting upon it from the outside. Later on, in Chapter 8, I will advance one such model, an "inside-outside" model of media-influenced foreign policy, and speculate on its impact on the international political system.

NOTES

[1] From interviews.

[2] *TV Guide*, April 1, 1979, p. 17.

[3] *New York Times*, October 5, 1988.

[4] Other nontelevision technologies such as computers, telephones, and air transportation have also played a part. Another critical technological development, the spread of the VCR, is rapidly becoming an important element in this equation, with 100 million videotapes traded legally and illegally across borders every year. A small but important fraction of this trade is in specifically politically material—instructions for subversion and guerrilla tactics, calls to arms, and other instructions. Ganley and Ganley report that VCR penetration is universal, with all nations having a significant number of VCRs and engaged in videotape tape trade. Gladys D. Ganley and Oswald H. Ganley, *Global Political Fallout: The VCR's First Decade* (Norwood, NJ: Ablex, 1987).

[5] This assumes advanced arrangements have been made for transponder time and for the technical details. These can be complex: The global *Sport Aid* coverage of 20 million runners around the world on Sept. 11, 1988, required 14 satellites and 28 transponders to reach viewers in 100 countries. *Live Aid* was even more complex in its preparations to reach 1.5 billion people in 150 countries. See *Broadcasting*, Sept. 5, 1988, p. 54 for more details on these programs. However, The Discovery Channel's 1988 *live* telecast of archaeological excavations from the bottom of the Red Sea with waterproofed minicams and portable microwave dishes came off without a hitch despite storms and sharks and wars in the region.

[6] Evan Thomas, John Kohan and Alessandra Stanely, "The Great War of Words. How the U.S. and the U.S.S.R. Sell Themselves to the World," *TIME*, Sept. 9, 1985, p. 3.

[7] Steven S. Wildman and Stephen E. Siwek, *International Trade in Films and Television Programs* (Cambridge: Ballinger, 1988), pp. 37–42. See "European TV's Growth: Cultural Effect a Worry," *New York Times*, March 16, 1989; and "Study: Cable on rise in Europe," *Electronic Media* June 26, 1989, p. 10, both of which predict that 44 percent of British homes will have dbs receiving equipment by 2000AD.

[8] Statistics on television taken from Wildman and Siwek, Op. cit., pp 42–59; Tapio Varis, "The International Flow of Television Programs," *Journal of Communications* 34:1 (Winter 1984) p. 143; *World Broadcasting Systems*, 1985; and *International Television Almanac*, 1986.

[9] "Guerrilla TV" *TV Guide*, April 1, 1989, p. 17.

[10] Ellen Mickiewicz, *Split Signals: Television and Politics in the Soviet Union*. (New York: Oxford University Press, 1988, p. 3)

[11] Conversation with Ted Turner, December 1988, Atlanta. This has been corraborated by conversations with other Turner Broadcasting executives and with CNN and Headline anchors who receive fan mail from countries that do not legally receive CNN.

[12] "TV Overspill in Europe," Table 3–2 in Wildman and Siwek, Op. cit., p. 39.

[13] *TIME*, Loc. cit. See also "Salvador TV Dares to Tell the News." *New York Times*, Oct. 27, 1988, p. 23.

[14] Describing this world trade in television programming is complicated by overspill, incomplete data, large amounts of bootlegging, and and a very large barter market in which little or no cash changes hands. The statistics come from a variety of sources, cited below, and while the relationships are accurate, no precise numbers can be cited for dollar value or number of hours of programming exchanged.

[15] *New York Times*, April 16, 1989, p. F8

[16] Wildman and Siwek, pp. 39–40.

[17] Tapio Varis conducted studies in 1973 and 1983 of international flows of television programming for the UN, which showed that the dominance of the U.S. has remained unchanged in that period. While the emergence of national production and cable systems in many nations has likely eroded the U.S. dominance somewhat, CNN and other U.S. news systems massive export of their product abroad has undoubtably held the U.S. position in news. We will have to await another study to verify this. See Tapio Varis and Karl Nordenstreng, *Television Traffic, A One-Way Street* (Paris: Boudin/UNESCO, 1974), and T. Varis, "The International Flow of Television Programs," 1984.

[18] Conversations with anchors and executives at CNN, including Bobbi Batista, Headline News daytime anchor, and Robert Seiber, Vice President of Research, Turner Broadcasting; "The Global Village Tunes In," *TIME*, June 6, 1988, p. 77.

[19] Global issues are defined in this context at those issues whose solutions lie outside of usual bilateral bargaining between nations, because their origins and/or consequences involve most or all nations, transcending national borders.

[20] Richard Halloran, "Calling for a Redesign of National Security," *New York Times*, April 2, 1989, p. E 4.

[21] This does not include the domestic lobbying operations and public relations paid for by foreign countries, estimated at $100 million per year by *US News and World Report*, March 29, 1985, p. 41.

[22] "UN. Dateline: United Nations," *United Press International*, Sept. 6, 1983.

[23] William C. Adams, *Television Coverage of International Affairs* (Norwood, NJ, Ablex Publishing, 1982), especially Chapters 1, 2, and 13.

[24] "Biases" is used throughout in the sense of the second meaning defined by *Webster's 7th New Collegiate Dictionary*: "an inclination of temperament or outlook; bent, tendency." It does not refer to "prejudice" or any reference to the slant of the content of policy to or away from any particular parties or ideological positions. "Biases" here refer to the postulated foreign policy characteristics such as accelerated speed, tendency to respond to individuals, and so on.

2
Sadat and Begin: Contrasts in Media Power

Three case studies were completed as part of this research, a comparison of Begin and Sadat during the Camp David era, the highjacking of TWA Flight 847, and the Intifada in Israel from its inception to March, 1988. The case studies were undertaken primarily to provide strong circumstantial data to support the self-reported responses obtained in the interviews. The cases also provided a look into the mechanisms by which various players use the mass media to move their agendas, and how the media effected those agendas for their purposes.

Case 1 covers the period November 9, 1977, to April 12, 1979, during which Egyptian President Anwar Sadat visited Israel, Sadat and Israeli Prime Minister Menachem Begin visited the United States, and the Camp David meetings took place. It highlights a number of specific media roles and influences during the Carter Administration, especially the use of the U.S. media by foreign leaders to affect U.S. policy and the ability of the media to globalize regional events and set agendas. It also focuses on the use of the media by the Carter Administration to influence other national leaders and to encourage domestic support for foreign policies.

Case 1 also provides an illustration of the ability of skillful national leaders to use the American and the world media to manipulate policy in other countries and to manipulate opinion in their home countries. Both

Sadat and Begin used the U.S. media with great skill, as did President Carter, but Sadat was by far the master of the media. He was especially adept at using television to stimulate favorable public opinion and then marshaling that good will into policy influence. Begin seems not to have had the savvy with the U.S. media that Sadat displayed.

The mass media, and the use of the mass media by Sadat, Begin, and President Carter, had three policy effects during this period of Middle East peacemaking. First, the media were very effective at shifting the policy advantage from one leader to another. Second, they influenced the character of the Carter Administration's foreign policy in identifiable ways. And finally, there were a few instances of direct media-policy links.

USING THE MASS MEDIA TO SEIZE THE POLICY INITIATIVE

The mass media shifted policy initiatives from one national leader to another as Carter, Begin, and Sadat each used it to his own advantage. All three national leaders saw the media as a tool to influence the agendas and responses of the other two. Sadat was especially skillful at this, and television was usually his medium of choice.

On November 15, 1977, Prime Minister Begin extended a formal invitation to Sadat to address the Knesset. Sadat accepted and visited Israel in an historic occasion televised globally.[1] While in Jerusalem, Sadat held a joint press conference with Begin, addressed the Knesset, and performed a number of telegenic symbolic acts for television audiences at home in Egypt and in the United States. Carter applauded Sadat publicly, calling him a great and brave statesman, while other Arab nations and the Soviets criticized the visit, calling it traitorous to the Arab cause.

Despite the initial public invitation from Begin, the visit was a flawless media coup by Sadat. The visit story first surfaced on November 9, 1977, in Sadat's comments to a Congressional delegation about gaining peace in the Middle East. Sadat said he would go to Israel if that was what peace required. This was the lead story on all three networks, but Sadat's remarks were a small part of a larger story on the Israeli-Palestinian conflict in Lebanon. Begin responded positively the next day at the end of a Middle East story carried on CBS. ABC ran the story a day later keeping expectations up. More important perhaps regionally was a television broadcast of Begin's speech beamed at Egypt. Sadat quickly began to capture the TV initiative on November 14 in interviews with CBS asking for a proper invitation from Begin.

Both leaders were interviewed, but Sadat was able to gain center stage with expressions of hope for peace and a request for permission to speak to the Knesset, and with his response to questions about the danger of retaliation from other Arab nations. He simultaneously portrayed himself as a brave statesman and asked for an expanded invitation from Begin during the same televised interview. Begin's response that he would greet Sadat and take him to Parliament was diluted by his statement that it was up to Sadat to make the trip come about. Network news reporter John Scali ensured Sadat's control over the agenda by comparing Sadat's possible trip to Jerusalem with Nixon's historic trip to China, a comparison that would reappear many times during this period.

The visit itself was the lead item on all networks and received from 3 to 15 minutes a night coverage during the course of the invitation, the acceptance, and the visit. It was also front page in the *New York Times* and other U.S. papers, as well as a major news item worldwide. Although the visit was planned and arranged behind the scenes by members of the Carter administration in cooperation with Israel, Sadat clearly used the media coverage to shift the Middle East peace policy initiative to Egypt.[2]

The media overnight made Sadat a world hero, and in doing so seems to have improved the U.S. perception of other Arab leaders. Sadat used symbols such as riding in an open car, praying at Al Aksa in Jerusalem, and personally greeting the Israeli people to change American images of Arabs as either greedy oil sheikhs or Islamic terrorists. By doing so in a highly visible manner, he firmly implanted images that he and other Arab leaders were enlightened men of reason who could and would negotiate fair political compromises. In terms of media impact on foreign policy, this was a skillful use of the mass media to accelerate the improvement of U.S.–Egyptian relations and help build support for arms sales to Egypt.[3]

During his February 1977 visit to the U.S., Sadat's media use was directed at the Congress as well as at the American people. He was aware that American attitudes toward Egypt and Arabs in general had to undergo substantial modification in order for him to make headway against Israeli's lobby in the Congress for approval of weapons sales and any future agreements that required Congressional cooperation. In essence, Sadat's visit was the beginning of a media campaign to regain American friendship and obtain American arms.[4] Among the tools he used were televised meetings with Jewish leaders and with members of Congress, an address to the National Press Club and a speech on Capitol Hill—both heavily covered in all media—and televised scenes from a meeting with Harold Brown—all very effective in establishing the image of a world leader worthy of American support and cooperation.

The full agenda-setting impact of Sadat's media use is difficult to measure because of the prior involvement of the White House and the

Israeli government in arranging the visit. The agenda was already set in both Washington and Israel, and Sadat was operating within this agenda rather than creating it, although he was pushing for Egypt's interests. On February 7, Sadat was effective in raising the issue of Russian arms supplies in Ethiopia, Somalia, Chad, and Sudan in Congress and on the networks to keep his case for arms on top of everyone's short list.

On December 5, following the Tripoli Conference, Sadat severed diplomatic relations with Syria, Iraq, Libya, Algeria, and South Yemen, citing attempts to disrupt the peace process. He also ordered several Soviet consulates and offices to close. The first public word of this came through network news broadcasts of Sadat's speech, followed by Vance's announcement that he would tour Middle East capitals to meet with Arab leaders. While Sadat's action surprised both the U.S. government and his own, the State Department learned of his decision sometime prior to the announcement, so the information was not critical for foreign policy formation.[5]

However it further separated Arab leaders, including generating a public disagreement between Iraq and Syria regarding the Geneva conference and UN Resolution 242. Egypt was reported as excluded from the Arab League. NBC characterized this as the biggest breakup of Arab unity since World War II. Again, Sadat used the media to send a message to the U.S. and Israel underscoring how committed Egypt was to achieving peace and how much this was costing him diplomatically and financially. The very public actions, including breaking diplomatic relations with Arab states, were calculated to convince Carter and Begin that Egypt needed visible concessions from them.

The television coverage also contributed to the administration's decision to announce the Vance meetings, accelerating the policy process at a pace that likely would not have occurred had the announcement been confined to the *Times* the next day.

The announcement was a masterful use of mass media by Sadat. In one stroke, the televised broadcast made Sadat a hero at home, moved American and Israeli policy makers to take quick action, affected other Arab governments, and strengthened domestic support for his policy.

Print media covered the story the following day and both print and television followed the story for nine days until Vance left Jerusalem on December 14, The heavy coverage of Vance in the Middle East, and of Sadat—both in network lead stories and front page in the *Times*—clearly kept the policy initiative with these two men, not with Begin (or Carter, who did not seek it). Begin appeared to recognize this in his acerbic comment to news reporters that negotiations should not take place in front of television cameras. Begin subsequently used the less visible *Times* to deliver a more positive statement in the form of a message to the United Jewish Appeal that "a real peacemaking process" was taking place.

On December 28, 1977, Begin submitted his 26-point peace plan to the Knesset for approval. The same plan was also presented to Sadat. Sadat rejected the plan at a press conference but expressed optimism and hope for U.S. pressure on Israel. President Carter used television to affirm U.S. opposition to a Palestinian state, a signal to Begin not to fear that America's support would evaporate in a media frenzy. The State Department announced that Vance would attend the Egyptian–Israeli foreign ministers meeting.

In this case, Sadat's use of television shifted the focus *to* the White House and virtually forced President Carter to respond. By using television to publicly complicate the peace process, Sadat made necessary an equally public response by Carter. Carter found it necessary to answer Sadat and reassure the Israelis and U.S. Jews of support in the highly visible environment of a televised interview, not just a newsclip.

The use of television by Sadat accelerated and personalized the policy process, generating a personal response from Carter in a matter of hours in a direct cause-and-effect relationship.

On March 23 the next year, President Carter and Begin concluded two days of talks in Washington after failing to reach agreement on any of the major points blocking progress in the peace negotiations. Carter told U.S. Senators that the diplomatic process had "been brought to a halt." Begin appealed directly to the American people on television news and during a now-famous Barbara Walters interview.

This is a clear example of the direct use of television by a foreign government to attempt to influence the policy of the United States. Carter chose not to respond directly, either on television or in the print media. Instead he briefed the Senate Foreign Affairs Committee, producing a print and broadcast news item that served as an indirect response. In this instance, Begin's attempt to use television to focus political pressure on the White House and regain the policy initiative failed, indicating that when the White House wants to control its agenda, it can do so regardless of the news media, at least in most circumstances.

Begin and Sadat arrived in U.S. for Camp David talks in early September, and signed two historic documents: "A Framework for Peace in Middle East," and "A Framework for the Conclusion of Peace Between Israel and Egypt." Jody Powell continued to enforce the media blackout while Carter addressed Congress.

Both leaders tried to use the mass media to shift the policy initiative to themselves and set the agenda in their favor before the Camp David meetings began. On the morning of September 4, Begin softened his image by mingling with people on the street in New York City during his stroll down Park Avenue, and speaking of Harry Truman before going to Camp David. However, he refused to make any substantial statements to the press, reportedly at Carter's request. Unfortunately, his refusal to talk with the press made him appear stubborn and uncooperative (even though he was cooperating with Carter's wish to deny the press speculative statements).

But even here, Sadat was able to share the stage with Begin on the network news that night, even though he had not yet arrived. Sadat was in Paris with President Giscard d'Estaing, and managed to get film of his meetings with Giscard on networks news, in some cases (NBC), ahead of the report on Begin. ABC covered Begin first, but gave Sadat almost twice as much time on the screen, reporting the French visit and them showing file tape of the Sadat visit to Israel, film of Palestinian refugees in the territories, and commentary on the need to involve Palestinians in any solution. NBC also reported on Sadat's departure from Egypt and his activities on the plane to Paris.

The following day, the networks covered the arrival of both leaders at Camp David, but Sadat again upstaged Begin. Sadat's arrival in the U.S. garnered highly positive coverage, complete with a preemergence interview while still on the plane with Vice President Mondale. Additionally, ABC ran tape of Sadat's departure from Paris with Giscard's support for Egypt's positions. CBS also noted Sadat's invitation to the Pope to visit Israeli-occupied Sinai and pray on Mt. Sinai, following Marvin Kalb's report on Israel's desire to maintain air bases in the Sinai.

Carter took control of the media environment by enforcing a blackout, preventing either Sadat or Begin from using the media to gain advantage. However, on September 6, 1978, while Begin was inside Camp David, Sadat took a tour of the countryside. There was no contact with the press because of the news blackout, but the networks ran film of Sadat, further enhancing his positive image. However, the locus of policy stayed with President Carter and the administration during Camp David because of the blackout; only Jody Powell had information the media needed. Had Sadat been available to the media, it is possible Carter would have lost the initiative to Sadat, angering Begin and complicating the negotiations.

MEDIA INFLUENCE ON THE CHARACTER OF POLICY

The media strongly enhanced Anwar Sadat's status in the United States, and, with it, brought a new view of Arab leaders. The mass media also focused the attention of policy makers on Sadat as a new player to be dealt with. While the substance of the negotiations revolved around the long-standing points of Egyptian-Israeli dispute, Sadat's rapid trans-formation of his image contributed to the softening of Congressional attitudes toward Egypt. Thus, he created a political environment in which a weapons sale to Egypt would be possible. Sadat's media tactics included:

- appearing on television with Jim Wright and other members of Congress
- a highly personable interview with Barbara Walters
- the countryside tour
- the speech at the Press Club
- the media coverage of the personality clash between Sadat and Begin (especially Sadat's warning of possible war after Israel rejected his peace plan) in which Sadat was almost always portrayed much more positively than Begin.[6]

The skillful use of American media by Sadat led to Israeli charges on March 13, 1979, that the Carter aide Gerald Rafshoon manipulated the media to pressure Israel to approve the agreement. While this was certainly true in some instances, it was Sadat who used the press to seize and hold the public relations initiative and retain the policy issue as much as possible. Begin's inability to use the American media to counter the Sadat media campaign or even to enhance his own image among Americans contributed to Sadat's success.

DIRECT MEDIA-POLICY LINKS

Two instances of media-policy cause-and-effect relationships were evident in *Case 1*. In the first instance, President Carter found it necessary to forcefully talk Sadat out of announcing a recall of Egypt's negotiations during the speech scheduled to be televised from the National Press Club in November of 1978. In all likelihood, Carter would have made the same effort, but the fact that it was televised made the need for action critically urgent.[7]

The second instance involves Prime Minister Begin's blunt statements to the media. Upon arrival in the United States in March of 1979, Begin told the media that the peace talks were in "grave danger." President Carter undoubtedly knew the status of the talks and of Begin's perception before Begin landed, but the media announcement (carried in both the print and broadcast media) stimulated Carter to decide to personally involve himself in the talks. He quickly announced he would fly to the Middle East to try and break the deadlock. Carter was apparently influenced to act by Begin's public announcement. Had Begin not announced his reservations through the media, Carter might have remained in the U.S. and worked through intermediaries.[8]

MASS MEDIA AS A CRITICAL INFORMATION SOURCE

The media was not a critical information source for the foreign policy process in this case. But one instance did occur when the mass media provided the U.S. government with information critical for a policy response. On January 18, 1978, the Egyptian and Israeli foreign ministers' peace talks were halted and Sadat recalled his foreign minister. Secretary of State Vance (who was in Jerusalem) and the U.S. government were apparently not told in advance or even concurrently of Sadat's decision. Vance was reported on CBS as stating he learned of the minister's recall from a person who heard a radio report. Vance announced plans on the 19th to visit Sadat the next day, after leaving Jerusalem.

An accident where the media might have provided immediate critical information, the seizure of hostages at Larnaca by anti-Sadat terrorists was not covered by television and not reported in the *Times* until February 19, long after the U.S. government was aware of it. The Egyptian raid to free the hostages was covered on television, but the U.S. was not directly involved. Moreover, the U.S. had people close to the scene and had no need for instantaneous information in most cases. Other than the minister's recall, the U.S. was intimately involved on a day-to-day basis with the events of case 1 and relied on the media for political information and political signals, but not for critical factual information.

Sadat's use of the media to transform his image was a classic example of television's power to create psychological and political environments in which previously unthinkable decisions can become politically necessary. Sadat's media objective was to convince the American people and their Congressional representatives that here was an Arab they could trust and do business with. His skill with television enabled him to initiate the "bandwagon effect" effect, the perception that he rode a sea change in public opinion that all media and all politicians had to quickly join or be left behind.

Sadat's "bandwagon" was the palpable prospect of peace in the Middle East, manifested in the visit to Jerusalem, a symbolic action that presented the image of a breakthrough and multiplied millions of times over by the small screen. The pent-up demand for peace among Americans focused on Sadat as the key, regardless of the realities of Middle East politics. Sadat's bandwagon could not be resisted by the anti-Arab Members of Congress, nor for that matter, the Prime Minister Begin.

The replays were too prevalent, the demand too strong, the sound bite too compelling: Give peace a chance.

NOTES

[1] Unless otherwise noted, all descriptions of events and policy decisions have been drawn from the *Vanderbilt Television News Abstracts* or the *New York Times* during the case study period.

[2] Interview with Robert Lipshutz, White House Counsel who set up the invitation. See Leon H. Charney. *Special Counsel* (New York: Philosophical Library, 1984) for details of the behind-the-scenes preparations.

[3] William Adams. *Television Coverage of the Middle East* (Norwood, NJ, Ablex, 1981). See especially pp. 1–3, 32–33, 25–26, and 155–156 for studies on how Sadat was able to use television to turn around American and Congressional opinion of Arab leaders.

[4] Coverage of Sadat's Feb. 1978, visit to Carter was comparatively light, partially because of the White House blackout on the talks. But the images were all positive; many pictures of Sadat with a smiling Carter, Sadat at the Press Club warning of a hardening of Israeli positions while Egypt struggles to remain reasonable, and so on. Sadat's goal with Congress was made explicit during televised interviews on Feb. 6, 1978, when he specifically asked the Congress for arms. He followed up the next day with a televised speech to Congress requesting arms to protect Egypt not form Israel, but from its African neighbors. See Vanderbilt, *Television News Abstracts,* for the dates indicated.

[5] Interviews with Robert Lipshutz and Hodding Carter for this study.

[6] Adams, op. cit.

[7] In his interview for this research, President Carter described his very frank private conversation with Anwar Sadat prior to Sadat's speech at the Press Club. Sadat had planned to denounce Israel and announce the withdrawal of Egyptian negotiators in this speech and Carter realized that the damage this would do would be magnified by the network coverage. He managed to convince Sadat to change the speech and continue negotiating.

[8] Unfortunately, time ran out during the interview with President Carter before this question could be asked.

3
TWA Flight 847: Terrorvision That Worked (Almost)

The hijacking of TWA Flight 847 and the response of the Reagan administration to the crisis were largely television events. Television served as
a direct and influential communication medium and critical information
source for the U.S. Government and as a policy lever the hijackers used
to clearly and directly influence the administration's actions. Television's role during this case was so visible that it was publicly criticized
by the administration and the print media. Television even repeatedly
examined itself and its role in the incident in several special documentaries.

However, an examination of the events of Case 2 indicate clearly that
without television and the other mass media's involvement in the situation the Administration's options and actions would have been severely
restricted. Without television and the other media it would have been
very difficult for the administration to assemble and interpret the facts
necessary to formulate adequate responses. The administration's ability
to communicate with the hijackers would have been substantially limited without a strong mass media presence. And the mass media also
directly intervened in a number of ways that are still subject to debate as
to their propriety.

THE MASS MEDIA AS A CRITICAL INFORMATION SOURCE

On the afternoon of June 14, 1985, TWA Flight 847 from Athens to Rome with 104[1] Americans and 39 others was hijacked and forced to land in Beirut, where 19 passengers, mostly women and children, were freed.[2] The plane flew on to Algiers where 18 more passengers were released and gunmen threatened to kill all the remaining passengers unless Israel released Moslem prisoners captured in Lebanon. The plane returned to Beirut and an American passenger was killed. The hijackers claimed to be the Islamic Jihad.

It is difficult to separate precisely the information the administration derived from the mass media from that which it received from direct contact with representatives of the hijackers and from diplomatic sources. The media reported that Robert McFarland was in direct contact with Nabih Berri on at least one occasion by telephone during the ordeal, and it is likely that routine communication was established with Berri at least part of the time.[3] However, the hijackers themselves used the media heavily to send messages to the administration independent of Berri. Moreover, vital information on the location and condition of the hostages was usually available principally through the media.

The first information the administration received about the hijacking came via television news reports, and all subsequent information was delivered that day by television. No official reports or print stories were available until the next day, and the wire services were usually several hours behind the satellite television transmissions. The news reports provided information on the location of plane and the passengers, the demands of the hijackers, some information on who the terrorists were, and a statement from an Israeli pilot attributing the impetus for the hijacking to a statement made earlier by a former Israeli negotiator on television.[4] Three instances exemplify the communication roles of the mass media during the hijacking.

President Reagan reacted immediately to the news reports by moving the Delta Force into the region and asking the Algerian government to allow the plane to land. The President responded to the hijackers on television by vowing no concessions.

Television provided the initial announcement and some detail in the interview with a released passenger and the Israeli pilot. Within a few hours the White House had established some information flows from the region, but the hijacking scene itself—the plane and the terrorists—was available primarily to the media. Television primarily was used by the hijackers to communicate their demands and to reveal their killing of an American passenger as a threat.

The first information on the murder of an American passenger came from television reports on June 15, 1985, from a broadcast of the pilot's voice inside the plane in Algiers. This news broadcast and the interviews with released passengers provided information on the condition of the passengers, the number of terrorists, and their weapons. The interview with the pilot functioned not only as critical information, but as direct communication between the terrorists and the administration; the pilot made clear the consequences of trying to use force to free the passengers.

The *Washington Post* added information on the Shi'ite militiamen at the Beruit airport and transcripts of conversation between the tower and the pilot. Some of this was available to the White House at the time, but much of it was not because the reporters had greater access to the hijackers than did diplomatic personnel. The White House staff was continually trying to assemble a picture of that was actually happening from news reports, television broadcasts, conversations with reporters, and diplomatic and CIA sources.

On June 24, Berri set new demands for hostage release, including withdrawal of U.S. warships from the Lebanese coast. Berri claimed the demand was made in defense of Lebanon and not in the name of the hijackers. Film of hitherto unseen hostages was shown, and the hostages' request to move the U.S. fleet was covered. The *Washington Post* reported Berri admitted that he controlled only 30 hostages.

The film and information on the hostages Berri controlled indicated to U.S. policy makers that the situation was more volatile and less under control than previously thought. The film followed an interview with a hostage the previous day who asked that no military force be used. President Reagan canceled his vacation to take charge of crisis (Secretary Schultz and National Security Advisor Robert McFarland had been more visible in the press previously), and called an unscheduled White House meeting. The policy focus began to shift to the White House although the role of the media in this shift is unclear.

The following day Reagan was reported to hold an unscheduled White House meeting with his advisors and to cancel his vacation plans. Larry Speakes announced that military action or a blockade of Beruit was under consideration. Berri insisted again that U.S. ships be withdrawn from the Lebanese coast, and increased the pressure on the administration by releasing a videotape of 12 hostages who were obviously tired and angry. The condition of the hostages was probed by the networks using interviews with medical experts and former hostages to detail the pressures on those shown in the tape. U.S. warships were careful to stay out of Lebanese territorial waters, but remained off the coast. Behind the scenes, the U.S. continued to negotiate with Syria and Israel for diplomatic help.

The focus of policy on the White House did not last long; a media blackout was imposed by the White House on June 26, leaving the State Department and Berri as the chief actors in the hostages drama.

On June 27, negotiations for movement of hostages collapsed due to problems with French, Swiss, and Austrian delegations. The hostages voiced sympathy for the terrorists' cause. CBS reported that the hijackers were actually aiming for an El Al flight. The White House linked the TWA hostages with others held in Beirut.

On June 28, the media reported unconfirmed reports that hostages were to be taken overland to Damascus. Berri met with hostages and allowed more live interviews.

The mass media were being used by Berri to pressure the administration to meet some of the terrorists' demands: to unlink these hostages from others held in the Middle East, and to prove to the terrorists and others in Lebanon that Berri can stand up to Uncle Sam. The television interviews with the hostages, who pressed for Israeli concessions, supported the terrorists' demands and appeared to underscore a hard line by Berri. At the same time, Berri sent messages via the print media that he was willing to shift some hostages to a Western embassy, thereby pursuing two strategies at two levels in two different media.[5]

While Berri was using the media to negotiate, information provided by the media to the administration became critical for the facts it provided on the condition, location, and number of the hostages. Even more valuable was the political information provided by the media that helped to shape the government's moves day by day.

The media increased the number of players here by enabling the hostages to in effect become a third party in the negotiations, actually bargaining with their own government either on their own or under the control of the hijackers. In the second interview, the hostages once again rejected military options and insisted that the White House restrict negotiations to them alone and not link their release to that of the other seven American hostages in Lebanon. This was critical political information for the administration and influenced its decision to drop military plans and link all hostages together.

MEDIA INFLUENCE ON POLICY LOCUS

The policy initiative shifted several times during this case, but the locus of U.S. policy remained with the White House. The hijackers initially took the policy initiative with the broadcasts from the plane in Algiers and Beruit. They lost it quickly to Berri because he was accessible to media and skilled in using them. The media found it much easier to invest Berri with the policy initiative than the hijackers even though he may never have been in control of more than a third of the passengers.

The U.S. policy locus stayed with the White House for most of the ordeal, but this was the strategy of the White House and not the result of the media's pressures. In fact, Washington press were so well controlled by the White House that the President's prestige was rarely at risk. The President went to Camp David on June 16, the day before Berri came on the scene as the terrorists' representative. Larry Speakes, Marvin Kalb, and Bob McFarland were the more visible players, rather than the President. Reagan saved his appearances for strong statements:

- On 6/17/85, he announced that there would be no deals with terrorists
- On 6/19 and 6/22, he met with hostage families
- On 6/19/85 and 6/20/85, he expressed strong criticism of TV interviews with hostages. (This resulted in criticism of Reagan by Peres, Tip O'Neil, networks, and the hostage families for inaction, but with little effect.)

The entry of the hostages into the negotiations at the June 20 news conference may have influenced Reagan's decision not to use force in a rescue attempt and to drop plans to link other American hostages to the TWA passengers, but focused on, rather than diffused, the policy making in the White House. By entering the negotiations, apparently as either a third party or as supporters of the hijackers, the hostages intensified press demands for White House responses. Hostage Conwell's demands that no military force be used were directed at the White House.

However, it was Shultz, not the White House, who replied. The White House responded to the pressure from Berri, the hostages, the hostage families, Peres, and others with a news blackout, refusing to be drawn into what could become a losing situation both potentially and in public relations terms.

MEDIA INFLUENCE ON THE CHARACTER OF POLICY

The media dictated the pace of policy during the hijacking. Daily reports of demands, positions, and responses were the lead story in all media from the first hijacking report until the hostages landed in Germany. Both the print and the broadcast media were used as vehicles for negotiations and speculated daily on the content of negotiations. Because the entire affair was essentially a media event, negotiations took place on a day-by-day basis through press conferences and new reports which often supplanted diplomatic communications and sometimes informed them. As a rule, the pattern that emerged was that a statement or speech at a press conference by the hostages or Berri would result in a White House or State Department response later that day or the next day, coupled with negotiations with third parties and phone calls to Berri.

The mass media impacted the agenda of U.S. policy at several points. The wider question of Middle East peace was buried in the media focus on the hostages, sidetracking any wider policy initiatives in the Middle East during the affair. More specifically, the June 19 interview with the pilot, where he warned the White House not to use force to free the hostages, effectively made that option very difficult for the Administration. After being warned against it on national television by a hijacking victim, any use of force that did not result in a virtually perfect rescue would inflict terrible political damage on the Administration.

The mass media were also a gatekeeper to the terrorists. The terrorists depended on the media to deliver their message to governments (until later telephone negotiations began with Berri), and to the world. This included their long list of demands. NBC, and later ABC, edited their demands, shortening the list to fit the time constraints of the news format, and emphasizing the release of Muslim prisoners held by Israel. The terrorists quickly understood that this emphasis gave them the ability to portray Israel as a proximate impediment to release of the hostages, and themselves focused on the prisoner release in their subsequent demands. Television created political reality.

The interviews with the hostages objecting to linkage with other kidnapped Americans helped eliminate that option, despite earlier press reports that the Administration and Israel had agreed on that course of action. The extent of administration frustration with media involvement in its agenda came to light when White House officials were reported to be considering asking the media to curtail its coverage of the crisis (this followed interviews with hostages on *Good Morning America* and on an ABC terrorism special). Senator Dole remarked that he would observe the Administration's request to black out all information on the hostages and negotiations.

President Reagan used his June 29 radio broadcast to deliver a speech in which he called the hijackers thugs and murderers. This prompted Berri to delay release of hostages and to make new demands. Had these remarks been confined to the print media, it is likely Berri would not have known of them or reacted if he did not know of them. As it was, the delay occurred as the preparations for release were underway, including an Israeli release of prisoners. The delay was temporary, but may have complicated the U.S.–Israeli agreement concerning release of Shi'ite prisoners (Peres met with reporters and denied a deal had been made).

THE CENTRAL ROLE OF TELEVISION

The TWA hijacking was a television event; the print media for the most part were a day behind the networks in both information and impact. There were a number of distinct differences between the role of the broadcast and the print media:

- Nibih Berri's influence and negotiating position was largely the result of television coverage. Berri used the print media only when he wanted to send less favorable messages to the U.S., in order to delay their arrival by at least a day, and to insure that the item would not be covered or read in Lebanon. Television was Berri's principal tool to effect the agenda and the pace of the negotiations. Examples of Berri's use of television include:
- A June 17, 1985 announcement that he ordered the hostages removed and hidden in Beirut for "security reasons." This was followed by a profile of Berri on the evening news. This established Berri as the negotiation point for the United States in a confused situation.
- A June 18 claim in a news conference that he controlled the hostages, followed by network speculation that he was behind the hijacking and that he was functioning in President Gemayel's place. This further established his authority locally and internationally.
- Televised interviews with hostages set up by Berri to warn the Reagan administration of retaliation if force were used. The message was more powerful coming from the hostages rather than from Berri himself.
- A televised hostage news conference on June 20 with Berri. This move allowed Berri to project a humane and sympathetic image while detailing the criteria for their release. The news conference was a "first" in journalism and garnered enormous coverage for Berri.
- A June 27 televised warning to the U.S. to stop overflights. Berri used the fastest and most direct way to make a demand and let all parties know it had been made.
- A June 23 interview with the hostages asking Reagan to refrain from military response. Berri described the hostages playing on the beach and detailed their cuisine.
- A June 24 release of film of hitherto unseen hostages, plus messages sent to families. The film guaranteed the wildest possible coverage.
- Berri's televised announcement on June 26 of hostage Palmer's release combined with details of demands for further releases continued to reinforce his control of the initiative.
- Interviews with Berri and hostages on June 27 and June 28 who state support for terrorists' cause, object to linkage with other hostages,

and deny brainwashing. Film of sick hostage with Berri waiting for doctor's report, expressing sympathy for hostages wives. Lunch for hostage Conwell and TV reporters.

- Television was the communication medium of the hostages and their relatives, and it provided them with their best leverage on the administration. Television also transformed the pilot into a hero, portraying him as somewhat in opposition to the administration. The print media utilized interviews and photos extensively, and were the only information source for passenger lists,[6] but they could not provide the immediate communication and powerful images that the hijackers, Berri, and the hostages used to influence the negotiating agenda.

- Television was much more critical of Reagan and the administration (and in some instances of Israel) than the print media. Not only did ABC air an embarrassing special on intelligence failures in the Middle East, the networks on two occasions showed tape which undermined Reagan's positions or contradicted his statements (ABC tape of candidate Reagan calling for preemptive strikes against terrorists, and NBC tape of Reagan criticizing Carter's handling of the Iran hostage crisis after Reagan denied he had criticized Carter).

Israel also used television to criticize and goad the administration. Israeli Prime Minister Begin complained to Reagan on network news about his inaction on the Shi'ite prisoners, and *Nightline* gave Peres the opportunity on June 20 to strongly criticize the President for inaction in the crisis. Similar criticism did not appear in the print media. The edition of the *Washington Post* that same day carried a favorable Joseph Kraft editorial, "Reagan's laid-back attitude better than Carter's personal involvement in Iran," and other editions of the *Post* editorialized sympathetically with the administration. The June 21 edition of the *Post* referred to Peres' remarks only in an analysis of the strain on Israel.

Television appeared more sympathetic and helpful to the hijackers than did the print media. For instance, the brutality of the hijackers was not highlighted in network news reports, but it was detailed in a *Washington Post* story. The initial television interviews with released passengers described the takeover and the beatings of passengers and the threats to kill them. As the story unfolded, the focus shifted to Berri and his ability to portray the hostages not only receiving good treatment, but sympathizing with the hijackers' cause. Television provided Berri, the hijackers, and the hostages significant time to explain their positions and demands and to criticize the U.S. and Israel.

DIRECT MEDIA-POLICY LINKS

The mass media were criticized by the administration, by media critics and observers, and by the media itself for involvement with U.S. foreign policy and negotiations.[7] It is true that the media played a key, if not the central, role in the event. The entire incident would likely not have happened had not mass media existed and its behavior been somewhat predictable by the hijackers and Berri. In that sense, the media effected every aspect of U.S. policy and negotiations, from diverting policy making energy from the larger question of Middle East peace to the minutiae of bargaining with Berri and the hijackers. Clearly, the media enabled the terrorists to usurp normal diplomatic communication and negotiation channels for their benefit. But, can cause-and-effect relationships be established linking the media to specific changes in policy? The answer to this question must be approached with care because of the difficulty in separating the effect of the substance of the media's message from the effect of their delivery.

However, two instances of direct media-policy impact appear to have occurred in Case 2:

1. *Television's introduction of the hostages as a party to the negotiations and their objection to linkage of their fate to that of the other seven American hostages.* The hostages were interviewed several times on the air, each time warning of consequences if force was used to free them, and objecting to joining their fate to that of other American hostages. In both cases the administration had these policy options under consideration, or had announced them. In both cases, the administration changed strategy. Larry Speakes announced the consideration of a blockade or intervention on June 25, 1985 and Secretary Weinberger publicly reserved the right to use force. Two days later, the hostages were interviewed on film stating sympathy for the cause of the hijackers and warning against military intervention. The warning was repeated in subsequent hostage interviews. No further mention of force was made in the media by the administration. Secretary Schultz talked about including all hostages as late as June 28, and then dropped it. Had not such a request been made widely and publicly through the media, the administration might have been tempted to bet on surprise and try a forced rescue.

2. *Nabih Berri's introduction on network news as the hijackers' negotiator on June 16, 1985.* Reagan returned early from Camp David for NSC meetings in response and McFarland immediately contacted Berri by phone. His appearance on the network news with some of the hostages and with a list of demands made him the focus of U.S. negotiations and

set the framework and the agenda for U.S. negotiating strategy. He accomplished this although he held only 30 hostages.

Had Berri not used the media to establish himself as the negotiating point for the Reagan administration, he might not have been taken seriously, or might even have been ignored. If this had occurred, the U.S. might have gone ahead with other, less successful strategies.

NOTES

[1] Number of passengers reported vary depending on the date and the medium.

[2] Unless otherwise noted, all descriptions of events and policy decisions have been drawn from the *Vanderbilt Television News Abstracts* or the *New York Times* during the case study period.

[3] ABC reported the McFarland-Berri phone call on its June 17, 1985 broadcast. The call likely took place the preceding day.

[4] The television accounts on June 14, 1985 were preceded by newsbreaks earlier in the day; the evening news broadcasts included recordings of the hijackers and the pilot, interviews with released passengers, tape of the plane, interviews with experts, lists of hijackers demands, and a review of U.S. policy regarding terrorism—a remarkable assembly of information in only a few hours.

[5] *Washington Post*, June 27, 1985. This was not covered by the networks although they covered Berri's press conference. There is no tape of Berri making this offer in front of television cameras, so it may be assumed he used the print media to pursue a second strategy.

[6] In other cases, television was the source of information on passenger lists. In the bombing of the PAN AM flight over Lockerbie, Scotland, a local Syracuse, NY, station obtained the passenger list. While this was a good news scoop, word reached relatives of passengers, forcing station managers to undertake the unhappy task of delivering the sad news of dead sons and daughters.

[7] The networks examined their role in the crisis on several occasions (6/21/85 CBS, 6/22/85 CBS, NBC, 6/24/85 ABC, 6/28/85 Ken Stein on CBS, 7/3/85 ABC.

4
The Intifada: Terrorvision That Didn't Work (Almost)

Intense media coverage of the *Intifada*, the Palestinian uprising and continuing revolt in the occupied Israeli territories, lasted from December 11, 1987 to March 15, 1988, the date the Israeli authorities cut off routine television broadcasts from the territories.[1] During this period of the *Intifada*, the mass media set agendas, stimulated domestic lobbying pressure, directly influenced policy actions, shifted policy initiatives, and globalized regional events so they gained international significance. The perceived power of television was underscored by Israeli army attacks on television crews (as well as attacks by protesters) and by an Israeli blackout on media coverage of the demonstrations and violence. It is clear from this case and from interviews with policy makers that the mass media were also a source of useful information to the U.S. foreign policy community.

Television was the most influential medium in this regard, although its influence, while broad in its reach, was often limited in its application. The mass media were not the sole source of information, but they did provide a form and quality of information that was valuable to the Administration. The media brought almost daily images of the violence in the territories to policy makers in Washington, allowing them to make judgments independent of what both Israeli and American diplomatic personnel were reporting. However, the visuals of the fighting and the interviews with protesters were also available to the people of the U.S., Israel, and various Arab countries at the same time, where they sometimes sparked independent pressures for foreign policy changes at odds with established U.S. policy.

The influence of the media coverage of the *Intifada* on U.S. foreign policy may be more important in terms of long-range changes in domestic support and governmental attitudes than in terms of immediate tactics or short-term policies. The mass media's relationship with the *Intifada* appears to have created a new political environment in the U.S. that is hospitable to advocates of a more critical appraisal of overall support for Israel, rather than nuts-and-bolts changes in the details of that support.

MEDIA AS A CRITICAL INFORMATION SOURCE

Media served as an information source to U.S. policy makers during the period of the *Intifada* studied, although in a more generalized manner than in the other cases. There were very few examples of the media providing information that was both unavailable through other channels and vital for decision making.

The first violence actually began on December 9, 1987, reportedly as a result of an Israeli truck that hit four Palestinians, but was not covered in the U.S. media until December 11.[2] Even then, it was hardly front page news: The networks uniformly reported the *Intifada* as the third story of the evening news, after a commercial and stories from the U.S. and Egypt; the *New York Times* ran a small story on page 15. The story did not receive top billing until the 18th when NBC led with the story (it had by then moved up to page 3 in the *Times*). By the 22, it was the lead story in both print and network news.

Over this period of 11 days, the mass media effectively globalized the *Intifada*. What could have been characterized as an internal Israeli problem might have remained such much longer had it not been covered internationally (as the Pol Pot/Khymer Rouge holocaust in Cambodia remained virtually invisible until the release of *The Killing Fields* and to some extent, even afterwards). Within a few days of the first network news story it was now the object of criticism by the Vatican, the U.N., and the U.S. government. It is debatable that these three institutions would have given it the attention and the recognition they did had not the mass media lifted it out of Israel's borders and disseminated it globally.

Politically critical information began to flow almost immediately. The first televised reports clearly positioned heavily armed Israeli troops in a David and Goliath stand-off against young boys throwing rocks and bottles. A televised report on December 15 that Israeli soldiers had stormed an Arab hospital in Gaza, combined with interviews with Palestinian youths saying they were not afraid of the Israeli Army, alerted U.S. policy makers that this was clearly not a short-lived flare-up created by outsiders, as the Israelis claimed.

Although U.S. officials were aware of the violence before the media reported it, the U.S. did not respond until the day of the first televised reports, and then in the form of a mild White House expression of concern for the treatment of Palestinian youths. This was a direct result of the media coverage and of the televised images of soldiers beating teenagers.

Regardless of Israel's protests that it was handling the matter in a humane way, the contrast between the Palestinian civilians and the Israeli solders in the nightly television images and the scenes of soldiers beating children gave the U.S. government little choice but to respond critically. Within only three days, the Palestinians and the media had succeeded in permanently characterizing the *Intifada* as "fearless rock-throwing youths versus Israeli troops,"[3] a characterization that stuck. Regardless of the facts or of the situation, that is how most Americans came to perceive the *Intifada* (aided by the American predilection for the underdog). The shift in popular opinion was obvious to the pulse takers in the White House, and Israel was not only powerless to stop it, but was doing a very poor job of trying to counter it.

The impact of the televised reports was not lost on the Israelis. The first Israeli attempt to control the press was reported by Peter Jennings and Tom Brokaw on December 18. The newscast included tape of soldiers being instructed not to hit demonstrators when cameras were around and of soldiers ordering camera crews to leave a demonstration area. This was followed on the same broadcast by further White House criticism, this time quoting the President. The *New York Times* covered the *Intifada* the same day, but did not report the attempt to exclude TV cameras in the following day's edition.

The media coverage of the *Intifada* impacted on the policy process in both the White House and the State Department in a way not found in other cases. In the TWA case, the policy process was almost totally dependent on the media for communications with Berri and for information on what was going on. During the *Intifada* Case, communication and information transfer moved at three distinct levels: Day-to-day media reports (in some cases hour-to-hour because of the presence of CNN and *Headline News*), which kept the White House, the State Department, and other players immediately informed of the situation;

cable traffic from the embassies and other diplomatic sources involving policy communications and descriptions; and face-to-face and telephone diplomatic conversations between U.S. and Israeli officials.

The injection of the media into this information stream had two policy-related consequences:

First, the immediate media reports gave the U.S. policy community an advantage over the Israeli government. The Israelis were not the information gatekeepers that the hijackers were in the TWA hostage crisis; they were essentially forced to react to what the Palestinians chose to do and what the media chose to report.

In dealing with the U.S., there was no time and little opportunity to frame events in terms favorable to Israel, or even to present them in what may have been the most factual manner. The pace was set by the media. The media's penchant for confrontation, violence, and the underdog delivered an immediate and powerful version of events to American policy makers every night on television and every morning in the *Washington Post* and *New York Times*. This created impressions and stimulated protests before the cables could arrive and go through channels.

The result was that the Israelis were routinely put on the diplomatic defensive. Israel had to respond to criticism almost daily as a result of news broadcasts.[4]

The Israelis were put in the position of responding overnight to American demands for explanations of actions covered the night before on the news. They could not frame their decisions in their own terms. In essence, the Israeli government was politically forced to react to an agenda created in large measure by the Palestinians through television. Normal diplomatic discourse was overwhelmed by the media.

Second, the media provided U.S. policy makers with day-to-day updates on events in Israel and the territories which demanded policy responses, some public and some private, on specific issues. Control of the pace of U.S. policy was taken away from the administration by the media. Three issues provide examples of this:

1. *Israeli tactics.* Israeli's tactics were criticized in statements issued by the White House on December 15 and 17; by President Reagan through Marlin Fitzwater on December 19 by President Reagan personally on the 22; by Phyllis Oakley on the following day and by the State Department in a statement a day later. Most notable was Fitzwater's strong condemnation Israel on December 18, following the release of CBS film of Israeli soldiers beating Palestinian youths.

The continuing scenes of Israeli-Palestinian confrontation, punctuated by film of Israeli brutality (and not balanced by film of Palestinian and PLO violence) put heavy pressure on the U.S. to complain to Israel and pressure Israel to change tactics.

2. *Deportation*. The networks broadcast coverage of the deportations and of protests over them in Jerusalem on January 1, 1988. Israeli spokesmen rejected U.S.criticism of its deportation policy, saying those deported were *Intifada* ringleaders. The next day, the networks and the *New York Times* covered a U.N. vote on the return of deportees, with tape of the U.S. abstaining. This was followed by news packages of the arrest of journalists covering deportation and lawyers defending those fighting being deported. Israel's objections were overwhelmed in the media coverage of the actual deportation and criticism of the policy. The coverage continued in both print and broadcast media until January 15.

The U.S. responded immediately to the deportation of four Palestinians on January 13 with a statement from the White House calling for an end to deportation. The coverage of the U.S. abstention on the U.N. vote regarding deportation led to administration statements to the effect that it had little influence over Israel on this matter. The response came both from the White House and the State Department; in addition to a White House statement, Ambassador Vernon Walters, National Security Advisor Colin Powell, Charles Redman, George Schultz, and Tom Pickering all appeared on various news media to explain the U.S. position, each referring to the news broadcasts of the *Intifada* and the deportations.

3. *Comparison of Israel to South Africa*. The first mention of a comparison between Israel and South Africa policies also surfaced in the network coverage of deportation, January 14, 1988. It was covered in detail on the 18th by Peter Jennings, and John McWethy on ABC spent over five minutes on the topic, a serious blow to Israel's image. Israel released a working paper the same day, rebutting the comparison point-by-point. The Israeli foreign minister met with reporters and American Jewish organizations on January 18 as part of the drive to squelch the comparison.

The information delivered by the media was not always crucial for policy making in terms of the data it contained, but rather for the political impact it carried. What was important was not so much what U.S. policy makers knew, as when they knew it and what and when the American people and other nations knew it.

MEDIA INFLUENCE ON POLICY LOCUS

As in the TWA hijacking, the Reagan White House used the media to control where it wanted the policy locus, rather than vice versa. The President rarely took the policy responsibility himself, but rather left it to Marlin Fitzwater when the White House did decide to involve itself. For the most part, the policy locus stayed with the State Department.

The locus of the policy initiative is more important in the *Intifada* case than the shift of policy focus from the White House to other agencies. The policy initiative clearly stayed with the Palestinians, subject to some gate-keeping influence by the media. The Palestinians knew they could generate media coverage by violence, and they knew they could generate positive media coverage through violence that provoked a confrontation with Israeli soldiers. Whether or not there was a clear and continuing strategy on the part of the *Intifada's* organizers to do this, the result was the same.

The Israelis never captured the policy initiative even though they attempted to do so several times:

- the tour of Gaza by Rabin on December 30, 1987
- curfews and lifting of curfews at various points
- the beating policy established on January 20, 1988
- attacks and controls on reporters on several occasions
- the eventual news blackout.

The ability of the Palestinians to control the issue agenda through the media did not mean they controlled the U.S. policy agenda. Once the Palestinians had established that the U.S.–Israeli policy agenda would involve the *Intifada,* the White House chose when and how to respond.

The larger question of the role of the occupied territories in the U.S.–Israeli agenda and how that question should be framed was the major shift in the character of U.S. policy effected by the media. If the *Intifada* had not been covered by the media, or even if it had been covered only by the print media, it is likely that the U.S. would not have allowed it to effect even short-term relations with Israel. The fact that the U.S. waited until televised and widely circulated print reports of demonstrations several days after they began before commenting is one indication of the effect of mass media.

MEDIA-POLICY DIRECT LINKS

Although the overall agenda was set by the *Intifada* and the mass media, cases of direct media-policy examples are rare, due to U.S. control of the pace of policy making. The White House refused on all but a very few occasions to act in response to media reports. The most obvious case was the criticism of Israeli tactics by the White House, and later by a reluctant President Reagan, and the refusal to veto a U.N. censure after continued televised scenes of soldiers fighting against unarmed teenagers.

A second example occurred on March 8, 1988, when CBS news revealed a meeting between U.S. envoy Vernon Walters and Yassir Arafat in Tunis. Walters denied the meeting the next day despite confirmation by CBS News President Howard Stringer. There is no indication of communication between the White House and the Israeli leadership concerning the story, but it is safe to assume that some discussions took place as a result of that report.

As it was, the short-term effect was much less profound than the long-term shift in U.S. attitudes. There are numerous indications that the mass media coverage of the *Intifada* and Israeli's tactics in handling it did lead to a permanent shift in U.S. and American Jewish attitudes toward Israel and its relationship with the occupied territories. American Jewish groups were initially angry at Reagan's criticism of Israel (12/24/87, network news), and were silent about deportations (1/13/88, network news), but this shifted as more images of Israeli tactics were shown on American television. By January 27, Israeli leaders were publicly asking American Jews "What else can we do?," and by March 14, American Jews in Los Angeles were demonstrating against Israel's tactics. Many credited (or blamed) the news media with influencing this change, compounded by Israel's poor handling of the media.[5]

THE ROLE OF TELEVISION

Television's role in Case 3 was far stronger than that of the print media. This was made clear by the numerous attacks on television crews by the Israeli army and the eventual Israeli attempt to black out television coverage. A reading of broadcast and print reports of the *Intifada* shows that television broke more stories and introduced more new elements into the story than the print media did:

- television brought Yassir Arafat into the discussion through a live interview on *Nightline*
- television showed striking images of Israeli soldiers breaking a Palestinian's arm with a rock
- television broadcast a tape of the hour-long beating of two Palestinians by four Israeli soldiers
- television interviewed medical personal on March 1, 1988 who charged Israeli soldiers with a policy of breaking bones (covered earlier in the *New York Times* 2/14/88)
- television broke the story of Vernon Walter's meeting with Yassir Arafat
- television introduced the comparison of Israel and South Africa

- the *New York Times* reported on March 5, 1988 that Henry Kissinger urged the Israelis to ban television from the territories and may have actually been responsible for the blackout

Finally, a review of television reporting from the period shows that it not only was the most rapid source of day-to-day information on the *Intifada*, but that the picture it presented was far less favorable to Israel than that presented in the print media.[6] There is no evidence that this slant effected U.S. policy toward Israel, but the constant presentation of damaging scenes, plus numerous specials on the Palestinians (some positive, most negative,) must have contributed to the shift in public attitudes and government policy toward that has occurred since the *Intifada* began.

NOTES

[1] Media coverage has extended beyond March 15, 1988, but at a reduced level and was included in this research. Unless otherwise noted, all descriptions of events and policy decisions have been drawn from the *Vanderbilt Television News Abstracts* or the *New York Times* during the case study period.

[2] Jim Mesada, NBC news, December 13, 1987, quoting government sources in Israel.

[3] CBS news 12/15/87.

[4] Incidents of defensive responses include:
- on 12/21/87 to world leaders
- on 12/22/87 to President Reagan
- to more world leaders on 12/23/87
- to Israeli citizens on 12/25/87
- to Israeli military reservists on 12/31/87
- on 1/15/88, when Peres felt obliged to justify the expulsion of Palestinians
- on 1/13/88 to the Reagan administration for deporting a group of Palestinians

[5] Likud member Begin called the media the "oxygen of the terrorists." Col, Efraim Laid of the Israeli army told networks crews that the media encourages Palestinians (denied by cameramen). Not only Jews credited or blamed TV for this attitude change; the Palestine National Council told the networks on 1/22/88 that it was the images from Israel that have made a lasting impression on the American people, including Jews. A Palestinian now living in the U.S. claimed on 2/5/88 on network news that the nature of the occupation issue had been changed by television.

[6] See William Adams, *Television Coverage of the Middle East* (Norwood, NJ: Ablex, 1981), pp. 32–33, 25–26.

5

Mass Media Roles in Foreign Policy

It has become obvious, in conducting foreign policy, that the press plays a critically important role. The press can either make or break a foreign policy initiative." (Cyrus Vance)[1]

"If the press can move policies forward, you also have to accept the fact that they can make it more difficult" (Henry Kissinger)[2]

Moving policies forward or stopping them cold is a role frequently mentioned by foreign policy officials when asked about the media and their work. But the mass media industry today—as opposed to the elite group of Washington print reporters known as "the press" in Cohen's time—do far more than just move or block foreign policy within an administration. The mass media today play distinct roles in the shaping and reality of American foreign policy. They function as:

- a rapid source of information useful for policy decisions
- an agenda setter which influences the agendas of the U.S. and other nations
- a proxy for diplomats
- a diplomatic signaling system with policy influence.
- a tool used by terrorists and non governmental organizations.

Television also plays distinct diplomatic roles through space bridges and on-air negotiations, sometimes called "television diplomacy."[3]

These roles and the special position of television which emerged from all elements of the research—the interviews, the survey, and the case studies—will be covered in Chapter 7.

A RAPID INFORMATION SOURCE

The mass media tell us about wars, disasters, highjackings, and elections around the world, often within hours of the event. In providing this near-instant notification of what is going on globally, the mass media serve four distinct roles as rapid information sources for policy makers: (a) policy officials' use the media for immediate useful information, (b) policy makers use the mass media in the early stages of an issue to make decisions, (c) media are often the only source of policy information in crisis situations, and (d) the media's information is often seen as critical for policy making, sometimes more critical than official data.

Fastest Source of Useful Information

There was almost no question in the minds of policy makers interviewed that mass media are the fastest source of information on politically important events around the world. There was some divergence of opinion on how useful this information is for substantive decisions. Some policy officials interviewed indicated that the immediate media information's usefulness was limited, while others attested to both the media's speed of information delivery and its importance in their work. Among the former was Carter administration National Security Council staffer William Quandt, who was very skeptical of the media as a rapid information source. When asked if the quickly delivered information provided by the media was useful, he replied:

> Not really on anything I was dealing with. The wires are often early sources of information, for instance in the 1973 Arab-Israeli War. I had dozens of other channels of information.[4]

Daniel Kurtzer, Chief of the Middle Eastern Affairs Staff of the Policy and Planning Division of the State Department, argued that the media provided information unavailable from the official sources, even when officials were on the scene:

> My answer would be yes . . . [the media's utility as an information source] would apply to cases where our access was limited to the media's access. For example, the last Arab summit meeting in Algiers. . . . The embassy had its people talking to participants. I know, however, that the media's

access to the participants was better than ours. So we were watching the media reporting more carefuly in some respects than we were watching our own embassy's reporting.[5]

Former State Department Spokesperson Hodding Carter felt that policy officials in general use the media heavily whether or not they admit it:

The answer is, of course. Most policy people, when they are not out there posturing and beating their chest in public about the effects of the media, would be happy to tell you how often they get information faster, quicker, and more accurately from the media than they got it from their official sources.[6]

Dennis Harter, Director of Press Operations at the Department of State, agreed, but differentiated among the types of data delivered by the media and by other sources, and their usefulness:

I agree [that the media is frequently the fastest source of information] for raw data, but not for analytical information. But raw information is also very important just to get a policy maker started on the right issue.[7]

President Carter also qualified the usefulness of media-delivered information, reflecting the perspective of the nation's top foreign policy decision maker:

Sometimes we would get a preliminary signal through a news report or Reuters or AP or BBC or American sources that precipitated questions from me as President to the State Department or to the CIA to give me a follow-up. The definitive information on which I would rely to make a decision will come from more competent sources and in more detail, but the original item will more likely be revealed to me before I got it through the entire bureaucracy. . . . a delay as of much as 24 hours sometimes.[8]

A majority of those interviewed clearly agreed with Hodding Carter and Daniel Kurtzer that the media frequently provide information most rapidly and that they can be a useful source of policy information. Eighty-seven percent of the interview respondents could recall cases when the media were the only source of information available for decision making, and 65 percent agreed that the media were frequently the fastest source of information for policy making. A small number of respondents, 8.7 percent, added that the media were the fastest information source only in crisis situations.

Media Are Used in Early Stages of the Policy Cycle[9]

A second aspect of the role of media as a rapid information source is the degree to which it is used at the earliest stage of the policy cycle, the Problem Identification Stage. Seventy-four percent of the foreign policy respondents to Linsky's survey indicated that mass media have some impact at this stage, compared to 28 percent who indicated no effect. Forty percent indicated that this effect was "large" or "dominant."

As shown in *Table 5–1*, 53 percent of the foreign policy officials who responded to Linsky's survey who perceive that the media have a large impact on policy at this stage rely on the media very much and 81 percent rely on it very much or somewhat, compared to 20 percent who perceive the media as having no impact on policy.[10]

Media Are Used in Crisis Situations

Foreign policy personnel often rely on mass media-delivered information during crises. A majority of 63 percent of the policy personnel interviewed indicated that media were frequently the most rapid source of information in crises situations. As shown in the TWA highjacking, mass media are sometimes the only source of information at the beginning of a crisis situation and may continue to function in this capacity throughout the crisis. Virtually all of those interviewed offered an anecdote or observation on the utility of the media in a crisis from their personal involvement. For example, former NSC staffer Robert Pastor pointed out that during a crisis, it is often members of the media who can make contact with key parties when official sources cannot:

> The news media is tremendously effective, more effective than anything else in following a fast-breaking violent crisis because the media can go to places that are under siege that the CIA can't go. [In] the reporting on the

Table 5–1. Media Impact at Earliest Stage of Policy Cycle Compared with Officials' Reliance on Media for Information.

Media Impact	Reliance on Media for Info		
	Very Little	Some	Very Much
None	52%	28%	20%
Some	21.8%	40.6%	37.5%
Large	18.4%	28.9%	52.6%

X-square = 12.39 @ 6 D.F., Sig = .05, R = .29, N = 95

fighting in Nicaragua in 1979, the U.S. Government couldn't respond to any of that, compared to what the news media was doing. And I'm sure that's true in Lebanon and of a lot of places.[11]

Dr. Judith Kipper, ABC consultant on the Middle East and an advisor to current and past administrations on Middle East politics, was more direct in her assessment of the need for media-delivered information during emergencies:

Any crisis where you need on-the-spot information, the media information is more accurate and the government relies on it.

Dennis Ross, Middle East staff specialist on the Reagan NSC, a foreign policy advisor to Vice President Bush during the 1988 Presidential election campaign and currently Director of Policy Planning at the Department of State noted that television can be crucial during a crisis, but one has to be careful of the information it provides:

CNN reports if something is happening now, where you are getting a lot more from CNN than you are getting from your own sources. That is something that has a relatively short life, however. The Kuwait plane hijacking [for instance]. During the re-flagging, when ships would be hit, some of the CNN reports were very accurate. Sometimes it turned out not to be true.[12]

The Media's Information Can Be Critical

Former Assistant Secretary of State Harold Saunders described as critical the initial information the State Department received at the outbreak of the 1967 war:[13]

At the beginning of a crisis, it is often the news media that provide initial reports, so that when situation began the input from the media is significant. The first hours of the 1967 war all we had were [media] reports from various Mid East capitals. In a matter of hours reports came in from embassies, which may have been more comprehensive and from more authoritative sources, and then our intelligence began to come in, later on you depend less on the media. But in a crisis, you depend on the media for some information.[14]

Saunders is not alone in this assessment. In cases of fast-breaking crisis situations, most foreign policy officials interviewed reported that the media can and often does provide highly crucial information. Former Assistant Secretary of State Langhorn Motley noted that during highjackings, CNN not only got information out before the other networks, but before official sources could get geared up to let Washington know what was happening and who the players were. Eighty-seven percent of those interviewed agreed with Saunders and Motely, and could recall situations wherein the media were the only source of information for policy making in fast-breaking crises or terrorist incidents.

MEDIA ROLE: TERRORIST TOOL

Much has been made in the academic and popular press of "terrorvision"—the successful use of the media by terrorists to influence U.S. foreign policy—such as described in the TWA 847 high-jacking case. But is terrorvision successful? Do all such media-terrorist relationships lead to changes in U.S. foreign policy? The policy officials interviewed for this research did not think so. They agreed that terrorists were often highly skilled and effective in using the media to provoke government responses to their actions, but they also felt that this did not necessarily result in significant policy changes in any more than a handful of cases.

In the *Intifada* case, Israel freed the prisoners demanded by the TWA plane's hijackers, who later dropped their secondary demands. The terrorists accomplished this by using the media skillfully to maintain the momentum of the hijacking and to hold the policy initiative. This was also true of the students who took over the American embassy in Tehran. But it is not true of other terrorists, such as the hijackers of the *Achille Lauro*, who did not understand the media and who had very limited access to it. Different terror groups have different agendas, some of which are more amenable to media manipulation than others. And they have differing levels of skill in dealing with the media.

Foreign policy officials indicated strongly that nongovernment organizations, such as terror groups, were able to magnify their visibility and influence and to gain attention from higher levels of government. Eighty-three percent of the foreign policy officials surveyed by Linksy responded that the media magnify the influence of outside organizations, and 64 percent said that the use of media by outside organizations would gain attention from higher levels of government (less than 11 percent saw no effect). However, this increase in influence is not necessarily seen as changing policy outputs. Table 5–2 shows that there is no relation between policy officials' perception of the increase in a group's visibility due to media, and its effect on policy outputs.[15]

Most of those interviewed agreed that terrorists who obtained coverage on the media and used it well were treated differently than those who did not, that is, while overall policy may not necessarily be impacted by terrorist use of the media, tactical response certainly is. Ninety-

Table 5–2. Perception of Media Ability to Magnify Outside
Influence and Impact on Foreign Policy Outputs.

Group's Influence Raised	Effect on Policy Outputs		
	Low	High	% of Total
Yes	66.6%	83.5%	82.9%
No	33.3%	16.5%	17.1%

R = .00867 Sig. = .1977
N = 94; χ-square = 5.77 @ 4 D.F., Sig = .2168

one percent of the policy makers questioned agreed that the media increase the visibility of terrorists and their power to invoke governmental responses, and 74 percent said the media increase terrorists' power.[16] Harold Saunders, for example, was very clear on this, "If terrorists were not on the tube, we would respond, but in different ways." Dennis Ross of the NSC expanded on Saunders' point:

I think they are a factor which has to be dealt with much more because of exposure. If they didn't have the exposure it's possible they would be a factor in the same respect. On the other hand if American interests are being targeted even if there wasn't a lot of exposure you would want a policy for responding to it regardless if there was exposure or not.[17]

Christopher Van Hollen of the Senate Foreign Relations Committee Staff insisted that it is media that is new, not terrorism, implying that whatever policy concessions that are made are the result of media access:

To some extent groups that may not have entered into the process [terrorism] enter the process because they have access to television. On the other hand, but even more importantly, groups that were part of the process before but were never able to assert a strong influence over the process or were not able to get a lot of attention. The most dramatic example is terrorism. Where terrorists always were part of the process, but part of their success in their view depends on getting access to the media.[18]

Phyllis Oakley, Deputy Spokesperson for the State Department, distinguished among the governments that had been subjected to terrorism, pointing out that nations differed in their susceptibility to terrorists and media influence:

It depends upon how receptive the government is to being influenced by it. Obviously, in the period of the Iranian Hostage Crisis, I think that is an example of a government letting this influence greatly. It's a different influence in Irangate; it's not the same thing. But then you look at something like the British Government with Terry Waite which is a very different thing. I think it varies with the policy of the government.[19]

Hodding Carter echoed this point, implying that the targeted government may have more to do with policy impacts of terrorist use of the media than either the terrorists or the media:

I used to say for years until the Iran Arms for Hostage deal that I knew of no government policy that was changed because of the heavy publicity given to terrorists. Now I have to say "yes" because of Ronald Reagan and the policy change that occurred because of the publicity received. But we did not change our policy in the TWA incident.[20]

In general, policy makers perceived that media are effectively used by outside groups and individuals to impact U.S. policy, but that it does necessarily change policy outputs.

The TWA hijacking provides a concrete example in which the media served terrorists in a variety of roles ranging from a globalization device to a communication and negotiation medium. It also exemplifies a situation in which a policy change may have occurred, although it was a private (and denied) agreement with Israel to release prisoners as part of a trade for the hostages. This was a shift from the public U.S. policy of no deals with terrorists. This policy has not changed for seven other U.S. hostages in Lebanon who have not had access to the media and whose captors have not shown either the inclination or the skill to use the media in the high-profile manner demonstrated by Nabih Berri.

It is clear that outside groups, including terrorists, are able to use the media to magnify their influence with U.S. policy officials and to bring their agenda to the attention of high levels of the U.S. government. The media also play a role in terrorism which impacts on the U.S. tactical response during an incident. That role involves the use of media by terrorists to globalize their action and their message, to communicate with the targeted government and others, and to seize and hold the immediate negotiation initiative.

The ability of terrorists to use the media to force changes in U.S. foreign policy is as much or more a function of the vulnerability of the administration to publicized terrorists tactics as to the skill of media use, and is by no means common. Poor use of media by terrorists, such as occurred in the *Achille Lauro* case, has little likelihood of impacting policy; skillful use of media, as in the TWA case has a higher likelihood of impacting policy, but is not the sole or always the most important determinant of lasting policy change. Other factors include the domestic political situation in the U.S., the skill of the U.S. administration in using the media, the emergence of domestic lobbies and their use of the media, and ongoing relations and discussions with other governments who may be involved in the incident and who are impacted by the policy.

MEDIA'S AGENDA-SETTING ROLE

"Agenda setting" is generally defined as the process by which problems become salient as political issues around which policy alternatives can be defined and support or opposition gathered.[21] In the context of mass media and policy, "agenda setting" refers strictly to the *salience* of issues, not to their policy position. In policy situations, this involves two elements:

1. Placement of an issue or region or country on the U.S. foreign policy agenda that was not already there
2. Movement to a higher level of policy consideration of an issue or region or country presently on the agenda (i.e., from a planning technician to an Assistant Secretary)

The agenda-setting question asked of policy officials in the interviews was: "Does the media set the agenda of U.S. foreign policy officials either by globalizing local and regional events and elevating their salience, or by any other mechanism?" The case studies also provided insight into agenda setting by the media; examples from the *Intifada* case demonstrated how the media may have caused a long-term shift in the character of U.S.–Israeli relations through their impact on American Jews.[22]

As noted above, a high percentage of those who responded to the survey perceived that individuals or outside groups who obtained media coverage were able to magnify their influence and gain the attention of higher levels of the foreign policy community. However, the interview transcripts revealed a variance in opinion among the officials on this question. Carter administration National Security Advisor Brzezinski saw the agenda setting going from the White House to the media, not the other way around:

I think in an administration, if it's activist—and ours was in the area of foreign policy, it tends to determine agenda for the press. Not exclusively, and certainly many events transpire over which you have no control. But by and large we set the agenda.[23]

President Carter saw a definite media role in setting agendas when it globalized regions or countries, and told of an incident when the media's globalization of a regional event that was not even news almost derailed a major policy initiative:

> The media, by concentrating on one particular event in the world, can exalt it to a preeminent status in the consciousness of the public and the consciousness of the Congress, and even among sometimes diplomats in the State Department. But that particular event may not warrant preeminent consideration, but because of the high publicity assigned to it, the government officials, including the President, are almost forced to deal with it in preference to other items that might warrant more attention.
>
> I mentioned [one such event] when reports of Soviet troops in Cuba were broadcast. This was a very disturbing thing to us and interfered with the ratification of the SALT II treaty, and caused us two-three weeks of research and the ultimate result was that it was not news but some candidate (Frank Church) made it a campaign issue with the help of the media.[24]

William Quandt, who usually downplayed the impact of the media in his responses, agreed with the President but saw the media as more of a distraction than an agenda setter:

> It [the media] hinders [policy] when the media disseminates misleading information which forces you to take positions that you'd rather not have or [creates] a distraction by [reporting prominently] a crummy little incident that isn't intrinsically important but everybody is screaming and shouting about.

In the State Department, Dennis Harter saw little agenda change because of media and implied that it was the other way around, the government set the media agenda:

> The areas [the media's globalization effect has] focused on are areas which are traditionally areas of interest, i.e. Korea, Philippines, Central America, etc., which would have naturally surfaced in the U.S. even without a great deal of media attention. Other areas where there could be equally important events going on, i.e. Indonesia, Brazil, etc. tend to be ignored.[25]

Hodding Carter agreed with Harter, perhaps indicating some communality of viewpoint among foreign policy press relations officials:

> With the Persian Gulf it was administration decision that brought this massive focus to bear, that then brought the cameras to the Gulf. It rarely gets on television without a government decision having been made first.

They may not play it the way we want it, but first we tell them, i.e. terrorism.[26]

The results from survey questions that asked to what degree negative or positive media coverage effected the importance of an issue in the foreign policy bureaucracy, shown in Table 5–3, indicate that a strong majority, 77 percent, of all foreign policy officials who responded to Linsky's survey perceived that positive or negative mass media coverage can increase the importance of an issue to the bureaucracy (the remaining 23 percent perceived no effect).[27]

This result was confirmed in the interview questions: A total of 82 percent of those interviewed for this study perceived that mass media attention to a regional event can put the region or the event on the nation's foreign policy agenda. A majority attributed this capability to media-stimulated domestic political forces, although some qualified this answer by saying this was the case only part of the time.

Additionally, the results of the "action" responses (those survey responses that specify that action was likely as a result of media coverage) provided an important qualification. They indicated that, while the media are perceived to be able to establish the importance of issues and often to move an item to a more senior person, it will rarely lead to a reassessment of a policy position on an issue already on the agenda.

Policy officials' narratives provided insight into the kinds of issues that the media can elevate on the policy agenda, and the conditions that raise the likelihood that an issue will benefit from media exposure. For example, Christopher Van Hollen and Jody Powell described in concrete terms the most often-mentioned news items that made their way onto the policy agenda because of mass media coverage—South Africa and Ethiopia:

(Van Hollen) . . . I can think of situations where the television coverage definitely created an additional element to an overall picture and contrib-

---

Table 5–3. Perceived Effect of Media Coverage on Foreign Policy Agenda.

Positive coverage affects agenda	15.5%
Negative coverage affects agenda	33.0%
Positive and negative coverage affects agenda	27.8%
TOTAL	77.3%

N = 89

uted to people's sense of what was going on. Pictures from South Africa, many of them which were broadcast around the time of the early South Africa sanctions legislation. It certainly played a role, the images of children being beaten. The images that came across were a factor.[28]

(Powell) . . . It depends on what you're trying to do on the policy making level. You may for example want more public interest. Yes, of course, the Ethiopian food crisis is a situation which television did do it [set the agenda.[29]

Policy officials often noted that it is issues like these—those involving "global issues", such as environment, hunger, or amnesty—that are most susceptible to agenda setting by the mass media. They also noted that important events or issues not covered by the mass media can suffer in their ranking on the foreign policy agenda.

Most of those who responded positively to an interview question regarding the agenda-setting influence of the media attributed this influence to mass media's ability to stimulate or maintain domestic political forces. A few noted that the mechanism is one of the media *creating a positive policy environment for policy initiatives to be brought forward.* Often, interviewees said that policies put on the agenda by media were under study but could not be moved for priority or political reasons. Media stories provided the positive environment necessary for them to be moved. Roman Papaduick, Assistant Press Secretary for International Affairs in the Reagan White House, used the drought in Ethiopia as an example of this:

What television did was bring the image home to the American public, but the policy had always been there. What happens is TV finds the problem, then finds the policy and marries the two. Therefore, makes it look like the policy evolved to meet the problem.[30]

Dennis Harter of the State Department pointed to other areas "discovered" by the mass media after the policy officials had spent some time working on them, such as the international drug trade. But the media's ability to do so is seen by policy officials as circumscribed by three conditions:

1. Media influence varies with the nature of the issue, with global, multilateral issues being more susceptible to media influence than bilateral or military issues.
2. Media influence derives to some extent from the media's ability to stimulate domestic political forces to support or object to a policy initiative.
3. Media influence varies with the prevailing political environment, although it can influence or create that environment.

MEDIA ROLE: DIPLOMATIC PROXY

The mass media have been often criticized for meddling in foreign policy. But policy makers see media involvement as an infrequent occurrence, although one that can have very serious consequences. The TWA hijacking case provided several examples of media intervention in a negotiation situation, both as an instrument used by all sides, and as an independent entity pursuing its own objectives. The degree of this involvement can be seen from the extreme level of complaints about it during and after the fact: Television was smugly criticized by print media for usurping diplomatic roles;[31] President Reagan criticized the media in general and television in particular for interference in the negotiation process;[32] and television criticized itself for its mostly inadvertent involvement in affairs of state.[33] Even the TWA hostages complained that the television networks were using them to boost ratings and in doing so, may have complicated efforts to free them.[34]

Whatever the actual involvement in foreign policy was during the TWA highjacking, it signals a basic change in the mass media–foreign policy community relationship. How much of a change can be seen by comparing John Scali's role as a backchannel interlocutor between Kennedy and Soviet officials during the Cuban missile crisis with the activities and criticism of television during the TWA 847 hijacking. Scali's role was kept relatively quiet, and when it did become widely known in the press and policy communities, it was generally seen as a positive, patriotic activity.[35] In the TWA case, television was virtually charged by government, other media, and even by itself with frustrating national policy.

Two aspects of the mass media's diplomatic proxy role emerged from the interviews: Diplomatic intervention by media in negotiations, and "television diplomacy"—the on-air meeting of national representatives. Policy makers were found to have strong perceptions and opinions about both.

Diplomatic Intervention

What are the perceptions of foreign policy officials about the involvement of the media in negotiations and diplomacy, either institutionally as in Case 2, or on an individual basis? Do they feel it is a widespread practice and if so, what is the impact on policy outputs? Does it lead to better or worse policies?

I found that policy officials interviewed for this study were generally aware of journalistic involvement in diplomacy: 74 percent of those personally interviewed knew of such cases or had heard of them. However, they rejected the media role as a positive one: 78 percent answered an unqualified "bad" when asked about the effect of this on U.S. policy outputs, and those that did not describe involvement as negative, gave a qualified answer indicating that it was justified only under special circumstances.

While the majority of policy officials indicated that they personally knew of such a case, a review of the interview transcripts reveals that most had heard of cases secondhand, rather than firsthand. Most of those interviewed also mentioned the same cases, that is, John Scali in the Cuban missile crisis and Walter Cronkite behind the scenes on the Sadat visit. The interview transcripts show that while policy officials are aware of the incidents, their perception is that journalistic involvement is an infrequent occurrence and not a significant part of the flow of diplomacy. The 78 percent negative response cited above was strongly categorical, that is, journalistic involvement in international relations was seen as bad for policy in all cases, as described by Hodding Carter, "There is no place in diplomacy for journalists or anyone not authorized by the government."

Other statements from the interviewees lend additional detail to these findings. Ambassador Herman Eilts felt that there was a contradiction in using a journalist for negotiations in terrorist situations:

> It would never occur to me to use a journalist for this kind of mission, simply because if you're dealing with terrorists, there is a period of time where the emphasis must be on secrecy. And I don't see how a journalist being true to his profession can maintain dual loyalties; the loyalty of secrecy and the loyalty of wanting the readers to know.[36]

The policy makers who qualified their answers referred to the kinds of information that journalists could provide or the contacts they could make which would be impossible for officials. Christopher Van Hollen of the Senate Foreign Relations Committee exemplified this line of thinking:

> As a general rule I would say not [positive for a journalist to be involved in diplomacy or foreign policy] but in extraordinary circumstances I would say yes. If an American journalist somehow gets a contact through his reporting in a particular country that enables him to have special access and knowledge and if the journalist is willing to cooperate.[37]

Robert Beckel, former Special Assistant to President Carter for International Affairs, recognized that journalists can sometimes play an information role, but he saw danger in anything else:

> This is very dangerous. I think there is a place for journalists, because journalists sometimes have better sources than the U.S. government does,

where they think it's appropriate to provide information to the government that might help in diplomacy; but to actively engage in diplomacy, I think, is a big mistake.[38]

Beckel used the Scali example as the way it can be done legitimately:

I think Scali's role in the Cuban Missile Crisis is a good example of what I'm talking about. There's a distinction between that and actively pursuing independent diplomacy. Scali received information and turned it over to the government and the government felt that he was the best avenue to pass information back and forth. That was a decision by the government; it was not an independent decision by Scali to engage in independent freelance diplomacy.[39]

Daniel Kurtzer of the State Department noted that sometimes journalists accomplish diplomatic feats that have eluded diplomats for years:

the Sadat peace initiative, where at a critical moment when the receptivity of both parties to committing themselves to peace was very high, it perhaps required a Barbara Walters (sic) to break the psychological logjam, which I don't think diplomats could have accomplished.[40]

President Carter's experience gave him a broader point of view when asked about situations involving journalists and diplomacy. While recounting instances of mass media involvement in diplomacy that had very serious negative effects, Carter recognized a valuable role for the mass media in certain circumstances:

those efforts by journalists can either be very beneficial or damaging. In some cases the journalists have access to terrorists' spokesmen and can receive proposals that might lead to a solution of a kidnapping or a hijacking of a plane when it is almost impossible for government policy to permit contact with criminals of that kind. Obviously, when the news is made known that the terrorists will accept these actions and the hostages will be released or the plane returned, then the government can decide whether it wants to accept terms of that kind without dealing directly with the hostage takers or hijackers.

But he added that the media can damage negotiations and put American lives and policies in danger:

There are other times when pressures from journalists have resulted in very very serious damage to the well-being of hostages and other citizens of our country. The most notable example of that is when Mike Wallace and other reporters went to Iran and interrogated Ayatollah Khomeini very forcefully and publicly on *60 Minutes* and news broadcasts, asking "will you release the hostages, will you direct the students to leave the embassy grounds?" and the inevitable response of Khomeni to the world public was "no, not unless the Shah is brought back."

Well, once the news reporters forced Khomeni, possibly against his will, to make a public commitment of that kind, it was impossible for him to meet with or talk to any intermediaries that we would want to send to explore the opportunities at least for the hostages.[41]

MEDIA ROLE: TELEVISION DIPLOMACY

Policy officials differed about the emergence of Ted Koppel-style "television diplomacy" in which national representatives are brought together on the air for discussions of the issues that divide them. Paralleling Koppel, networks and independent producers have begun to broadcast "space bridges" which link policy officials and citizens of different countries together by television to discuss issues that divide them.

What are the ramifications of this new use of the television medium? Do televised interactions between U.S. and foreign leaders impact foreign policy, and if so, is the influence positive or negative? Television diplomacy was examined extensively in the interviews, both in specific questions and in the unstructured discussions.

Interview respondents were mixed in their view of TV diplomacy's effect on policy, but the weight was toward a negative perception: Only 26 percent said it helped sound policy, 35 percent said it both helped and hindered, 17 percent said it hurt, and 22 percent thought it was irrelevant. Harold Saunders, who agreed with the majority, summarized the perception that television diplomacy is not generally useful:

> I think television diplomacy generally hinders foreign policy. If you take
> NIGHTLINE etc., I don't think those dialogues are particularly useful
> because they are not very well prepared . . . I think to have a productive
> exchange, people need to spend some time learning to talk with each other
> about sensitive issues. Learning how to handle sensitive issues creatively,
> finding common ground, not shying away from sensitive issues, rather
> than engaging in debates and scoring points.[42]

Phyllis Oakley exemplified the minority. She pointed out the valuable education that "television diplomacy" can provide both for policy and the public, and indicated that it can sometimes articulate what policy officials have been unable to get across:

> I think the Koppel Arab-Israeli show was well done. It was useful in
> presenting the passions of both sides and how difficult it is to make an
> agreement. In a sense this is what Schultz has been saying. Talking to the
> Soviet legislators before the summit [is] useful for information sharing.[43]

MEDIA ROLE: DIPLOMATIC SIGNAL[44]

In his book, *Communication and Diplomacy in a Changing World,* former Vietnamese Ambassador Tran Van Dinh wrote in 1987:

> Since World War II, the extensive use of the mass media in diplomacy, the so-called "public diplomacy," has transformed both the appearance and the substance of diplomacy.[45]

A political problem resulting from this transformation was foreseen almost a decade earlier by George Dalley, Deputy Assistant Secretary of State for International Organization Affairs:

> The explosive growth in communication technology in last two decades coincided with the process of decolonization. The increasing penetration of Western communications into the Third World has come to be perceived by some as new attempt to reassert the domination of former colonial powers.[46]

Influencing Other Governments

This perception in the Third World may not be without a basis in fact. It is certainly not without a basis in the perception of American policy makers. Those interviewed agreed that the most utilized and most effective technique of media use by foreign policy officials is for signaling American preferences to other nations. Dennis Ross of the NSC summed up the preference signaling role of the media from a policy official's point of view:

> Yes, the idea is you're trying to make it clear to another government that there may be a cost or benefit, more like a cost, in what they are doing.[47]

President Carter also pointed out the usefulness of the media to a head of state attempting to influence other governments.

> I used international media broadcast in several cases, we had nationwide broadcast to Poland and to Germany, including East Germany, and to Japan, where I would respond to questions from a fairly large audience in a town meeting forum. And with arrangements, even Communist governments [allowed] that the telecasts would be live and nationwide.[48]

Diplomatic aspects of this transformation were frequently mentioned in the interviews, ranging from the use of the media as a communications device to negotiate with governments who cannot be contacted in other ways, to sending influential signals to the people and the agencies

Table 5–4.   Policy Maker Influence of Media.

Placed 10% or more of stories on agency	72.4%
Sought to influence media coverage	85.7%
Felt appropriate to leak to media	50.0%
Leaks ok to consolidate support	66.7%
Leak ok to force action on issue	41.7%

N = 94

of other governments and receiving signals back from them. Examples of this use of the media include Presidential satellite addresses to foreign audiences, exchanging messages with foreign leaders through press conferences and news programs, and satellite conferences with embassy personnel in several countries simultaneously.

Former Presidential Assistant Robert Beckel described one such attempt to influence other governments through the media:

> On Panama. We were having a great deal of trouble with Torrijos near the end of the treaty debate because we needed to add some reservations and conditions onto the treaty that he didn't like; and we were trying to explain that, how difficult it was; and we simply had to have it. And we tried to get the press operations to ratchet up to the networks to talk about the political difficulties facing the treaty ratification.[49]

Table 5–4 presents the results from analysis if foreign policy officials response to Linsky's survey related regarding government influence on media for policy purposes. The results clearly show a willingness on the part of foreign policy officials who responded to Linsky's questionnaire to obtain press coverage and to use the press for policy purposes: 86 percent of the survey respondents sought to influence media coverage of their agencies, and 72 percent indicated they or their staff were responsible for at least 10 percent of the actual coverage.

Table 5–5 presents results from the interview questions concerning the use of the media to influence foreign governments. These results essentially confirmed the survey findings that the use of the mass media is widespread among the policy officials interviewed: 78 percent reported using the media, many responding that the practice is constant. *Table 5–5* also echoes the indications from the transcripts that print is the medium most often used to influence foreign governments (numbers indicate the percentages of respondents who answered positively in each category).

Table 5–5.   Policy Maker Perception of Media Use to Influence Other Nations.

	Used to Influence Other Governments	Used to Influence Other Peoples
Print	44%	33%
TV	22%	56%
Wires	22%	0%
All media	33%	11%
Radio in 3rd world	11%	44%
Depends on nation	11%	22%

Numbers are % of N. N = 23. Totals add to more than 100% due to multiple answers.

Influencing the People of Other Nations

Seventy-eight percent of those interviewed agreed that mass media communication with other nations' peoples is a useful policy tool. Several volunteered that media communication with other nation's peoples has become a fact of life in the foreign policy process. A few also referred to President Reagan's use of WorldNet to broadcast to European audiences, and to the Christmas message broadcast exchange between the U.S. and the Soviet Union, as well as media events and televised speeches by U.S. officials on tour overseas.

Table 5–5, which quantifies the responses to interview questions asking policy officials which media are most effective in influencing other governments and other nations' peoples, shows a sophistication in media use. Print is the most favored medium of choice when using media to influence other governments, but television is the medium used to go over the government's heads. The wire services and a mix of all media are employed significantly to reach governments, but not significantly in reaching people directly. And finally, radio is seen as still as very important as television in reaching mass audiences in the Third World.

The narrative from the interviews fleshed out the quantitative response shown in Table 6–5. Dennis Ross, the NSC Middle East staff specialist, noted that television is an excellent medium for public diplomacy, and when directed over a government's head can rapidly get its attention:

> Public diplomacy is most easily conveyed on TV and is most instantaneously seen. . . . TV is used to communicate in a sense over the heads of Governments in a way that makes them feel a need to respond in some fashion.[50]

Jimmy Carter did not have access to a global television news industry that today reports almost every word the President utters, but he sees it as very important to the Presidency. He said that if he were President now he would expand the use of television as a diplomatic tool to reach into other countries through more over-the-air contact:

> That kind of television can be done now not just within a nation, but across national boundaries, and I think this is a very fine opportunity for a President to let American views be disseminated to the world.[51]

Foreign Government Use of Media To Influence U.S. Policy

The evidence is also overwhelming that U.S. policy makers perceive that foreign governments try to use American mass media to manipulate American foreign policy. Ninety-two percent of the interview respondents reported that they could recall or had heard of cases of foreign government use of media to influence U.S. policy. The perception was strong in all agencies and in all government rankings. Many of the policy officials interviewed noted that other national leaders have been increasingly turning the media tables on the U.S., using American media to influence American public opinion and policy. Hodding Carter stated it bluntly:

> Certainly foreign governments used the media to influence the US Government. Officials would constantly bring reporters in to get a message across. Sometimes overtly. I know very few sophisticated governments that didn't do it. I have known of reporters that have been used as carriers of messages. The media used the most is print.[52]

Phyllis Oakley noted Gorbachev's skill at using the media as a negotiating tool by charming the people of the U.S. on television:

> The Gorbachev interview with Tom Brokaw last year before the summit was an important introduction to the American people before the Summit. It was a smart thing for the Soviets to do. The overall impression was positive, that he was a forceful, energetic determined man.[53]

President Carter recalled both Sadat and Begin's use of the media to influence U.S. policy through U.S. public opinion, and according to Carter, despite Sadat's brilliant use of television in the U.S. during the Camp David period, Israeli Prime Minister Begin had mastered the art of media manipulation of U.S. public opinion on a day-to-day basis:

Menachim Begin was a master at it. He was able through his eloquence and his intelligence and his knowledge of the American attitudes to make statements through the media that promoted Israel's on controversial issues.

I had to be quite careful with Mr. Begin in the Oval Office to address every single issue he raised because I found that if he raised 15 issues and I responded to 14 of them, he would assume I agreed with him on the 15th issue . . . and he would immediately after he left the White House either through direct news reporters or through his speeches to Jewish audiences [covered by the media] interpret what I said in a very effective fashion.[54]

Several policy officials interviewed noted that Third World leaders have also gained skill in using the media to influence American policy. Robert Beckel described past Panamanian President Torrijos' attempts:

But Torrijos used television to take some people into the streets to show us that he had a lot of influence. . . . you know, he encouraged the U.S. television news outlets to cover rallies, stuff in Panama.

Hodding Carter described similar tactics by Daniel Ortega of Nicaragua:

I recall the media used by foreign governments to influence the U.S. press, largely print and radio. Danny Ortega uses his radio addresses to communicate to the U.S. government in hopes of influencing our foreign policy.[55]

William Quandt described the very effective use of the media by Israeli officials to influence U.S. policy.

Sure [I recall the media being used by other governments to influence US policy], both the Arab and Israeli government. Particularly the Israelis who are leaking information to their own press and that would get picked up by the American press. All of a sudden something that Vance had said 24 hours earlier in Jerusalem would be fed back to us in a slightly distorted form and we would have to react to it. The leaks were often with a purpose, they weren't innocent leaks . . .[56]

Harold Saunders described the Israeli use of the media as not only purposeful, but also somewhat out of control:

The Israeli government is notorious for every member of the cabinet having his own favorite reporter or newspaper and during negotiations, across the board they were leaking and I am sure it was designed to influence American policy.[57]

Harold Saunders' quote in the *Introduction* describing the use of mass media as a fact of life in foreign policy sums up mass media's roles in foreign policy:

> international relations today is a continual process of policy making and policy influencing communities on both sides of the relationship, and television is a significant part of that interaction, and so are other forms of communication.[58]

NOTES

[1] Unpublished transcripts of Martin Linsky's research interviews.

[2] *Ibid.*

[3] All quotes in this chapter are from my interviews with policy makers unless indicated otherwise.

[4] Personal interview, Summer 1987, Brookings Institution, Washington DC.

[5] Personal interview, Summer 1987, Department of State.

[6] Personal interview, Summer 1987, Washington DC.

[7] Personal interview, Summer 1987, Department of State.

[8] Personal interview, Fall 1987, Carter Center, Atlanta, GA.

[9] See Linsky, op. cit, pp. 140–142, for a complete description of the stages of policy making used in this study.

[10] Linsky's survey asked, "In your experience how significant was the impact of the press [the identification of the problem] stage of policy making?" and "To what degree did you rely on the [mass media] organizations for information about your policy areas?"

[11] Personal interview, Carter Center, Fall 1987.

[12] Personal interview, Brookings Institution, Summer 1987.

[13] It should be noted that Saunders was critical of the media's role in foreign policy in most of his other interview responses.

[14] Personal interview, Brookings Institution, Spring 1987.

[15] Linsky survey questions cross-tabulated: #II.–10, "Overall, how great do you believe the effect of the media is on [foreign] policy?" and III.–3, "In your experience, did the ability of an individual or outside group to gain attention in the media magnify the group's influence?"

[16] Interview questions #1, 2, and #13: $N = 23$.

[17] Personal interview, Summer 1987, Washington DC

[18] *Ibid.*

[19] *Ibid.*

[20] *Ibid.*

[21] Lutz Ebring, Edie N. Goldenberg, and Author H. Miller, "Front Page News and Real World Cues: A New Look at Agenda-Setting by the Media," *American Journal of Political Science* 24 (Feb. 1, 1980): p. 17. Since this research involves the foreign policy process in which policy officials are engaged around specific issues, we will also consider the position of an issue within the policy structure,

as well as its political salience, in measuring agenda setting. In this way, we will capture not only a measure of the political interest in an issue, but a measure of its likelihood in obtaining an output from the policy process.

[22] The television images from the *Intifada* may have had a more profound effect on the relations between American Jews and their national lobbying organizations. Michael Lerner, editor of *Tikkun,* pointed this out in an editorial in the *New York Times,* Feb. 24, 1987, p. 27.

[23] Unpublished transcripts, *op. cit.*

[24] Personal interview, Fall 1987, Carter Center.

[25] Interview cited.

[26] *Ibid.*

[27] Question II.3a, "When an issue in your office or agency received what you saw as positive or negative coverage in the mass media, did that coverage increase the importance of the issue within the bureaucracy?"

[28] Interview cited.

[29] *Ibid.*

[30] Personal interview, Summer 1987, Washington DC.

[31] *Washington Post,* June 20, 1985

[32] *Washington Post,* June 21, 1985.

[33] CBS News, 6/21/85; ABC, CBS speicals, 6/26/85; CBS, 6/28/85, with Ken Stein accusing network correspondents of engaging in diplomacy instead of journalism.

[34] CBS News, 6/28/85.

[35] For more information on Scali and opinions about his role, see *New York Times,* Jan. 13–16, 1989, for stories on meetings between Soviet, Cuban, and American officials involved in the crisis.

[36] Personal interview, Fall 1987, Boston.

[37] Interview cited.

[38] *Ibid.*

[39] *Ibid.*

[40] *Ibid.* Barbara Walters did not break the logjam; that was accomplished by White House counsel Robert Lipshutz and Special Consultant Leon Charney. See Charney, 1989, *op. cit.*

[41] *Ibid.*

[42] *Ibid.*

[43] *Ibid.*

[44] Signal is used here similar to "semaphore," defined as "a system of signalling by human or mechanical means" (*Webster's New Compact Format Dictionary,* 1985, ed.) In railroads, a semaphore is used both to signal information to an engineer, and to direct the behavior of the train.

[45] Tran Van Dinh, *Communication and Diplomacy in a Changing World* (Norwood, NJ. Ablex, 1988), p. 37.

[46] Quote recorded in 1979; Op. cit. p. 39.

[47] Interview cited.

[48] *Ibid.*

[49] *Ibid.*

[50] *Ibid.*

[51] In fact, Reagan did just that. President Reagan made extensive use of the WorldNet satellite system to broadcast to specialized groups, national polities, and State Department personnel around the world. See Michael David and Pat Aufderheide, "All the President's Media," *Channels*, September, 1985, pp. 20–24.

[52] Interview cited.

[53] *Ibid.*

[54] *Ibid.*

[55] *Ibid.*

[56] *Ibid.*

[57] *Ibid.*

[58] *Ibid.*

6
Mass Media Influence in Foreign Policy

there is a question as to how much policy should be made with public input and how much should be simply handed down to the public. And I'm inclined to think that the public should be allowed to participate more in the process (Robert Pierpoint)

Mass media are a *pervasive influence in the foreign policy process*, shaping the tone, style, and emphasis of U.S. policy outputs in various ways and to varying degrees, both in specific situations and across the board. This influence stems from policy officials' perception of the roles the media play in policy making and international relations in general, and from the media's injection of biases into the policy process.

Television appears to be an important component of these biases, or influences. As television (and to a lesser extent radio) has replaced print and wire services as the major conduits of national news,[1] it has profoundly changed the political impact of information around the world. Some of these changes are the result of television's more critical[2] and cynical[3] coverage compared to that of the print media. Others flow from the result of television's technical requirements, such as of its tremendous truncation of messages. Most important may be the broad reach of television, which can sharply effect policy by moving otherwise low-priority stories onto front pages of the elite press and onto policy agendas.

This influence and how it effects policy was specifically examined in both the interviews with foreign policy officials and the policy-maker survey. Two primary mechanisms emerged through which the media influenced policy outputs, domestic politicization of foreign policy decisions, and fast-forward policy making.

Additionally, a third mechanism was apparent in some circumstances: The ability to shift the focus of foreign policy to the White House and the President—a mechanism that depends as much on the White House as on the mass media.

DOMESTIC POLITICIZATION
OF FOREIGN POLICY DECISIONS

As live foreign affairs coverage has proliferated, interested publics have increased their involvement in domestic actions designed to influence foreign policy decisions.[4] An indicator and possibly an effect of this is the increase in the number of organizations devoted to lobbying international causes before various branches of the U.S. government.[5] Robinson and Sheehan call this combination "The New Two-Step Flow of Media," in which they argue that the original Katz and Lazarsfeld theory that news flowed from the prestige press to opinion makers and thence to the public must be modified to show a flow from the prestige papers to the networks to the public.[6]

The new two-step flow theory replaces local opinion leaders with network news anchorpersons. No longer does the flow of information go from the prestige press to national and local opinion leaders, and thence to the public. Now it goes from the New York Times to Dan Rather, and then to the public. More recently, news now flows directly from the TV networks to the public and the government simultaneously. The networks have brought the vocabulary of the New York Times and the Washington Post to the American hinterland, with policy results.

This new two-step flow also goes from the elite press and the broadcast media to constituency organizers and policy makers. The policy officials attempt to manipulate and influence the flow of press information to domestic constituencies to gain support for or to generate opposition against policies. The research question formulated to test this proposition is: "Is there evidence that the mass media contribute to domestic pressures for policy change?"

The survey results were more mixed, but still showed a strong use of the mass media to effect domestic opinion. When asked, "When an issue in your office or agency received what you saw as positive coverage in the mass media, did that coverage galvanize outside support?," 56 percent of the responses indicated that it did, while 44 percent said it did not. However, 67 percent of the same sample indicated they had leaked information in order to consolidate support outside the government. Since only 50 percent felt it was ever appropriate to leak (see *Chapter 5*), this indicates a high value was placed on using the media to obtain domestic support for foreign policy initiatives.

The interviews with policy officials revealed a very strong perception of the power of the media to stimulate domestic support. Ninety-five percent of those interviewed agreed that mass media stimulate or contribute to domestic pressures for foreign policy decisions.

Attitudes of the policy officials interviewed toward media-stimulated domestic pressures were mixed, but mostly negative. Only one respondent, a senior White House policy official heavily involved in Middle East negotiations, felt it helped development of sound policy. A little over half of those interviewed said it could either help or hinder, depending on the case at hand, and about one-fourth expressed that it was irrelevant to policy in almost all cases.

South Africa was mentioned a number of times in the interviews as a case of domestic pressure generated by the media. Hodding Carter and Harold Saunders typified the comments:

(Hodding Carter) The media's globalization has created domestic pressures for foreign policy action that would not have surfaced otherwise. The pressure is always there once the camera is there.

Again, South Africa, TV globalized a reality which has been there forever, it forced actions of Congress. The pressure was always there but the camera jelled that pressure. Television can make a minority issue a heavy majority or plurality issue.

(Saunders) South Africa is an example of the media generating a domestic pressure for a foreign policy action that might not have been taken otherwise.

Robert Pastor pointed out that the media and democracy were intertwined in the domestication of foreign policy issues, which is good for democracy but may not be good for policy:

Agree [the media can stimulate domestic pressures on foreign policy officials]. Here the problem is democracy, not the media. The media permits more people to participate but so does democracy. We're in favor of that. To the policy makers, especially people in the State Department, it's a hindrance. It's a pain in the neck, both democracy and the media.

Christopher Van Hollen from the Senate and former Ambassador Eilts both noted that the capability of the media to stimulate domestic pressures was conditioned on the issue, the length of coverage, and other considerations:

> I agree [that media can stimulate domestic pressure] to the extent that there is a strong constituency in the U.S. that may have had a particular interest in that region, or the issue is a strong humanitarian one. Then that constituency is universal. . . . Americans don't like to see people starving on television. Americans don't like to see people beaten on television. Whether the sort of public emotion about the issue actually spills over into a concrete policy change depends on the longevity and depth of the coverage. If it was a sustained barrage of television coverage. I certainly think it can have effects. Look how *Nightline* got started . . .
>
> The starvation in Africa [did become a domestic issue due to media coverage], but only marginally so in the sense that it created an impetus for relief aid. As for American policy toward South Africa, yes. As for *Intifada*, yes in an indirect sense. And it is not the Israelis' handling of it. It is the sustained nature of the uprising. . . . That was a surprise for everyone.

The effectiveness of the media's capability to stimulate and sustain domestic pressures is related to the length of the media coverage and to the nature of the issue, with global environmental and human rights issues having the highest likelihood of media impact. Policy officials frequently also use the media to consolidate support for policies (or opposition against undesired policies) across the board and consider this an appropriate and useful technique of the foreign policy process for any category of policy.

FAST-FORWARD POLICY MAKING

The emergence of global satellite delivery[7] enabled television and radio to flash news of events and the statements of national leaders or terrorists immediately to media outlets around the world.[8] Tran Van Dinh notes that the speed of diplomatic messages has increased from week-long ocean crossings to near-immediate telephone calls. The media have further accelerated this pace by providing information on events to embassies and to their host country counterparts, constituents, and enemies, before diplomatic communication can take place via cable or phone.[9] Almost all of those interviewed said that this pace has become a way of life in policy making, and as such, profoundly changed the nature of international relations. Seventy-six percent of the foreign policy officials surveyed responded positively to the question, "Is there evidence that the mass media [both positive and negative media coverage] accelerate foreign policy making?" Results from the interviews agree with the survey finding that policy officials perceive that the media accelerate policy decisions; 91 percent agreed that it does. Of those interviewed, 14 percent responded that it depends on the event and 77 percent agreed without qualification. Respondents were not unanimous in their opinion of the impact of this speed-up on foreign policy, however: 43 percent felt it was an unqualified negative; 22 percent said there were some benefits; 13 percent felt it was positive; and the remainder did not know. The interviews indicated that while policy officials generally agree with the proposition that the mass media have accelerated policy, a significant minority perceive that the fast-forward effect is not universal and does not effect some kinds of issues.

Governments can avoid the fast-forward effect. Prime Minister Thatcher accomplished this during the Faulklands Island War by sending the British fleet to fight Argentina's forces. By using an essentially 19th-century gunboat strategy, she forced the media—and the Argentines—to work on a 19th-century timetable. She delayed the military encounter for two weeks, and kept the media away from the news area for that time, while hoping for a diplomatic resolution. While this worked for Ms. Thatcher in the Faulklands, and for the U.S. in the invasion of Grenada, the media are expanding their satellite capability, which may eventually enable them to report on military activity in remote areas.

The media usually cannot effect particular kinds of issues, for instance, those involved with arms control. Harold Saunders explained that arms control is usually not subject to press acceleration because of its own internal calendar:

> I would generally argue that the media accelerates the pace of policy; there will be exceptions in some cases like arms control. It will still take time for complex bureaucracy to take a position on a complex issue. Arms control moves may depend on scheduled negotiations, meetings, routine things like that. More often than used to be the case, probably the media precipitates things.

Several interviewees noted that the government may be working on a policy matter for some time before the press reports it. Then, depending on the issue and the stage of decisions, the policy pace may or may not pick up. Harold Saunders again:

> If you have been working around a problem for months in secrecy and had discussions with the President and something leaks and you do something, advancing your timing by a day or two or a week, its usually no big deal. If you are working on policy from scratch, it makes for less good policy.

Others interviewed noted that the rapid flow of information may not ultimately change policy outputs, but it complicates the policy process. The Senate Staff's Christopher Van Hollen:

> It means more distractions which take people's eyes off a long term goal. People end up spending a lot of time fire-fighting on issues that probably wouldn't have been raised to a high level in earlier days because there wasn't that much information about it that quickly. But I certainly don't think it has done any real damage.

The narratives indicated that the policy officials interviewed were less negative in their perception of the impact of the fast-forward effect than their categorical answers suggest. (Forty-three percent said it had a negative impact). When their comments are reviewed, the results are much more conditional. Robert Beckel's description of "a mixed bag" is more typical:

> Oh, I think it's a mixed bag. I think it probably exposes problems more quickly that if left to fester would probably get worse, so I think there are some advantages there; but I think it tends to accentuate a dangerous situation that might otherwise not be as volatile . . . it causes response that may not be as well thought out as it should be.

Others offered similar conditions on their initial judgment of negative effect on policy:

> (Phyllis Oakley) It depends. The tendency would be [to say] it harms foreign policy because it doesn't allow for enough time to think things through and to consult. You have to give quick answers and whatnot. But it is not inconceivable where facing the media having had something to say forces a decision, which if allowed to drift might be different or not as good. . . .

> For example, the coup in Haiti. The media was talking about it and we didn't have much time so that my first reaction was the statement I made on Monday saying, 'If this is a military coup, we would condemn it.' And so you are conditioning it because the media is reporting various things on Haiti you don't know anything about.'

> (William Quandt) The media have contributed to that trend [of accelerating the pace of foreign policy] but it is not the only element. For example, the democratization of foreign policy—[the rapid pace—] that's the way it is. You don't always make better decisions because you have a lot of time.

> (Hodding Carter) Television has, because of the impact of the fast arriving picture, has forced or driven governments to respond more quickly to events than its own information would have deemed prudent, to say

something to counter these images. These images thus effect posturing, but not policy, if we make the distinction.

A few people replied that the fast-forward effect was entirely negative, not because it had no impact, but because it did. William Ingle, House Foreign Affairs Committee Minority Counsel, offered an example with an important point:

> It's a major problem. It's very common. They [Members of Congress involved in foreign policy] have very little time to respond because it will be literally within an hour, a half-hour of an event, in some cases. It is difficult for anyone to get information at that point. So what you are responding to are very superficial facts of an event. Unfortunately, *most people share their view of the situation at that point in time when they have to say 'I think this is good, this is bad.' And then it's difficult to change that view even six hours later when more information can come in.* (italics added for emphasis)

While the mass media have accelerated policy making, other forces have also contributed to the more rapid pace of policy making, including increased democratization of policy and the fact that there are more players in both international relations and policy making. The overall effect in the perception of policy officials is that the fast-forward effect has become a fact of life.

PRESIDENTIALIZATION OF FOREIGN POLICY

Lloyd Cutler wrote in *Foreign Policy*, in 1984, that the mass media, especially television, had virtually invaded the White House and become a significant factor in foreign policy decisions. He wrote that:

> it came as a distinct surprise how much television news had intruded into both the timing and the substance of the policy decisions that an American president is required to make. TV news now has a much greater effect on national policy decisions—especially foreign-policy decisions—that print journalism has ever been able to and more than most experienced observers realize.[10]

Cutler went on to describe in detail numerous instances of TV effecting foreign policy decisions, including ratification of SALT II treaty, response to the Soviet Invasion of Afghanistan, and the decision to invade Grenada in 1983, among many others.[11]

Cutler argued in the article that the administration felt obligated to respond to events by the next TV news deadline in order to prevent the news media from reporting that the President was unsure or the administration was divided. He also observed that TV set White House agendas. "If it's not on TV it's not important," he wrote.[12] David Stockman described the same phenomenon in the Reagan White House when he detailed the nightly White House ritual of watching the national news as "reality time," when the President and his top advisors decided what they thought was important.[13] Others have noted similar influences.[14]

Pressure from the mass media to shift policy focus to the White House was clear from the interviews, but the success of this pressure also clearly depends on the White House's ability to resist it, its own agenda and tactical moves to use the media, and the nature of the issues involved. Some issues raised by the mass media must be answered by the White House, especially those involving human rights, suffering, and global problems ("Why aren't you interested in this?"), while others, both bilateral and multilateral, can be controlled by the White House regardless of media pressures. A slight majority of the Carter Administration respondents, 55.6 percent, agreed that this shift occurred.

The interviews revealed a wide range of opinion on this question. There was no pattern in the narrative responses as there was in the categorical answers—responses did not relate to the respondents rank or agency. Robert Pastor of the NSC was typical of the affirmative end of the range of answers—those who saw a mass media-driven policy focus shift to the White House:

> Yes, absolutely. There has always been a tendency in Latin America to turn to the U.S. for a major problem now you have the whole world [turning to the U.S. to solve problems]. The reason is the American media are there. The next day the White House press asks "what are you doing about this?" They wouldn't ask the question if the agenda wasn't being set. It's hard for an American President, even a conservative Republican President, to say 'this is none of our business, we are doing nothing, why should we do anything?' . . . the American people wouldn't accept such an answer. Marginally, you would have to say you are looking into it, we're monitoring it, etc. . . .

William Quandt, also a former NSC staffer, perceives the media influence on the White House completely differently:

> No. If the White House wants to duck the issue they can push it back to the State Department. The White House usually likes attention, the people like to get the President on camera, they like to show that he is in charge and so they invite it. If they don't want it, they don't have to have it.

Hodding Carter of the State Department agreed with Quandt:

> The White House has complete control over that, where the focus of the camera is . . . If you resist the pressure, if you simply say that is not our

priority no matter what you think is a priority, and the Reagan Administration proved it to a tee for the first four years, that government still has
by far the upper hand in the contest . . . it is only when it [the White
House] has no real sense of direction itself, no clearly articulated goals
[that the press can shift policy focus or control the agenda].

Phyllis Oakley agreed with the proposition, but took a more thought-
ful approach, noting that the media are not the only pressure impinging
on the White House:

I agree [with the proposition], but that is not the only factor. The other
factor is that so often there are competing views on foreign policy issues
. . . so that you get the Pentagon, State Department, agencies, civil service, Post Office, etc. views and the only coordinating element is the
White House because of the National Security Council structure, and so
that it is in a sense the change in foreign policy issues and their complexity
as well [as the media] that put them over into the White House.

It appears clear that, while Presidentializing policy may be a mechanism effected by the media which influences policy, the President and
the White House can have extraordinary influence on the media. The
contrast between Carter's handling of the Iran hostage situation and
Reagan's handling of the TWA hostages clearly demonstrated that a
media-wise administration determined to control its agenda can do so
regardless of the media.

NOTES

[1] Bower found in the 1970s that television was replacing print as the major
medium of news. Others note that radio, especially drive-time news programs,
also constitute a large share of the average American's daily news diet. Television has greatly increased its position as the major news medium since the 1970s
according to much research. Robert Bower, *Television and the Public* (New York:
Holt, Rinehart and Winston, 1973).

[2] Michael J. Robinson and Margaret Sheehan. *Over the Wire and On TV* (New
York: The Russell Sage Foundation, 1983), p. 262.

[3] *Ibid.*, p. 278.

[4] There has been an explosion in international news on all television outlets.
CNN instituted an hour a day of international news in 1986 and has expanded
coverage constantly since then; local news now devotes 40 percent of its cover-
age to national and international stories, according to *U.S. News & World Report*,
March 16, 1987, p. 54; many major market independent and affiliate stations
created foreign bureaus or traveling bureaus to cover everything from the fall of
Marcos to the Mexican earthquake; and the emergence of services like CONUS,
Newsfeed Network, ABC Newsfeed, and CNN's syndication service now give

any local station the ability to cover foreign news as quickly and deeply as the networks. In the top 30 markets and in markets with large foreign-born populations, this coverage has increased significantly in the past 10 years. See the 1988 and 1989 issues of The *Tyndall Report* for a tracking of foreign news.

[5] Robinson and Sheehan, *op. cit.*, pp. 268–269. The authors list seven movements as of the early 1980s. Since then several national movements have emerged supporting and opposing U.S. intervention in Central America. The seven movements are: civil rights movement, the women's movement, the nuclear freeze movement, the antiwar movement, the abortion rights and the right-to-life movement, and the Central American movement, pro and con).

[6] See Katz and Lazarsfeld, *Personal Influence: The Part Played by the People in the Flow of Mass Communication* (Glencoe IL.: The Free Press, 1955); Robinson and Sheehan, *op. cit.*, pp. 228, 286, regarding the combination of prestige press and network news in media impacts. See also Paul Lazarsfeld, Bernard Berelson and Hazel Gaudet, *The Peoples' Choice* (New York: Columbia University Press, 1948) for the seminal writing on this theory.

[7] Because satellite delivery from proprietary uplinks was and is faster than print media story filing by phone or telex (both subject to censorship), radio and television frequently beat print coverage and are usually the first word of important events.

[8] As noted in Chapter 1, this was not the case during the Vietnam War when news tape from Viet Nam routinely took two days or more to get on the air.

[9] Bobbie Battista, Headline News daytime anchor, reports that her fan mail increased "dozens of times greater" when Headline News was made available overseas by satellite in 1986. She said that she noticed "quite a few" letters from embassies and government offices around the world.

[10] Lloyd N. Cutler, "Foreign Policy on Deadline," *Atlantic Community Quarterly* 22 (1984): 223–232; (Reprinted from *Foreign Policy* 56, (Fall 84), p. 223.)

[11] Examples described in *op. cit.*, pp. 224–227.

[12] Cutler, *op. cit.*, p. 228.

[13] Stockman, *op. cit.*, p. 178.

[14] Robinson and Sheehan, *op. cit.*, pp. 265–266. The authors do not distinguish between domestic and foreign affairs coverage; the focus on foreign affairs coverage is mine, based on observation. See Robinson and Sheehan, *op. cit.*, Chapter 8. Michael Grossman and Joyce Kumar, *Portraying the President: The White House and the News Media* (Baltimore: Johns Hopkins University Press, 1981), argue in Chapter 12 that the White House focus on television strengthens the incumbent. See also David Paletz and Robert Entman, *Media Power Politics* (New York: The Free Press, 1981), Chapter 4. Observation of the Carter and Reagan administrations indicates that it depends on the person and circumstances.

7
Television's Special Role In Foreign Policy

You can sit and watch it on CNN, and know what's happening. Off in the crisis center . . . they're watching it. Sometimes the other foreign leaders will get on— you can sit and watch things faster than you would get an official report . . . (State Department Deputy Spokesperson Phyllis Oakley)

Television news now girdles the globe. CNN's news signal is broadcast to 82[1] countries, and according to CNN executives, fan mail sent to the CNN and Headline News anchors, is pirated by government agencies and private distributors in virtually every nation.[2] It is used regularly by diplomats, foreign ministers, even heads of state to get their messages across borders into the homes of their allies and their enemies.[3] Israelis watch Jordanian TV, Arabs watch French TV, East Germans watch West German TV, and everybody watches American TV.[4] And if this were not enough, each year, 100 million videotapes, many containing political propaganda and instruction in political subversion and guerilla warfare, move across national borders in an unprecedented video black market.[5]

The total picture of the political ramifications of this movement of images and information across borders every day is far beyond the scope of this book, but it is clear that television, separate from other news media, effects U.S. foreign policy and the people who make and execute it, as well as the global international system. TV has become a source of information important to foreign policy makers, second only to news-papers. However, its direct use for policy purposes and its subsequent impact on policy outputs depends largely on the issue at hand and the official involved. The information it provides is used by policy officials in circumstances when it is most timely, most accurate, or has high visual impact.

USE OF TELEVISION NEWS BY POLICY OFFICIALS

Bernard Cohen wrote in 1963, a year when TV news was still a 15-minute long network stepchild, that the *New York Times* and the *Washington Post* were the major information sources in Washington.[6] Since then, network news has gone from 15 minutes to a half-hour, in-depth documentaries and newsmagazines occupy prime time, Ted Koppel interviews foreign ministers and heads of state, and CNN and Headline News put instantaneous reports from around the world into homes and offices around the world. How much of this video information is used by foreign policy officials, and how useful is it? The answer to both questions is "very much."

Watching television news appears to have been a routine for a majority of the government foreign policy community at least since 1981, when they were surveyed by Martin Linsky. Officials questioned reported watching a significant amount of TV news, as shown in Table 7–1. Altogether, 87 percent of those responding said they watch television news, and 63 percent said they watch it often, while only 4 percent reported not watching television news at all.

Moreover, those in the interview sample utilized television routinely within the time they spent gaining information from the mass media, although as a distant second to print media. The results of interview questions regarding time spent gathering information from media are

Table 7–1. Policy Maker Use of Television; Report from 1982 Survey.

TV Use Frequency Scale		Percent of Sample
Never	1.0	4.3%
↗	2.0	7.6%
Sometimes	3.0	9.8%
↘	4.0	15.2%
Often	5.0	63.0%

N = 92

Table 7–2.   Policy Maker Use of Media.

0–1 hr/day 30.4%
1–2 hr/day 43.4%
2+ hr/day 26.2%
don't know 0%

mean = 1.32hrs N = 23 (from interviews)

presented in Table 7–2, which shows at 70 percent spent one or more hours with the media per day (mean = 1.3 hours per day). Table 7–3 shows that 74 percent of those interviewed spent 20% percent or more of their time with media on television. Approximately three-fourths of the interview sample spent one-fifth of their mean media time on television, approximately 16 minutes per day, or about half of a network news broadcast.

The interviews found that 83 percent[7] of those questioned replied that they knew first- or second-hand of a case where TV directly impacted policy by providing information that either contradicted official information or provided a visual element so powerful it effected policy officials who saw it. Those that did recall such an incident noted that the majority of their television information for policy making came from either the nightly network news or CNN/Headline News, indicating that the visual power they referred to was derived from reportage of actual events, rather than from conversations on intellectual programs. In analyzing the respondents' anecdotes, it is clear that the majority of those interviewed had in mind powerful visual images, principally from Lebanon, Ethiopia, and South Africa.

The survey data also provide evidence on this point. As Table 7–4 shows, the sources of media information most heavily used by policy

Table 7–3.   Policy Maker Use of Television:
Television Use as a Portion of Time with Media.

TV Use % of All Media	Percent of Sample
0–5%	13.0%
6–10%	4.3%
11–20%	4.3%
21–30%	34.7%
31–74%	34.7%

N = 23

Table 7–4. Media Sources for Foreign
Policy Information.

Newspapers	81%
All TV news	39%
Network news	15%
Wire services	1%
Summaries	0%

N = 100 (from survey)

officials are print followed by television. Print is used twice as frequently by officials, but television serves as a primary information source to almost 40 percent of the survey sample. Sixty-three percent of the respondents reported watching television news "often." Anecdotes indicate responses for wire services and radio may be understated.

The interview transcripts revealed anecdotal evidence that the rapid and routine transmission of politically sensitive information by television around the world, largely by CNN and signal overspill in Europe, dilutes the central control over policy and diplomatic activities abroad. Ambassadors and other embassy and intelligence officials remarked that television disseminates sensitive information that effects negotiations or relations, and often requires that policy decisions or diplomatic moves be taken before instructions can be obtained from the State Department or foreign ministry.

The interviews also revealed anecdotal evidence that television, primarily through videotapes, has become an avenue of generating and guiding political activity in various countries. Most often-mentioned cases involved the use of audio and video cassettes and television broadcasts by the Ayatolah Khomeni to incite and organize followers. Other examples appear in the literature of similar uses of television in El Salvador, Afghanistan, Peru, and elsewhere.[8]

TV'S INFLUENCE: MEDIATED OR DIRECT?

Is TV's influence direct or is it transmitted through other media? When asked this question directly, 63 percent of those interviewed agreed that television's impact reached them for the most part through other communications media. Seventy percent also perceived that the *mass media* could force an item onto the foreign policy agenda, reinforcing the mediated response. However, the interview transcripts indicated that almost all the respondents were thinking primarily of television when discussing mass media in this context.

Additionally, when asked if they could recall a case where the television image contradicted official reports or added a touch of reality so powerful that policy was changed, 83 percent answered positively, indicating a widespread perception among foreign policy officials that television information is independent from that of other media under certain circumstances.

The interviews indicated that this independent impact was episodic, occurring in special circumstances when vivid visual information effected a policy decision, or when television provided high visibility to new players or terrorists in a particular circumstance. Circumstances mentioned most frequently in television's independent impact on policy were terrorist incidents, human rights, environmental and other global issues, and responses to specific personalities.

TV IMPACT ON U.S. FOREIGN POLICY

TV impacts U.S. foreign policy principally through three individual mechanisms:

1. TV increases the number of players in international policy events
2. TV accelerates the pace of policy
3. TV sets policy agendas.

TV Increases the Number of Players

Television complicates policy making by opening the door to new, usually nongovernmental players. From the policy makers point of view, the use of television by groups such as Greenpeace or terrorists introduces more unpredictable variables into an already complex diplomatic world, and dilutes agreements, customs, and alliances that have been built up over decades.

Policy makers' perception of this mechanism is very strong: 81 percent of the policy officials interviewed agreed that TV increases the number of players involved in foreign policy questions. However 25 percent qualified this response by noting that other factors than media were involved.

TV Accelerates Policy Pace

Policy officials also perceive that television accelerates the pace of policy. Seventy-one percent of those surveyed perceived that media coverage speeds up issue consideration and policy decisions. The interviews found the same response; 73 percent of those interviewed agreed with the fast-forward theory of television-driven policy pace. Anecdotal information also showed clearly that those policy officials who use television routinely, especially CNN and Headline News, do perceive that television is a leading component of what was often characterized as a much faster world of international decision making with shorter lead times and ever more rapid transmission of messages. An example of this fast-paced diplomacy was visible during the TWA hijacking and subsequent hostage negotiation via television interview, news conference, and telephone.

TV Independently Sets Agendas

The interviews elicited numerous remarks that television has a limited but important independent impact on policy agendas involving the following circumstances:

1. Television can place global issues on the U.S. foreign policy agenda. These include starvation, famines, environmental problems, and human rights abuses, and the countries that are involved in these circumstances.
2. Television's ability to put items on the policy agenda is related to the visual impact of the issue and its longevity on the air. It will have an impact if there is film or tape continually available, and if the issue remains on television news for an extended length of time.

Robert Beckel's comment on television and the policy agenda sums up the comments on this question:

> The television coverage of Afghanistan moved it up on the agenda. South Africa, too, I think. What television does, particularly television, it forces things up on the agenda that policy makers may know need to be up on the agenda but didn't want to deal with it. South Africa is a good example of that . . . it's such a difficult problem. I'm convinced the Reagan Administration would not have sent Schultz back to the Middle East two or three times in the last three months if it had not been for the disturbances in the occupied territories that they saw on television every night.

The determinants of TV agenda setting are the nature of the issue, its visual impact, the availability of visuals, and the longevity of the coverage.

Despite TV's influence, there has been little change in government attitudes toward television. Reagan-era policy officials are somewhat less likely to see television as useful than are those from the Carter era,

Table 7–5. Indicators of Policy Use of Media Over Time.

Degree of Reliance on Media		1972–1977	1977–1982	Change
Very much		11.3%	19.3%	+6.0%
Somewhat		11.3%	13.6%	+2.3%
Very Little		6.8%	20.4%	+13.6%

	'62–67	'67–72	'72–77	'77–82
Time with Media (Average hours spent with media per week)	1hr	1.42 hr	2.07 hr	2.4 hr
Perception of impact on agency agenda: percent of those who perceived impact	6.7%	11.2%	30.3%	51.7%

Tables 7–5 and 7 are based on responses to survey Question II.–10. Table 7–6 displays the time series responses to question II.–5a.
N = 94–98

and are also less likely to perceive that television influences them to respond to personalities in the foreign policy process. This may flow from a more sophisticated use and view of television . . . the Reagan-era policy officials had more experience with the medium and were more knowledgeable about the real limits on its influence capabilities.

Policy makers interviewed reported that they have not increased their reliance on mass media since 1972, but that they have increased the time they spend with mass media, their perception of its impact on policy outputs, and their attempts to use it to influence other nations (see Tables 7–5, 7–6, 7–7).

TV'S SPECIAL ROLE

Television plays a special role in the American foreign policy process, but that role is limited and diffused. However, when it plays that role— as it did in the TWA hostage drama—it exerts a power over events and decisions that surpasses all other media combined. More important,

Table 7–6. Use of Media for Foreign Policy Purposes.

	'82–77	'77–72	'72–67	'67–62
Try to influence media (%)	47.7	23.0	10.9	4.3
Use media to galvanize support (%)	29.2	14.6	8.9	3.3

(N = 97, 96 from survey)

Table 7–7.   Change Perception of Media Effect on Foreign Policy Over Time.

	'82–77	'77–72	'72–67	'67–62
Some effect 2.0	1.1	1.1	0	0
Some effect 3.0	17.9	11.2	4.5	1.1
High effect 4.0	29.2	NA	NA	4.5
Dominant effect 5.0	3.4	0	0	0
TOTALS (%)	51.7	30.3	11.2	6.7

N = 89 (from survey)

perhaps, than the occasional made-for-TV policy episode—recognized by 90 percent of policy makers—is the steady pressure television exerts on the policy agenda and the more subtle effect it has of engaging a mass constituency in America's affairs around the world.

Foreign policy officials have integrated television into their usual information input; 90 percent of them report watching it as part of their routine. But this electronic information input into the policy process is far less than that of print, which is used four times as much by policy makers as television for news. Thus it is not surprising that most of the influence TV has on policy is mediated through other media, especially through print.

Foreign policy officials have significantly increased the time they spend with TV, up 45 percent since the Kennedy administration, and up 21 percent since the end of the Vietnam War. However, reliance on TV as an information source does not appear to have changed appreciably between 1972 and 1981. While the survey and the interviews indicate that a significant percentage of foreign policy officials at all levels and in all agencies perceive that the impact of the *mass media* on foreign policy is substantial, this attitude does not necessarily apply equally to television. Neither the survey nor the interviews enable television's impact to be reliably separated from that of the mass media as a whole, except in special circumstances, such as emergencies and environments that admit the press, but not diplomatic personnel.

The Reagan administration saw less utility in television and less impact from it on foreign policy than earlier administrations. This is a surprising finding given the Reagan administration's reputation for adroit and voluminous use of television for policy purposes. Other than a possible methodological artifact, two explanations occur for this finding:

1. The experience and expertise in television acquired by the Reagan White House led to a cynical view of the medium, that is, the

Reagan media advisors were better acquainted than their critics with the limitations of television, or at least government-generated television.

2. The impact of television on the Reagan White House staff was overlooked due to the confidence of the communication staff and advisors; they felt they knew the medium so well that they could prevent it from influencing them.

Television's Impact on Foreign Policy

Television is not used to a significant degree by other nations to effect U.S. policy except in certain circumstances and by a few foreign national leaders who are adept at its use. Sadat provided an example of such expertise, as has the Iranian government and Soviet Secretary Gorbachev.

TV has increased the number of players in international politics, but it is one of many factors that do this, some of which television reinforces. However, TV is not seen as an independent source of policy acceleration, but as only one of many factors in the fast pace of policy. Television can be a key factor under certain circumstances. Its impact is not routine, but is frequently rapid and dramatic.

TV can set policy agendas, but does so only in certain issue areas and under certain conditions. Issues most likely to gain visibility on the U.S. foreign policy agenda are global issues such as environment, amnesty, drugs, and human rights. The circumstances that are most likely to result in television influence on policy agendas are those that produce visual confrontations that can be taped and broadcast, and those involving issues that are compelling enough or visually exciting enough to obtain sustained television coverage.

TV may influence foreign policy making and diplomacy in other ways, such as reduction of central control over diplomatic and political activities, reduction of secrecy in diplomacy, provision of amounts of information to policy officials and diplomats worldwide that are beyond their capability to assimilate and verify (especially in the case of CNN), and facilitation of political movement through the use of spillover signals and videotapes.

NOTES

[1] Source: CNN Research Department, July, 1989.

[2] "The Global Village Tunes In," *Time*, June 6, 1988, p. 77.

[3] "Even Revolutionaries Smile for the Camera," *New York Times*, Oct. 4, 1987, p. H3.

[4] Steven S. Wildman and Stephen E. Siwek, *International Trade in Films and Television Programming*. (Cambridge, MA: Ballinger Books, 1988).

[5] Gladys Ganley and Oswald Ganley, *Global Political Fallout: The VCR's First Decade*. (Norwood, NJ: Ablex, 1988). See also "The PLO's Many Voices Differ," *New York Times*, May 2, 1989, p. A12, for an example of the use of videotape for political purposes.

[6] Bernard C. Cohen, *The Press and Foreign Policy* (Princeton, NJ: Princeton University Press, 1963).

[7] YES = 78.3%; NO = 17.4%; NO, BUT KNOW IT OCCURS = 4.3%

[8] Gladys Ganley and Oswald Ganley, *Global Political Fallout: The VCR's First Decade* (Norwood, NJ: Ablex, 1988), pp. 98–197.

8

The Insiders' Model of Media and the Policy Process

We spend so much effort trying to think how to spin the media, how to effect it, how to manipulate it, that after a while we become victims of our own sort of construct (State Department Spokesman Hodding Carter).

News is a product of all the roles of the press, and since the government depends on this news, the press is a participant in foreign policy making and needs to be brought into theory (Bernard Cohen).[1]

In 1963, Bernard Cohen's research indicate a junior partner status for a small press group involved with government in foreign policy. Cohen's unit of analysis was the interaction between reporters and their sources, an appropriate focus at a time when both the foreign policy and foreign affairs news communities were part of the same small clubby Washington establishment.

Cohen depicted a symbiotic media-government relationship, with the press as the helpful cooperative partner in the policy press. He found this relationship understandable because he saw minimal public interest in and attention to foreign affairs at the time:

The chief market for foreign affairs coverage in the American press is a small policy and opinion elite, and a somewhat larger attentive public whose persónal characteristics and interests are much the same as the policy and opinion elite, although the roles are not as specialized.[2]

Neither of Cohen's assumptions are valid any longer. Since Cohen's study we have seen the publication of the *Pentagon Papers*, the televising of the Vietnam War in American living rooms and the U.S. retreat from Vietnam, the on-screen toppling of two U.S. Presidents, the transformation of a hearing on a Defense Secretary nominee into a virtual televised trial, a highly successful President who was more comfortable with cameras than with facts, and the installation of media planners and public relations experts in the White House. Clearly, the media have become much more than the handmaiden of the foreign policy establishment. Something has changed.

Co-evolution, Not Symbiosis

Part of what has changed is that the mass media foreign policy relationship has outstripped the reporterpolicy-maker link Cohen studied. The fraternal symbiotic relationship he described has been replaced by two distinct global institutions—the worldwide U.S. foreign policy and diplomatic community, and the global media industry. Each of these organizations is dedicated to creating its own version of reality around the world, and both are adept at supporting, manipulating, or attacking the other for their own purposes. Analyzing today's media-foreign policy relationship requires comprehending the impact of thousands of daily, complex, multilevel transactions that occur between these two international giants.[3] The symbiosis described by Cohen and others has been replaced by *co-evolution*, the process by which the two entities grow and develop with each other, incorporating one another into their own existence, sometimes for mutual benefit, sometimes for mutual injury, often both at the same time. The resulting relationship is one of *interdependent mutual exploitation*. From the policy makers' perspective, a significant element of policy making involves using and influencing the media; policy making cannot be done without the media, nor can the media cover international affairs without government cooperation. The media today are indeed part of the policy process, as Cohen declared almost three decades ago, but the government has also become part of the media process. The result is something new and unprecedented.

The Evolution of Mass Media in Foreign Policy Theory

Recognition of this co-evolved interdependent mutual exploitation and of the growing importance of mass media's role in foreign policy and international relations has been very slow in coming. Cohen's observation that few outside of the Washington policy community cared about international news or foreign policy echoed the "mood theory" advanced in 1966 by political scientist Gabriel Almond. This theory held that interest in foreign policy reporting was generally low and fluctuated in times of crisis, which resulted in an unstable support for policy.[4] The Mood Theory flowed from the now abandoned "two-step flow-model" which held that the media's influence on public opinion (and hence, on policy) was transmitted through elite "opinion leaders" who, in turn, influence less interested masses.[5]

Journalist James Reston further denigrated the media's role in his influential book, *The Artillery of the Press*[6], which argued that any influence of the press on foreign policy was "usually exaggerated" and was exercised primarily through the Congress, which "confuses press opinion with public opinion."[7] Reston also postulated that the press had strengthened the government's hand in gaining domestic support for its international polices, repeating Cohen's assertion of a natural alliance between the foreign policy press corps and the policy makers.[8]

State Department Spokesman Charles Bray broached the view in the early 1970s that the symbiotic media-policy relationship was plagued by an increasing amount of friction, making it less symbiotic and more an adversarial coexistence, a conclusion supported by empirical studies.[9] He focused on problems of classification, Freedom of Information Act inquiries, and the pressure for the broadcast media to follow the AP and UPI news agendas despite their desire to analyze and use their own material.[10] By this time the structure of this relationship had been virtually codified in a series of written and unwritten rules to which, for the most part, both reporters and policy makers adhered. New entrants were socialized by their peers and by the structure of both the media institutions and the policy-making apparatus to follow these rules.[11]

But it was a decade before the subject of direct mass media influence on foreign policy was raised with high visibility by an insider. Lloyd Cutler, in *Foreign Policy* and the *Atlantic Community*,[12] described in detail many instances where mass media—especially television—exert a direct and substantive effect on foreign policy decisions. His impressive list of media-impacted policies included the ratification of the SALT Treaty,[13] the invasion of Grenada[14], the White House response to the Soviet invasion of Afghanistan[15], and Reagan's decision to open negotiations with Assad following Rev. Jackson's visit to free the hostages.[16] In addition, Cutler pointed out that television had a unique effect on foreign policy because it forced an administration to satisfy mass audiences about foreign policy initiatives, as well as the interested elite. President Ford later warned in *TV Guide*[17] that mass media opened the door to domestic lobbying on foreign policy goals, a complaint born out by empirical studies.[18]

James Larson documented the coevolution process in a monograph for the Foreign Policy Association that noted "the intrusion of television into every phase and level of the negotiation process [which] changes the whole spirit and nature of diplomacy."[19] He noted that political scientists have characteristically thought of foreign policy as an area apart from domestic social forces, with the mass media acting as intervening variables between domestic and foreign policy making, a situation that no longer exists. Larson dates this change from November 1979 with the takeover of the U.S. Embassy in Teheran, calling it the "watershed event in the evolving relationship of media and foreign policy."[20] The paradigm of media and foreign policy was beginning to shift from symbiosis to not always peaceful coevolution. But this change would not be apparent until mass media became a truly global force.

MASS MEDIA TODAY

What is seen, heard, and read about the world by publics and policy makers around the world is a product of a complex and largely independent industry. Although this industry depends on government for much of the news information it disseminates, it is driven by the motives of professionalism and profit, and operates according to rules, traditions, and limitations that have evolved with little regard for policy needs.[21] More important, vast changes in this industry in the late 1970s and throughout the 1980s have made it a completely global phenomenon.

The Global Media Industry

Mass media are now ubiquitous around the world. The mass media have evolved to the point where worldwide transmission and broadcast and tape distribution of news and entertainment programming can be accomplished easily and cheaply to and within almost any country. Media personnel travel and work around the world, hopping a jet and "parachuting" into a news hotspot with cameras, sound equipment, and even "fly-away" uplinks that beam signals directly to satellites. TV executives mingle at international trade shows and conventions, such as MIPCON in France or NATPE[22] and RTNDA[23] in the United States, exchanging stories, resumes, and tips. As a result, the information movement into and around media organizations, and the outlook of those organizations is increasingly global rather than national. Even local television stations in the U.S. and other Western nations send their own crews around the world when the story touches their local audience or is so important they want personal coverage.

Not only is news gathering global, but news transmission is now global. Every country is penetrated by the media of other countries, from international magazines and newspapers brought in by tourists and business travelers to news and entertainment directly broadcast from satellites to homes, offices, and cable systems in dozens of countries simultaneously. The global media industry is disaggregated,[24] with most countries supporting state-owned or private radio and television systems and newspapers, and thousands of independent international producers, distributors, syndicators, and publishers churning out millions of hours and lines of news and entertainment that is sold on a world market. Overlaying this are global media conglomerates, such as Time-Warner, Turner Broadcasting, ABC, NBC, CBS, and Rupert Murdoch, that own media properties in multiple countries and sell media products worldwide. Finally, a fledgling global advertising industry is emerging to take advantage of loosening restrictions on commercials in a soon-to-be united Europe, as well as the growing opportunities for print advertising in media that circulates in multiple countries.

Although radio, wire services, and print media have circulated information globally for years, it is television that has proliferated internationally at an explosive rate, giving mass media an unprecedented reach and penetration in virtually all nations. Wildman and Siwek found in 1983 that over 591 million television receivers existed worldwide (even in the countries with no broadcast system), a figure some industry observers say may have doubled by 1990.[25] By 1988, at least 90 countries had either public, private, or governmental television networks, not including the cable networks that have emerged in Europe, Asian, and the Middle East, the global reach of CNN and MTV, and the new networks, channels, and satellite systems in Europe.[26]

The globalization of mass media has been a particularly American process, so much so that due to its sheer reach and its volume, American mass media have become a worldwide cultural form[27] as well as a ubiquitous communication tool for American policy makers. The American media industry dominates the world mass media in reach, programming, and revenues. It is by far the largest supplier of films and television programs internationally and the leading provider of international news.[28] The influence of American news forms will be strengthened in the 1990s as CNN opens new bureaus and minibureaus throughout Europe, Asia, and Latin American, and NBC begins its drive to become a competing global news, information, and entertainment service.[29]

The VCR has also become part of the global media, and a major instrument of American cultural influence. The trade and smuggling in of videotapes is a multibillion dollar enterprise that is frequently enlisted to circumvent government censorship.[30] Ganley and Ganley[31] found that the most-watched videocassettes worldwide contain programs exported or bootlegged from the United States.

The VCR has also become an important tool for transmitting political messages across borders. Videotapes have been used for political training and subversion by Iran, the Salvadoran guerrillas, the USSR, the United States, the government of Peru, dissident army officers in Pakistan, the Amal Militia, the LNRF militia in Lebanon, and the Afrikaner Resistance Movement.[32] In an early use of cross-border taped media for political purposes, the Ayatollah Khomeni skillfully employed both video and audio tapes as tools to organize the overthrow of the Shah of Iran. Samzidat video magazines with snippets of Western news bootlegged from illegal satellite dishes proliferated throughout the USSR and Eastern Europe, part of the Western media invasion that is credited with accelerating the opening of the Iron Curtain.

Media Are Independent Actors

The media are independent entities functioning to meet their individual self-interests. They resemble policy agencies in that the daily media activity is a product of the capacities and political outcomes of numerous individuals and institutions all operating with their self-interest primarily in mind.

For the most part, the major mass media share elements of a common culture, such as professional ethics, training processes, journalism schools, and awards. However, they also operate under many different agendas and incentives. A grasp of the influences that result in the daily media outputs is helpful in understanding the "outside" role of the media in government politics. The behavior of the media is the aggregate sum of these cross-cutting influences, of which government and politics are a very small part, even in the reporting of foreign policy news.

Media organizations share the limitations and advantages of their technology, the incentive structures of ratings and profits, and the cultural dimensions of journalistic ethics and comradeship. News organizations utilize similar hiring and training processes, draw from the same labor pools, and have old boy and old girl networks that trace back to college. Sigma Delta Chi and other journalism organizations, and national and international conventions, bring members of the news profession together periodically to reinforce their shared cultures.

These elements are common throughout the news world and set media organizations apart from the governmental organizations they cover. The cultures are different, the ethics are different, the incentives are different from those in government. And while a very small percentage of journalists may enter government and vice versa, the people are different and do not frequently exchange places.

Additionally, the adversarial relationship of the media to government has grown significantly since Cohen described the cooperation between media and government in 1963.[33] From forcing diplomatic negotiations into the open[34] and revealing both embarrassing and injurious information, to actively opposing policies such as Contra aid or support for the Marcos' reelection, the mass media have advocated modifications or reversals of U.S. foreign policy on many occasions in the past two decades.

While the media share common attributes and culture, the individual media institutions also differ in many ways. Rewards often differ from outlet to outlet, that is, from CNN and Headline News to the network news organizations, to daily print reporters to wire reporters and editors.[35] Competition for audiences also separates the news organizations at the reportorial, editorial, and the business levels. Print reporters aim for regional or local audiences, looking for the angle for local readers. Wire service reporters are selling to editors and radio news directors, giving them a different slant. Network news producers aim for a mass audience, while the cable news outlets wire and shoot for audience niches, usually more educated and affluent individuals.

At a business level, the different outlets are increasingly competing for each other's audiences and advertisers, injecting a strong reporting incentive to get the story first, but an equally strong incentive to get the story that will grab their audience and allow them to attract viewers or readers from the competition.[36]

International News and the U.S. Media

Both global news and entertainment production and distribution are controlled to a great extent by U.S.-based or -owned industries, a circumstance which raises issues of bias, slant, and a Hobbesian vs. Panglosian portrayal of global reality.[37] The publication of such American institutions as The *Wall Street Journal* and the *International Hearld Tribune* have been the tip of the U.S. media iceberg for many years. Beneath the surface has been the power of the AP and UPI (now diminished), as providers of raw news material to other nation's print and electronic outlets. This Western flavor was reinforced by the other major news sources, the British Reuters News Services and BBC.

The most visible Americanization of the world's news flow is CNN's 24-hour global network. CNN's lease of transponder time from the Soviet Union now enables it to direct-broadcast to hotels, home dishes, and cable systems anywhere in the world. This has opened up new questions regarding the widespread availability of instantaneous American-style news information that in many countries was either unavailable, restricted to a governing elite, or subject to delay.

There are also questions of the impact of American news reporting on American audiences and policy makers. Studies of American coverage of international events invariably criticize the media for presenting an inadequate picture of the world[38] and providing international reporting with staffing, coverage, and placement that is second to local coverage, and rarely covering the Third World.[39] Content studies of evening television news found that from the 1976–1979 period, all three networks gave an average of 40 percent of their time to international affairs, a substantial figure.[40] However, certain countries and regions took the bulk of the time, notably the Middle East, Soviet Union, Western Europe, and Cuba.

Other influences also effect the nature of the news disseminated by American and Western organizations. The difficulties Western reporters have in merely gathering and transmitting information from locations, such as Beirut, China, and South Africa, shape the reality they portray often as much as do editorial decisions and reporter–diplomatic source relationships. It is the tape that can be shot and smuggled out that makes it to the screen, whether or not it is representative of the nation in question or even of the situation that is being reported. And, given that the preponderance of resources needed to gather, edit, and transmit news from trouble spots or from the world in general is controlled by Western media organizations, world information by logistical and financial necessity will have a strong Western and American slant.[41]

Media's Sources of Power

Another consequence of the globalization and evolution of the media is the solidification of their independence, which gives them a uniquely powerful position in the policy process. Their power results from their ability to locate and reveal positive and negative information which, under certain circumstances, can severely damage policies and careers or increase the likelihood of success. Insiders perceive that both positive and negative information could increase the visibility—and thus the vulnerability—of policy officials, but that negative media coverage had the strongest effect.

Media's power of global reporting is underpined by sources of power inherent in the media industry, including their constitutioal protection from governmental control, their role as a valuable source of operating information during crises and during the Policy Adoption and Evaluation Stages of the policy cycle, and the nature of the media-government mutual need/exploitation relationship.

Media's role as a check on official governmental information also provides them with power, based both on fear and on usefulness. Policy makers reported that the media helped keep other agencies honest, or at least provided the information they needed to know when they were not honest. But they were candid in saying that it hurt when the media applied the same reporting zeal to their own outputs. But the most important aspect of this power is the fact that the media are needed as an output to communicate with and influence other nations and various segments of the U.S. foreign policy community.[42]

GLOBAL MEDIA AND INTERNATIONAL RELATIONS

The mass media's American bias and inherent power have evolved conjointly with several other international forces to shape both the structure of the news and world information fluxes, and the structure of the international system. The other forces in this coevolution process include the increase in the number of nations, the spread of multinational corporations, technological change, growth in population and the resulting strain on ecological and economic systems, the rise of new international centers of finance and industry, the emergence of a global market in sophisticated arms. The growth of the global mass media industry has paralleled these developments, reinforced them, and brought them to the attention of the policy processes in capitols around the world. The mass media have three effects on the international system as part of this coevolutionary process. The media have opened the policy agenda to nonstate players, added global issues to national agendas, and accelerated and reinforced the political impact of interdependence. The result of these effects is a transformation of the international political system.

A Transforming Influence in the International System

The world media function as a transforming influence on the international system of sovereign nation-states. The thrust of this transformation is a globalization of the international system, that is, media have redirected some of the system's attention from national to worldwide issues. The media have done this by the increasing visibility and political salience of issues that transcend national borders, and of the presence of players other than nation states working for their narrow national interests. The new players include nongovernmental organizations (NGO), terrorist groups, and international environmemtal, human rights, and relief organizations, among others. In many cases, the principal source of influence these players have is through the media. By bringing to various publics around the world stories and images of global problems and trends, these organizations are able to exert new forms of political leverage on policy outputs. Additionally, by using the mass media as marketing vehicles, many are able to raise funds and coordinate resources at a scale that enables them to create action-outputs internationally. National television "p.i." advertising,[43] national and international televised rock concerts,[44] international sporting events such as the Goodwill Games, entertainment programming that transmits purposeful or subliminal political messages,[45] "space bridges" and dual-nation radio and television interview and talk programs have given nonstate organizations the resources to become players, however small, in an international system increasingly populated with nontraditional organizations. Policy makers made the point forcefully in the interviews that the media were most successful in effecting the foreign policy agenda in issues that were neither bilateral nor multilateral, but transnational and global. The global and transnational issues heavily covered by the international media, which have become visible on the agendas of both nation-states and multilateral organizations, include:

- global warming
- endangered species
- toxic waste exports
- human rights
- proliferation of chemical and biological weapons
- ozone damage to the atmosphere
- the spread of AIDS
- international refugees
- international drug cartels.

All of these issues are now politically salient in the developed nations, and most nations have responded to at least one of them. These issues are the product of interdependence, technological change, and other forces in world society; none are the *product* of the media. They would merit government attention without media coverage. What the media have done is invested them with an urgency and a reality such that the nonstate organizations advancing them have gained active roles in the international system. This has transformed the international system from one almost exclusively dominated by nation-states whose political intercourse centered on bargaining bilaterally and multilaterally for national advantage, to a more diverse system in which nonstate players introduce nonnational issues into the bargaining. The bargaining is still done to gain national advantage, but media's presence, both as an observer and as leverage for nonstate players, broadens the agenda and the decision values beyond strictly national advantage.

Media As a Transforming Force in U.S. Foreign Policy

Policy makers strongly agreed that one important change wrought by the global mass media is a significant increase in the complexity of the U.S. foreign policy process. While many factors have contributed to this complexity, policy officials saw that the media are a major contributor to complexity in international relations and they amplify all other factors. Insiders attribute this to three effects: media introduce new actors into the policy process, media constantly add new information to the process, and media broaden the range of goals and criteria used for policy making. In effect, policy makers perceive that the mass media have upset historical incremental change characteristics of foreign policy and opened it up to "shocks" in the form of issues and players which appear on the foreign policy agenda with little historical background, requiring new policies as well as changes in existing positions.

The new media-delivered information brought from outside the traditional foreign policy channels was seen to expand the range of intelligence available to policy makers. Media give them a larger, more detailed image of the world that was also closer to real time. However, media were seen to limit policy makers' ability to control information to gain advantage and power. Media-delivered information also serves as a check on the habit of agencies to rely on information selection that contributes to a parochial view of goals, objectives, and constituencies. To some degree, media may mitigate against the natural parochial tendencies of government by increasing awareness of and attention to cross-cutting issues and integrative policy needs.

Media are also seen to broaden the range of goals and criteria used for policy by interconnecting causes and effects that normally operate outside agency purview or perceptions, for instance, military and diplomatic policies in Central America may create refugees in Texas and California; trade negotiations with Japan may create jobs in Georgia and destroy them in Michigan. These effects of interdependence are daily headlines and nightly new packages, putting the issues on agency agendas whether or not they fall within normal agency policy areas.[46] Criteria for policy selection and evaluation have and will continue to become broader as the mass media make the connections between global issues and security, and bi- and multilateral policy responses and domestic impacts.[47] The bottom line of this expansion of policy criteria and added constituencies for foreign policy makers is a need for more staff, more review, and more tools to select from to operate in a more complex world.

In addition to increasing the overall complexity of policy making, policy officials perceive that the mass media have introduced five specific, identifiable transformations into the policy-making process, each with sharply discernable impacts on policy outputs. These are:

1. Globalization of the U.S. foreign policy agenda
2. Introduction of new players to the policy process who accelerate the domestication of foreign policy
3. Accelerated pace of foreign policy (fast-forward effect)
4. Use of media as a significant foreign policy output
5. Reduced central control over diplomacy.

Globalizing influence on the U.S. foreign policy agenda. As media have expanded globally, they have influenced the international system to include nonstate actors and to consider global issues. This has in turn influenced an expansion of the U.S. foreign policy agenda. The interviews with policy makers revealed that the list of issues meriting senior-level attention now routinely includes most of the global issues listed above. A key element in the salience of these issues is the intensity, duration, and type of media coverage they can garner. Those that are able to acquire coverage in prestige media or widespread and lasting television coverage are defined as politically important and receive attention.

This transformation is an expansion of the foreign policy agenda, not a change in its issue content. The media have little ability to force policy reviews or changes in established policies. The accomplishment of the media is seen to have been the expansion of the foreign policy agenda to bring global issues into the decision process and elevate them to the highest levels of decision making. Thus, media-influenced foreign policy contains more elements, is more complex, and has a more global outlook than it would without media, but it still focuses day-to-day on traditional bilateral problems and the advancement of national interest.

Media have added new players to U.S. foreign policy politics. The media have provided visibility and entry to new players in U.S. foreign policy politics, just as they have in the international system. Organizations, such as the British-based Amnesty International, terrorist groups, and a variety of nongovernmental narrow interest organizations based in the United States and other countries, are now players in certain specific issue areas in the U.S. foreign policy political process. They lobby the Congress and the White House and attempt to influence the State Department, mount advertising and public relations campaigns aimed at voters, and otherwise use modern methods to achieve foreign policy goals. Their issues are largely global, although in some cases they impinge upon bilateral relations, such as the U.S.–Soviet relationship or U.S.–Central American policies.

Insiders perceive that the strength of these groups comes from their ability to publicize their issues widely through the mass media, and to use the media to develop the resources necessary to operate multi-laterally.[48] The media coverage gives these issues salience and occasionally becomes a channel for political influence. Insiders also see that domestic groups are able to use the media to provide a check on official government information and to generate political input from constituencies. While these organizations are occasionally effective through political means, insiders perceive that the existence of their issues on the foreign policy agenda was due to largely to the media.

The entry of domestic interest groups into the foreign policy process is a relatively new phenomenon in U.S. policy making, where "politics stopped at the water's edge." While there have always been a few national organizations that sought to influence U.S. actions abroad, the past 20 years has seen a growth and a legitimation of domestic interest groups in the foreign policy process that is new in our history. Their existence and the influence they have developed is seen in large measure by policy officials to result from their ability to generate mass media coverage.

Organizations such as the Committee in Solidarity with the People of El Salvador, WorldWatch, Asia Watch, Common Cause, the American Enterprise Institute, the Fund for the Republic, the CATO Institute, Greenpeace, and others now routinely use the mass media in attempts to influence the American foreign policy agenda. While the political effect is only rarely visible, policy officials perceive that these organizations are effective in placing *global* issues on the U.S. foreign policy agenda and maintaining their salience. Domestic interest groups force consideration of the domestic impacts and global side-effects of traditional policies. Examples include union involvement in trade issues, environmental involvement in drug eradication plans, and humanitarian organizations involvement with Central American policy.

Environmental organizations, for example, have been so effective in raising the issue of the Brazilian rainforest that the Brazilian government has complained of an insult to its sovereignty.[49]

The ability of organizations such as the Conservation Foundation, Nature Conservancy, and the International Union for the Protection of the Environment to work with the U.S. government, international banks, and Latin American heads of state in debt-for-nature swaps is due in large part to the visibility given the rainforest issue by the media in the U.S. and worldwide.

The new players in the U.S. policy process are limited in their influence and in the issue-aras they effect. The influence they have developed through the media usually results in agenda setting rather than immediate policy change. Some of the policy officials interviewed noted that many of the issues they are concerned with have been under study in the government before they were publicized in the media. They see that the contributions of the media and the domestic political organizations are the creation of a political climate in which advocates inside the policy process can place those issues on the active agenda.

Media have accelerated the pace of foreign policy. Policy officials strongly agree that the media have significantly increased the pace of the policy process, although many note that other factors also contribute to the speed up of decisions. This "fast-forward effect" has mixed ramifications. The fast-forward effect can prevent problems from being ignored while they worsen, and force politically unpopular problems to be confronted, or at least talked about. But the increased speed of information delivery and the pressure of quicker decisions often results in reduced long-term thinking and in policy decisions reached without adequate research and consideration of other options. This is not universal; policy decisions made at leisure are not necessarily more productive than those made under pressure. As William Quandt pointed out, "You don't always make better decisions because you have more time."[50]

Many of those interviewed offered the opinion that good or bad, the fast-forward pace is the reality today within which foreign policy must be made and implemented. Actions and decisions are adjusted to the pace of events. The fast-forward effect is put to use to gain advantage when possible. Staff and resources have grown in response to acceleration of policy to provide the White House and the State Department more capability to function faster and to deal with incoming and outgoing media messages that drive policy deadlines.

Use of the media has become a foreign policy output. Media are seen by policy makers as powerful and pervasive enough to be used effectively by government to shape opinion and stimulate action in specific domestic and international audiences and constituencies. Government has added this capability to its repertoire, making media output the second most important category of output ("action-output" being the first).

Government has built an enhanced capability to use the mass media in the past decade under the Reagan Administration. Communication staffs, polling operations, and public relations consultants are now standard fixtures in the White House and other agencies. USIA has been strengthened and acquired some of the new technologies of global mass communications, such as satellite conferencing. The techniques of marketing have also entered the policy process especially in the White House, from audience surveys and media planning to video press releases and narrow-casting on cable television.

The Communication staff under Dennis Harter in the State Department has also strengthened its capabilities beyond that of just serving the Washington press corps. Harter's staff produce interviews, press guidances, columns, features, op-ed pieces, backgrounders, tours, and the other outputs to influence opinion beyond the beltway. Part of this has been in response to the increase in the number of media outlets and the greater education and experience of the reporters. More reporters from more news media are demanding better and faster information on international affairs.

Additionally, the ideological thrust of the Reagan administration, especially in Central America, led the foreign policy officials to use the media often to go over the heads of Congress and the career Foreign Service Officers to gain public opinion for initiatives that were not necessarily popular in Washington. This in turn required more media capability and sophistication in the foreign policy apparatus, much of which remained after Reagan left the White House.

Global media has reduced central control in diplomacy. Graham Allison characterized foreign policy bureaucratic routines as operating with central control and coordination.[51] However, mass media may reduce central command and control over policy in some circumstances involving embassy staff. The immediate delivery of issue-sensitive information to embassies and consulates and to the people and the leadership of host nations poses an interesting problem for the consular staff. They must decide whether to withhold response to media inquiries locally before getting guidance from Washington, and be called indecisive, or to respond without knowing what the policy response is being developed in their capital (which received the same news but may move slower because of a larger bureaucracy), and risk embarrassing their government.

THE INSIDER MODEL OF MASS MEDIA
AND FOREIGN POLICY

It is clear from the study data and from policy outputs that foreign policy officials operate inside the system with a model of media roles in policy that is much more active and complex than the models described by Cohen and Allison. How does this "Insider" model compare with existing models of the foreign process process? To answer these questions, I used the study findings to modify Allison's classic three-dimensional model of foreign policy making to bring a concrete shape to the insider's implicit model of media and foreign policy making.

Allison's Models of the Foreign Policy Process

Many existing models of the foreign policy process assume and predict the behavior of nation-states in terms of rational actions taken in what governments perceive to be the best-interests of the state. National governments appear in these models as monolithic actors interrelating with one other almost as individuals interrelate in society. They determine what is to their advantage under the existing rules of competition and act on those decisions. Graham Allison in his classic study of the U.S. foreign policy process, *Essence of Decision*, calls this explanation of foreign policy making the Rational Actor Model.[52] This model assumes that governments are black boxes whose policy outputs are the products of weighing and balancing alternatives and choosing those which advance the perceived interest of the nation in the most efficient and effective manner. Inside these black boxes are the gears and levers of analysis and decision, plus a number of built-in determinants like Stanley Hoffmann's "deep choices" of national character, ideology, the existing international system, history, and so on.[53] Authors such as Hoffmann, Schelling,[54] Morgenthau[55] and others have explained the actions of nations as just that—actions of unitary nation-states that presuppose purpose, intention, and reasonable choice. Although Allison and others have expanded this model, even today most popular and much professional analysis of international relations rely on it.

Allison develops two alternative models of nation-state behavior, Models II and III. Model II is based on organization theory and economics, and Model III is based on bureaucratic politics. These two models, the *Organizational Process Paradigm* and the *Governmental Politics Paradigm*, depict nations' behaviors in international relations by examining the internal dynamics of their governments, that is, by looking into the black boxes.

In these models, Allison opens the black boxes and examines not only the size and structure of the gears and levers, but also the competition among those vying for their control. He explains the actions of nations in the international realm in terms of the internal capabilities, processes, and limitations of the organizations that make up nation-states; and of the outcomes of the political bargaining among the different subunits of the national government.

But Allison's prototype models and virtually all subsequent models of the U.S. foreign policy process ignore the media, or at best, relegate them to a tertiary position as an observer with diffused input through "opinion leaders." The role of the media as an information source, a tool to influence national behavior, a venue for new players and new issues, or a door for domestic influence to enter the foreign policy areas are generally overlooked. As a result, these models cannot completely account for the emergence of global issues transcending national borders and national interests, the variety of new players who wield influence without military or economic power, and other aspects of modern international relations. But policy makers—"Insiders"—have a definite model of the media's relationship to the foreign policy process. They see the media as dual actors, effecting the policy both *inside* as a player or a tool of the inside players, and *outside* as part of the environment shaping policy, both overtly and covertly.

Insider Model of Media-Influenced Foreign Policy

The Insiders Model echoes Allison's two alternative models. It analyzes media's role as part of the nation's foreign policy levers and gears, and the media themselves as a set of active influences on the outcome of internal political struggles inside the U.S. government. In more graphic terms, as in Roger Hilsman's description of the policy-making process as represented by concentric circles,[56] the Insider's Model of Media-Influenced Foreign Policy assumes that the media simultaneously occupy locations in all of the policy process's inner circles and operate outside of the circles to influence actors on the inside. It assumes that in the continuing process of conflict and consensus building, the media are used by other parties to bargain for advantage and that the media actively join in the competition for their own interests.

Inside-Outside Players

Insiders perceive that media compromise a new category of player in international relations and foreign policy, one that functions both inside and outside the foreign policy process. The media operate inside by informing other players' decisions and lending themselves to other players' uses. They operate outside by acting according to their own incentives, standards, and self-interets, lending themselves to foreign governments who try to influence U.S. policy.[57]

This contrasts with Allison's models of the foreign policy process which describe it as one in which multiple actors function in a "constellation of loosely allied organizations on top of which governmental leaders sit."[58] His model (and most others) assumes that the foreign policy process operates inside of the policy environment and everything else is outside. The "inside" comprises the elements of the U.S. foreign policy community, such as the White House, NSC, Department of State, and other agencies. The "outside" is populated by actors who interrelate with an act upon U.S. policy, such as the media, think tanks, lobbies, and the public.

Insiders Model: Media Influence Inside the Policy Process

In the Insiders' Model, the mass media operate "inside" the policy process by influencing the players and governmental agency operations through five principal mechanisms:

- informing the policy process
- defining acceptable performance
- effecting policy makers' attention to goals
- constraining the use of other outputs
- setting the pace of policy making.

These "inside" mechanisms do not operate at all times and in all cases. They vary with issues, personalities, other elements of the policy environment, the nature of the Administration, and the timing of the issue at hand.

Mass media inform policy choices. The mass media inform the decision-making process at every stage of the issue cycle, and especially in those cases involving global issues or immediate crisis. Foreign policy officials perceived that the mass media provide useful information at the earliest stage of policy development, with most attention paid at the "Adoption of Policy" stage and the least at the "Solution Formation" stage. Policy officials also perceive that this informtion not only effects their cognitive perceptions, but is often translated into U.S. foreign policy outputs.

Insiders' perception of mass media's policy-informing role was demonstrated dramatically in the TWA hijacking cases, wherein the media were the primary sources of operating information. President Carter's use of television to communicate with Bani Sadir also typified this role of the media.[59]

Mass media can define acceptable policy performance. Allison proposes that the goals of each organization in the foreign policy process are not formally stated, but rather emerge as a "set of constraints defining acceptable performance," including the health of the organization itself.[60] According to Allison, this set of constraints derives from statute law, the expectations of other organizations and constituencies, and bargaining inside the organization. The constraints are not permanent, but rather quasiresolutions of competing forces within a bureaucratic matrix, resulting in imperatives to avoid roughly specified discomforts and disasters, such as budget cuts, policy rebuffs, or slot reductions.

Insiders see media involvement in this process primarily through the Evaluation stage of the issue cycle, which is the second most heavily media-informed issue stage. The media exert a significant influence on policy officials' perception of the effectiveness of their policies, although after the fact. However insiders perceive that media input in the Evaluation stage of an issue can effect policy makers' goals and standards. There are two possibilities for explaining this.

1. Issues are rarely completed neatly. Issues last months, years, even decades or centuries (i.e., conflict in the Middle East over the territories). The Evaluation Stage of one aspect of an issue often immediately precedes the Problem Identification Stage of the next aspect. Or, the supposed solution does not work and the decision makers return to "square one" with evalutions from the media and others in hand to set new goals and standards and look for new solutions.

2. The Evalution stage of the issue cycle is the final step. In those cases where an issue is resolved, the information carried by the media on what worked, what did not, and why will enter into the cognitive map of the policy officials for use in setting standards and goals in later issues.

Mass media are only one of the sources used by those working in the policy process to determine standards of acceptable policy performance. Its influence will vary from issue to issue and person to person. Following Allison, however, it is reasonable to predict that in many cases, the policy chosen will be the one that provides maximum avoidance of media criticism—a sort of self-censorship by policy officials caused by the media. A number of those interviewed, such as Hodding Carter, indicated that this did indeed happen.

Mass media effect agency attention to goals. Allison describes the goal-seeking behavior of foreign policy agencies as sequential, relying on standard operating procedures, and stressing uncertainty avoidance. Policy makers perceive that media disrupt this process through their agenda-setting function. Media coverage puts regions, countries, organizations, issues, and situations on the agenda of policy officials out of sequence. Insiders reported that this media impact is eventually absorbed or compensated for by government through press relations routines: standard operating procedures, such as press guidances and daily briefings for dealing with press inquires.

What is not compensated for is the degree of uncertainty the media's agenda-setting function can add to decision-making processes. Insiders noted that under certain conditions, media can change the priorities of foreign policy agencies. They reported—or more often, complained— that media are capable of influencing the diversion of resources from designated targets to new ones the agency has previously determined it does not want to address or to new issue-areas that are beyond its usual expertise.

As a practial matter, the agenda-setting function is only rarely seriously disruptive of foreign policy making, a point made by most of those interviewed. In occasional cases the media may have lasting impact by introducing a new player or an issue which remains on the agenda or redirects resources to a new crisis. Insiders perceive that global environmental and human rights issues are among those that have been added to foreign policy agendas partially as a result of media coverage.[61] However, issues that are added and which remain are then "handled" by the agency through new standard routines in the decision-making process. In other words, even in the case of long-lasting issues added by the media, Insiders see that the foreign policy process tries to return to an "inside" equilibrium

Media constrain government's options. President Nixon once complained that the TV coverage of the war in Vietnam was "probably the single most significant factor limiting our options there."[62] This typifies Insider perception of media operating within Allison's policy-making constellation to constrain the range of options that can be considered for policy.[63]

The *Intifada* provides an example of media constraining the policy options of another government, Israel. The videotape from the *Intifada* constrained Israel's response to the Palestinians and added control of Israel's domestic riot tactics to the U.S. agenda. In turn, this impinged somewhat on other issues between the two countries. Israel's initial response was to change the policy, that is, drop the beating orders. Later the Israeli government shifted policies to try to remove the media constraint by eventually blacking out news from demonstration areas.

In the TWA hijacking, Nabih Berri constrained the U.S. use of force to rescue the hostages by putting (or allowing) the pilot on television to warn against any attempt to use force. If the warning had come privately from Berri, unknown to the public and other governments, it would not have had the same impact and might not have deterred that option. But after a public warning with global media exposure, any attempt to use force that was not 100 percent perfect, that is, no American lives lost and all hostages returned, would be politically devastating for the U.S.

Media set the pace of policy (fast-forward effect). Timing can sometimes be as important as substance in foreign policy. A leader who does not act swiftly is criticized for indecision or worse; one who acts too quickly may be criticized for recklessness. But the mass media deliver new issues daily to the doorsteps of the White House, the State Department, and the embassies, all requiring action. They also deliver the same information to U.S. policy makers' counterparts in other countries and in Washington, to constituencies in other agencies, and to interest groups, and to the public, as well as to enemies and allies. As former Vietnamese Ambassador to France Tran Van Dinh noted, the speed of diplomatic messages has in this century gone from weeks to minutes.[64] Insiders perceive that this puts pressure on government to *do something* because the problem has become public information and constituencies want to know what is being done, in effect, setting deadlines that the policy process would not have set.

This pressure to make policy and respond in hours or minutes, or at least by the deadline of the next television newscast, can be very powerful at some levels of policy making and in some issues, although Insiders perceive that the power it exerts is related more to the Administration's skill in media-handling than in any inherent media power.

In effect, they see the media getting "inside" the policy-making process and reducing time for thought, planning, and strategy. By doing so, they eliminate options that might have been perceived and examined had there been more time. This media-accelerated policy pace is seen by Insiders as a two-edged sword when combined with media as output. Policy response through the media can be used to move issues forward which other governments have been ignoring by forcing them to respond quickly. Adversaries can be denied time for planning and full option review. Israel found itself in this position during the *Intifada*—it had to devise riot tactics and army control policy rapidly in response to media images of mistreatment of Palestinians.

Insider Model: Media As Governmental Output

The basic unit of Allison's analysis is government-action-as-output. He characterizes as government's organizational output actual occurrences—the actions government is able to take to effect the external policy environment. The range of possible outputs is limited to the government's physical capabilities and the organizational routines for employing them. Additionally, Allison notes that these outputs structure the situation within the narrow constraints which leaders must use to make their decisions: "Outputs raise the problem, provide the information, and determine the initial steps that color the face of the issue that is turned to the leaders."[65]

Insiders perceive government use of mass media's coverage as an output in itself, regardless of actual occurrences. Media techniques[66] are seen as an important part of the repertoire of the foreign policy process and their use constitutes a category of foreign policy output in themselves to effect the external policy environment. This media repertoire includes:

• communication plans
• press conferences
• op-ed page pieces
• leaks

- official reports released to the media
- events staged for the media
- media tours
- arrangements for traveling media
- features
- background meetings
- video press releases
- print press releases
- meetings with columnists
- meetings with editorial boards
- meeting with reporters
- press guidances
- press briefing books
- polls.

As with other policy outputs, media coverage may not necessarily be the result of a policy maker's intention; it can be and often is the sum of behavior of separate individuals with different intentions. Media output by government requires the cooperation of a separate set of independent and powerful entities—newspapers, networks, wire services, and so on. Media are not a neutral communication channel; it inserts its own biases into the final output, something Insiders are well aware of.

At the simplest level, Insiders use media as a signaling system employed to create perceptions in other nations or to transmit specific messages. President Carter's use of television news to communicate with the Prime Minister of Iran is an example of this level of media as output. At a more sophisticated level, Sadat's interview with Barbara Walters, his televised "country drive" and televised National Press Club speech, are also examples of the use of media output as governmental action. Each of these was a deliberate use of the mass media to *influence policy*, and not necessarily to transmit information or to publicize an actual occurrence. The reach and power of television was harnessed to influence decisions of another government. The Egyptian government took no *action*, but used the media as an output to help create a political environment that would allow a change in U.S. policy regarding selling military aircraft to Egypt.[67]

Insiders perceive mass media as an effective policy output. Eighty-six percent of the survey respondents sought to influence the media coverage of their agencies, and 72 percent reported that they or their staff were responsible for at least 10 percent of the actual coverage. They were generating outputs.

Insiders also see that the mass media have extended the range of output options available to foreign policy officials. In addition to moving troops, providing aid, initiating talks, and other actions, governments now have a wide range of techniques they can employ to generate stories or project images intended to influence policies and actions in other governments, as both President Reagan and Secretary Gorbachev have done very skillfully. A government foreign policy media campaign is designed and run like a battle, with as little left to chance as possible.[68]

To the degree that Presidents and other foreign policy leaders personally attend to the media, Presidential decision options are seen by Insiders to be expanded rather than constrained. In his interview, Jimmy Carter described his morning routine of reading the news summary and firing off notes to the Secretaries of State or Defense or the National Security Advisor or the Director of the CIA asking for information or action on items he saw in print or television stories. David Stockman described the evening news ritual in the Oval Office with President Reagan and his top aides watching all three news networks (now four) to see how their actions played that day and what would be politically "hot" the following morning. The next step in both the Carter and Reagan White House was discussing a media response to advance a specific policy.

The extent to which U.S. government will go to use mass media as action-replacing or action-paralleling output is evidenced by the tremendous growth in press offices and communications staff in both the White House and the State Department since the Vietnam War, including the increase in USIA's budget during the Reagan years to fund such innovations as Radio and TV Marti and WorldNet.[69]

Insider Model: Media Output as an Insider's Political Tool

In Model III, Allison depicts the foreign policy outputs of the U.S. government as the "result of bargaining along regularized channels among individual members of the government" who have separate and unequal powers and separable objectives in distinguishable subgames.[70] He says it is important to recognize that governmental actions on some issues are really an agglomeration of relatively independent decisions and actions by individuals and groups of players in a broader game.

In this paradigm, "governmental actions" are collages of independent decisions; "formal governmental actions" are a combination of the preferences and relative influence of central players; "formal decisions and actions" represent a combination of preferences and the relative influence of a special subset of players.[71] The players in Allison's depiction of this game are:

- *Chiefs*: Generally the President, Secretaries of State, Defense and Treasury, the Director of the CIA, the Joint Chiefs of Staff, and the National Security Advisor.[72]

- *Staffers*: the immediate staff of each Chief
- *Implementers*:[73] the political appointees and permanent technical staff inside each department.

He assigns media to the generalized category of "Ad Hoc Player," along with Congress, lobbies, and the people in general, noting that organizations or groups can be treated as unitary players as long as the dynamics of their outputs are kept in mind. He notes that each player has a different vantage point, set of misperceptions and expectations, goals, and styles. Politically, the actions of nations effect each other so that they result in advantages or disadvantages to the players in each nation. This impels the players inside of each nation who wish to achieve an international objective to attempt to obtain outcomes from their own intranational set of bargainings that add to the advantage of countries that advocate an analogous principle. This builds allies and creates positive political climates within which to move policy.[74] Thus foreign policy is a multilevel process both within and among nations. Media are involved in each of these levels, both within intranational policy-making processes and in international relations.

In the intranational process, media have evolved from *ad hoc* players to "inside-outside" political players which are also used as tools by the policy process's players—an "inside" role. The media also operate "outside" in the policy environment as independent influences and actors effecting government outputs. Additionally, media are used by players at all levels as an information input to provide operational information sources upon which tactical decisions can be made in both the international and the intranational bargaining processes.

Chiefs' Use of Media as Output

The priority of the "Chiefs"—the President and others who select and order the implementation of action-outputs—is to preserve their opinions until time clarifies uncertainties, and then select an option and build a consensus behind it. As Allison notes, these two priorities often conflict: Holding open options and building consensus requires fuzziness so that different people can interpret the Chiefs' statements in their own interest; action requires clarity to prevent the inertia and centrifugal forces of the policy machinery from diluting implementation. Chiefs continually use media to meet these objectives through three key mechanisms:[75]

- to keep options open while establishing agenda priorities in government

- to create domestic support for issues and policy priorities
- to signal other nations about the policy in order to build international support.

To keep options open while establishing agenda priorities in government. Media as output enables a Chief to present the image of activity while not choosing action. In this use of the media, the messages are aimed both domestically and abroad. The major thrust is domestic, however. Press conferences, press guidances, travel, televised speeches, and interviews all enable the Chiefs to outline the agenda priorities of the Administration while postponing action choices. This builds public and political confidence while buying time.

In aiming the message abroad, administrations can use the media to define the agenda they wish to focus on, while keeping options open for action on each issue. Prenegotiations take place in the media without commitments being made by any of the parties. The media facilitate the preliminaries necessary to specific bargaining situations to take place in a relatively risk-free manner. Without the signaling role of the media, much more difficult and potentially contentious face-to-face meetings would be required to settle agenda questions, with the risk of prematurely limiting options.

Secondly, the media enable the Administration or parts of the Administration to test options while (hopefully) avoiding political damage—the classic trial balloon. Again, this use of the media as output is aimed both domestically and internationally. Action options tested in the media can be disavowed, or their origins separated from the Chief. The media provide a tool for testing options and for evaluation of the test through reactions of other elements of the government, other countries, and various members of the media whose knowledge and opinions are respected in foreign policy circles.

Media enable the Administration to gauge the political salience of issues and action-output options with reduced political risk. The level of media play in the elite press, general print media and wire services, network and cable news, Sunday morning programming, or news specials all indicate different degrees of salience of an issue among various constituencies. By exposing a trial balloon in a particular medium, such as Ronald Reagan's weekend radio broadcast, or an interview with a particular reporter or domestic or overseas outlet, an Administration can gauge the response in certain audiences and political circles. The degree to which the item moves beyond the initial outlets and is covered in other media also indicate the political salience or liabilities of a position. The addition of polling to this technique makes it even more powerful.

This puts the media in the inside role not only of output, but also in the outside role of "salience gatekeeper." The aggregate decisions of a few network and wire service news editors can determine the salience of an action item, either killing it or giving it some of the political space necessary for implementation.

To create domestic support for issues and policy priorities. There exists among policy officials a widely held perception that the media can and do stimulate and help maintain domestic interest groups on foreign policy questions. Presidents and other Chiefs in the past two decades have made liberal use of the media to go directly to the people with appeals for support on foreign policy questions, from Kennedy during the Cuban Missile Crises to Ronald Reagan's television and radio addresses seeking support for his Contra policies.

As international mass media coverage has increased, the linkages of economic and political interdependence have increased the international impact of national economic, diplomatic, and military policies. As a result, both the general and the interested publics have paid closer attention to foreign policy questions, and have stepped up involvement in foreign policy issues. As Congress has asserted its role in foreign policy development, the importance of domestic support and lobbying for foreign policy issues has increased. Media provide an excellent tool for Chiefs to assert control by painting policy agendas in broad brush, stimulating popular support for the general policy thrusts (useful for pressuring Congress), while keeping the details vague to maintain flexibility in operations and tactics.

A second aspect of Chiefs' use of media to build domestic support for foreign policy initiatives is signaling the foreign policy establishment— the agencies, interest groups, think tanks, and others who influence the policy process. This signaling, in the form of interviews, press conferences, and speeches that are excerpted or quoted in the media, enables a Chief to establish the general agenda needed inside the Beltway to begin the process of creating a politically hospitable climate, even if the implementation details are unresolved.[76]

This is generally done through the prestige media—the *Washington Post* and the *New York Times*—although the interview research found significant use of "Sunday morning intellectual ghetto" television programming for this purpose. Programs such as "Meet the Press" or "Face the Nation" were frequently mentioned as important communication devices for The White House seeking to build internal support for policies. The White House Communications Office includes the Sunday morning shows in any "full court press" to generate governmental support for a policy, along with weekday morning news programs, *Nightline*, and CNN's *Crossfire*.

To signal other nations on U.S. policy and build support internationally. Policy makers strongly agree that the mass media are used by Chiefs to influence other nations' policies and other nations' peoples.

The use of the media to influence other nations' policies was seen to be strongest in the White House and least strong in the State Department, although the perception among policy makers was significant across the board. Many of those interviewed said that they used the mass media to send messages to other nations to establish political priorities or lay groundwork for more formal conversations.

Staffers Use of Media as Output. Allison notes that the priority of the staffs of the Chiefs is to get others committed to the coalitions they must build to support policy decisions.[77] Most day-to-day oversight, policing, and pushing is not done by the Chiefs, but by their staffs. It is their responsibility to create the necessary critical mass of support in the bureaucracies, the Congress, other nations and international organizations to implement a policy. To accomplish this, they utilize the media in two principal ways: to build support for their policies and undercut competing initiatives, and to create the political climate needed for success.

Staffers utilize the media to deliver specific messages to specific audiences as a part of a strategy to create a positive political environment and build support—a kind of political niche marketing. Staff outputs, like those of Chiefs, are part of a directed communication strategy drawn up utilizing specific media outlets to achieve specific goals with specific audiences. The strategies combine both domestic and international mass media, and use wire services and television to transmit messages around the world with the highest efficiency and speed.

These strategies include interviews with the prestige newspapers, release of information and reports to mass media, op ed page pieces in various newspapers, staff interviews in the foreign media. Staff also arrange for interviews with sympathetic citizens, members of Congress, and opinion leaders from education, business, and even the entertainment industry are part of the process at some time or another.

The goal of these media-use-as-output strategies is same as that of the advertising and public relations industry: to achieve maximum "reach" and "frequency" among targeted audiences, and to get the "bandwagon effect" started. Media outlets are chosen to provide targeted "reach," that is, a large number of people in each audience who will receive the message. "Reach" is used primarily for support-building. By reaching the right audiences, whether they are "inside the beltway," or in capitals across Europe, or in the Wall Street and Tokyo stock markets, political support can be cultivated through accurate media strategy and outlet selection.

Multiple messages are sent to increase "frequency," a technique used to build a positive political atmosphere. If the issue is chemical weapons and the White House wants to create the environment necessary for gaining support in the Pentagon and industry as well as in Europe for controls over its export to developing countries, daily stories are generated by staffers on chemical weapons. These are placed in prestige papers and targeted magazines to reach interested and influential audiences. Events, press conferences, interviews, and so on, are set up on television to reach a wide audience to generate the "bandwagon effect"—the point at which all media must "jump on" by running the story. At that point a critical mass of government support is likely to form because the frequency of the issue makes it important and one to be on the "right side" of.

Media stories then take on a life of their own in the mass and the targeted media and will generate general public and interested public support for positive policy initiatives. This makes the "timing" right for the White House and wrong for opposition.

A media strategy can also involve no mass media outputs, a policy Jody Powell followed during the Camp David negotiations. By keeping the media away from Begin and Sadat, Powell was able to prevent them from using the media to build and rally support in the U.S., as well as from posturing instead of bargaining. In this way, Powell was able to keep the spotlight focused where he wanted it, on the President and the President's program.

However, media campaigns as outputs can backfire by exposing the Chiefs and staffers to questions they are not prepared for and cannot answer adequately. A mistake or an "I don't know" can serve as the basis for a opposition media campaign against the policy and the staff involved with it.

Implementers' Media Outputs

According to Allison, Implementers' top priority is to give Chiefs confidence to do what must be done. Implementers are often advocates who have solutions in search of problems. Since chiefs often have problems in search of solutions, successfully implemented policies are usually the result of a lucky encounter of Implementers and Chiefs. Chiefs are often confronted with a deadline for a solution to a problem, so they focus on the problem and look for a solution. Implementers often are committed to a solution developed for an earlier problem, or one which they see as answering a number of policy and personal needs simultaneously, so they attempt to find a problem important to a Chief that their solution can be fitted to.[78] Implementers use the mass media to accomplish this in three primary ways:

1. To get Chief's attention and add to or change Chief's agendas
2. To alter the political environment and build confidence for solutions
3. To stake out positions for solutions.

All of these are directed almost exclusively at the domestic media and intragovernmental politics. The techniques are similar to those of Staffers, although rarely if ever, as well strategized. More often, the prestige print media are used as an outlet for a report or a leak, or a special interest or research group is the channel for providing information to the press to make the Chief aware of a solution.

These differentiations in roles are not always clear-cut; uses of media by Chiefs and staffers often overlap. The media strategies are also usually short term and highly reactive. While an issue or action may be selected and a media strategy drawn up to advance it, reaction from opponents and other interests, or from the media itself, often dictate that the strategies change. Finally, use of the media as output carries inherent risks in that, unlike governmental action-outputs, the government is not in control of the final result (although some would argue that the White House Press Corps gave a good imitation of a captive body under President Reagan).[79]

Outside Player: Media As Part of the Policy Environment

Insiders perceive that media are continually influencing foreign policy decisions, both by what they report and how they report it, and through reporter–policy maker contacts. This influence is particularly outside because the motivations and operations of the media in this influence are detached from the policies at hand, and derive more from the nature and motivations of the various members of the media.[80]

The Insiders Model includes media's inadvertent coloring the "face" of issues because of their peculiar requirements of space, continuity, drama, or editorial bias. Allison proposed that each player in foreign policy politics sees a different face on each issue, that is, how an issue effects their individual interests. For example, the *Intifada* is seen as a threat to Israeli security by the Implementers at the bureau level of the State Department, a potential opportunity to break diplomatic logjams by the Secretary of State, and an example of Israeli transgressions by members of Congress impatient with Israel.

Insiders see that media can frame these issues so that the face of the issue seen by one or another player becomes the face of the issue that the public perceives, and therefore, has to be dealt with by all the government players. In the case of the *Intifada*, the media largely presented the face of Israeli force in controlling the demonstrators. This presented a problem for the White House and the State Department and offered opportunities to Israeli critics in Congress and within the Administration.

This issue-face was presented not because the media is anti-Israeli or pro-Palestinian, but because it met the requirements of good television—conflict, exciting visuals, underdog success stories, and continuing material. Some would argue that it also tapped a latent frustration with Israeli influence over American Middle East policy and therefore attracted wide audiences, but the appeal would have been there regardless.

The impacts of these dynamics range from portrayals of the world as more violent and dangerous than it may actually be, to distorted American perceptions of certain religious groups, races, regions, and countries.[81] In policy terms, the mass media create a policy environment which may not match that familiar to policy officials but which stimulates domestic and international forces for policy changes Insiders perceive the media operating as a powerful "outside" force in foreign policy through three principal mechanisms: Mass media use by terrorists to directly effect policy outputs; foreign government use of media to influence U.S. foreign policy; outside agenda setting

Outside Player: Media Use by Terrorists to Effect Policy Outputs

The most striking example of outside use of the media to influence U.S. foreign policy cited by Insiders is that of terrorism. Modern terrorist organizations have become highly skilled and effective in the use of the media to attempt to influence U.S. policy. In some cases the media themselves have become actors in terrorist incidents, as they did in the interviews with the pilot and the hostages from the hijacked TWA Flight 847.

The ability of terrorists to use the media to force changes in U.S. foreign policy is a function seen by Insiders primarily of the vulnerability of the administration to terrorist media tactics and secondarily to the skill of terrorist's use of media. Amateurish media outputs by terrorists, such as occurred in the *Achilie Lauro* case, have little chance of effecting policy. Skillful media use as in the TWA case, while not the sole or the most important determinant of lasting policy change, has a higher likelihood in minds of Insiders.

Factors determining the degree to which this outside media influence will effect policy outputs are seen by Insiders to include the domestic political situation in the U.S., the skill of the U.S. Administration in using the media, the emergence of involved domestic lobbies and their use of the media, and ongoing relations and discussions with other governments who may be effected by the incident. The nature of the incident will also impinge upon the utility of the media in the Insider Model. A hostage situation will remain in the news longer than a single bombing, especially if the hostages are American and are allowed access to the press. Accessibility of the site to cameras is also important; a lack of film or tape will downgrade television coverage and the overall impact of the incident.

The most important determining factor in the Insider Model appears to be the strategy selected by the acting administration to manage the situation in the face of terrorist media outputs. Jimmy Carter's Rose Garden strategy, for instance, failed in the case of the Iranian embassy hostages, but Reagan's more detached strategy with Nabih Berri and the TWA hostages was successful in political terms.

Outside Player: Foreign Use of Media to Influence U.S. policy

As dramatic as the terrorist is on television, a more pervasive outside media role in the Insider Model is that of a conduit for influence by other governments. Just as the media operate inside the U.S. policy establishment to provide an additional range of outputs, Insiders are aware that other governments use the U.S. and international media as outputs to effect U.S. policy.

The classic example of Sadat's effective use of American television and media has been described earlier. In another case, General Torrijos of Panama used television to demonstrate his support in the face of U.S. pressure against him. Nabih Berri and the terrorists holding the TWA hostages routinely employed the mass media to gain and hold the policy initiative. Berri used interviews with his captives to unlink Administration demands for release of the TWA hostages to the release of other Americans. Berri was also able to use the televised interview with the pilot, who warned against using force to block any White House military moves to free the hostages militarily. The Israeli custom of leaking to the media supposedly confidential diplomatic discussions to undercut policy initiatives is notorious among Insiders.

The impact of this influence is difficult to gauge, but Insiders feel it is significant. Eighty-three percent of those surveyed and 91 percent of those interviewed perceived that foreign governments used the mass media to influence U.S. foreign policy, and at least half of each group perceived that influence to be effective. The anecdotal information gathered in the interviews indicated that U.S. policy officials considered this a significant factor in foreign policy decisions, and an important element in the international policy environment.

Outside Player: Agenda-setting

In the Insider Model of Media Influenced Foreign Policy, mass media's outside influence only rarely changes policy or even initiates a policy review. Its power lies in its ability to direct government's focus to an issue. By doing so it can place an issue on the government's foreign policy agenda by giving it overall political salience as usually defined in the literature of agenda setting. But Insiders qualify the agenda-setting capability of the media in three ways:

- It varies with the nature of the issue; global and multilateral issues being more susceptible to media influence than bilateral or military issues
- It varies with the prevailing political environment; although it can influence or even create that environment
- It derives influence from domestic political forces; media's ability to stimulate support or opposition to a policy initiative.

Insiders see that the ability of the media to effect the foreign policy agenda within these constraints has led to the addition of a number of issues to the U.S. foreign policy agenda that might not have received the attention they merit now, including global environmental problems, famine and starvation, torture and "disappeared" people, and AIDS. Some bilateral issues are seen as subject to media influence, especially those which could involve U.S. troops in battle. The trauma of Vietnam and the images of that war brought by television into American homes may have made it all but impossible for the U.S. to consider the policy option of risking an extended foreign military involvement—an "outside" media influence left over from an earlier decade.[82] The inability of the Reagan Administration to generate a majority of popular support for its military policy regarding Nicaragua and El Salvador was seen by Insiders interviewed as one product of this "leftover media images" influence.

Insiders also see that the media's ability to bring multilateral and global issues onto the agenda is paralleled by the proliferation of and increased attention to multilateral organizations. As a result, multilateral organization leaders from OPEC to NATO to the U.N. now find their way to U.S. TV screens, along with coverage of various U.N. peace-keeping forces and successes. The media creates a positive political environment for the growth in American support and involvement in multilateral organizations. The media expose the historically isolationist U.S. population to these issues and to other countries, leaders, and organizations.

In doing so, the media are only one of many factors. Those interviewed often ventured that the media reinforce other ongoing trends, such as faster and cheaper travel, a growth in the number of nations, and increased immigration around the world. Mass media chronicle these trends, making Americans aware of multilateral and global changes and the issues they bring. The media coverage provides existing popular organizations with visibility and political leverage that enable them to press for policies in response—a significant shift from the Cohen study era when media cooperated with government in foreign policy issues and the audience was rarely interested.[83]

A Continuing Evolution

The interdependent mutually exploitive mass mediaforeign policy relationship is a continuing dynamic that does not end with the Insiders' Model. Mass media are constantly undergoing technical, managerial, and political revolutions. And the media are being joined by other communications technologies like direct dial telephone systems, fax machines, and ISDN wiring—all of which will effect the foreign policy outputs of governments, and the relations between nations.

The Insiders Model is also only half of the picture; Cohen interviewed both sources and reporters. The Insiders Model reflects only the world view of the global foreign policy structure and its relationship to mass media. The global media may have a much different view of its relationship with the foreign policy process, and they will behave according to their world view, effecting reality in the process. A complete model of the foreign policy process may also have to include inside-outside roles for domestic and international political organizations, new organizational dynamics that reflect management changes in the foreign policy structure, and new sophistication in other governments and NGO's. Most, if not all of these elements will be dutifully reported by the media with responses from Department of State and White House spokespeople, depending on the communications strategy for that issue.

NOTES

[1] Bernard C. Cohen, *The Press and Foreign Policy* (Princeton, NJ: Princeton University Press, 1963), p. 46. See also Bernard Cohen, "Mass Communication and Foreign Policy," in James Rosenau (ed.), *Domestic Sources of Foreign Policy* (New York: Free Press, 1967) pp. 21, 199–200. For an updated study of this, see Robert Oldendick and Barbara A. Bardes, "Mass Media and Elite Foreign Policy Opinions," *Public Opinion Quarterly* 46 (1982): 368–382.

[2] Cohen, *op.cit.*, p. 259. See also Robert Bledsoe et al., "Foreign Affairs Coverage in Mass and Elite Periodicals," *Journalism Quarterly* 59 (1982): 471–474.

[3] Additionally, by focusing on the small percentage of mass media time and resources that are spent on reporting U.S. foreign policy, analysts overlook the undercutting impact of the other 90 percent of U.S. media output has on the U.S. foreign policy (and domestic policy) establishment. The entertainment output of mass media instills perceptions, values, and expectations in the public

that are often counter to those promulgated by government. Moreover, it contributes to a continuing lack of interest in government, especially in foreign affairs. Despite the vast potential power of government to shape opinions through the mass media, it is remarkable how little it succeeds. A small, but lively industry has sprung up in Hollywood to insert certain "global themes" into entertainment programming, primarily values of environmental protection and world peace, for instance, The American Ocean Campaign devised by "Cheer's" star Ted Danson to insert "protect the international ocean" themes in prime time network dramas.

⁴ Gabriel Almond and G. B. Powell, *Comparative Politics: A Developmental Approach* (Boston: Little, Brown & Co, 1966). This notion was contradicted in later empirical studies which found growing public interest in foreign policy and U.S. involvement in other countries' affairs. See William R. Caspary, "The Mood Theory': A Study of Public Opinion and Foreign Policy," *American Political Science Review* 64 (1970); 536–547, and Bruce Russett and Donald Deluca, "Don't Tread on Me: Public Opinion and Foreign Policy in the Eighties," *Political Science Quarterly* 96 (1981): 381–399. This is despite a reduction in the international print "newshole" from 10 percent to approximaely 2.6 percent in the same period documented by Michael Emery in "An Endangered Species: The International Newshole," *Gannet Center Journal* 3: 4 (Fall 1989): 151–164. Television appears to made up the difference, especially with the addition of the 24-hour news coverage of CNN and headline news.

⁵ For a review and critique of the two-step flow theory, see Robert Savage, "The Diffusion of Information Approach," in *Handbook of Political Communication*, pp. 101–119, and Doris Graber, *Processing the News: How People Tame the Information Tide* (New York: Longman, 1984).

⁶ James Reston, *The Artillery of the Press* (New York: Harper and Row, 1966).

⁷ *Ibid.*, p. 63.

⁸ *Ibid.*, p. 6 and p. 70. See also W. Phillips Davidson, *The News From Abroad and the Foreign Policy Public* FPA Headline Series No. 250. (New York: Foreign Policy Association, 1980).

⁹ Charles W. Bray, "The Media and Foreign Policy," *Foreign Policy* 16(1974): 109–25; William O. Chittick, *State Department, Press, and Pressure Groups: A Role Analysis* (New York: Wiley-Interscience, 1970). This was based on his earlier study, "State Department-Press Antagonism: Opinion Versus Policy-Making Needs?" *Journal of Politics* 31(1969): 756–771. See also "The Press, and Foreign policy," *Foreign Service Journal* (July-August 1982): 22–33ff (several articles). Lee B. Becker,"Foreign Policy and Press Performance," *Journalism Quarterly* 54 (1977): 364–388. Robert M. Batscha, *Foreign Affairs News and the Broadcast Journalist* (New York: Praeger, 1975), pp. 229–231. See also Stuart J. Bullion, "Press Roles in Foreign Policy Reporting," *Gazzette* 32 (1983):179–188.

¹⁰ Charles W. Bray, "The Media and Foreign Policy," *Foreign Policy* 16(1974): 109–25.

¹¹ W. Phillips Davidson, "Diplomatic Reporting: The Rules of the Game," *Journal of Communication* 25 (1975): 138–146. Timothy Schiltz, Lee Sigelman, and Robert Neal, "Perspectives of Managing Editors on Coverage of Foreign Policy News," *Journalism Quarterly* 50 (Winter 1973): 716–21.

[12] Lloyd N. Cutler, "Foreign Policy on Deadline," *Atlantic Community Quarterly* 22 (1984): 223–232. (Reprinted from *Foreign Policy* 56 (Fall 84).

[13] *Ibid.*, p. 224

[14] *Ibid.*, p. 225.

[15] *Ibid.*, p. 224.

[16] *Ibid.*, p. 227.

[17] *TV Guide* (Sept.-Oct. 1981): 58. For another popular view of media influence on foreign policy, see also Karen DeYoung. "Understanding U.S. Foreign Policy: The Role of the Press," *USA Today Magazine* (January 1985): 66–69.

[18] Bernard Cohen, "The Influence of Special Interest Groups and Mass Media in American Security Policy," in C. W. Kegley and E. R. Wittkopf (eds.), *Perspectives on American Foreign Policy* (New York: Martin's Press, 1983). See also Kevin Phillips, "Media Elite's Influence on Foreign Policy," *TV Guide* (August 23, 1975): A3–A11.

[19] James F. Larson, *Global Television and Foreign Policy.* Foreign Policy Headline Service 283 (New York: Foreign Policy Association, Feb. 1988), p. 5.

[20] *Ibid.*, p. 6. Others date the beginning of the media foreign policy relationship from the Vietnam War in the late 60s, or from the arrival of the half-hour news broadcast in the early 60s. Interestingly, after documenting the penetration of television into the policy process, Larson rejected Chittick's empirical evidence of press policy antagonism and argued that they worked so closely together they were virtually indistinguishable.

[21] Numerous authors have explored this topic. See Erik Barnouw, *Tube of Plenty: The Evolution of Television* (London: Oxford University Press, 1975); Steven Hess, *The Washington Reporters* (Washington DC: Brookings Institute, 1981); Mark C. Miller, *Boxed In: The Culture of TV* (Evanston, IL: Northwestern University Press, 1988); Ron Powers, *The Newscasters: The News Business as Show Business* (New York: St. Martins Press, 1978); and Tony Vera, *Live TV: An Inside Look at Directing and Producing* (Boston: Focal Press, 1987). Local television is also part of the global industry, with "parachute news crews" that cover global events. See "The Long Arm of Local News," *U.S. News and World Report*, (Mar. 16, 1987), p. 18.

[22] National Association of Television Programming Executives.

[23] Radio and Television News Directors Association.

[24] TV news production and news writing is disaggregated; distribution and entertainment production is concentrating.

[25] Steven S. Wildman and Stephen E. Siwek, *International Trade in Films and Television Programs* (Cambridge, MA: Ballinger, 1988); and Tapio Varis, "The International Flow of Television Programs," *Journal of Communications* 34: 143. UNESCO, *Statistical Yearbook 1985* (Paris), Table 10.

[26] *Ibid.*, Table 10-7; CNN information from conversations with Ted Turner and Bob Sieber, Vice President for Research TBS; European information drawn from *Channels 1989 Field Guide to the Electronic Environment* (Dec. 1987). Wildman and Siwek, *op. cit.*, Table 3-10 describes satellite systems globally. See also "Q&A: Cable's Top News Boss," *Electronic Media.* (January 30, 1989), pp. cover ff.

[27] American rock and roll, spread by radio, audio cassettes, and now television and video cassettes has become a *de facto* global culture. See Associated

Press, "United by Common Language of Film, U.S. Soviet Crews Work on Rock Video," *Atlanta Journal* (Oct. 15, 1988); p. A 20.

[28] UNESCO loc. cit.

[29] "NBC: Today America, Tomorrow the World," *Electronic Media*, (January 30, 1989: pp. 1ff.

[30] Wildman and Siwek, *op. cit.*, pg. 23; Chapters 8, 9, 10.

[31] Gladys Ganley and Oswald Ganley, *Global Political Fallout: The VCR's First Decade* (Norwood, NJ: Ablex, 1988), Chapters 6, 7.

[32] *Ibid.*, pp. 98–107.

[33] James Larson makes a strong case claiming that the opposite is true in *Global Television and Foreign Policy* (New York: Foreign Policy Association, 1987), describing the news media and the foreign policy establishment as acting in unison. While his case deserves respect and careful study, I disagree, arguing that the media act with the government on the "inside" and according to their own agendas and incentives on the "outside." While Larson cites two examples of media reinforcing U.S. foreign policy actions, numerous examples from the case studies, and others can be cited to show divergence.

[34] Larson, *op. cit.*, p. 5.

[35] There is a large literature on the independent role of the media in our society and its attitudes, incentives, hiring and training processes, and the culture of the media. Informative works include: Eli Abel, *What's News: The Media in American Society* (San Francisco: The Institute for Contemporary Studies, 1981); David Altheide and Robert Snow, *Media Logic* (Beverly Hills: Sage, 1979); Stephen Hess, *The Washington Reporters* (Washington DC: Brookings Institute, 1981); Ron Powers, *The Newscasters: The News Business as Show Business* (New York: St. Martins Press, 1978); Timothy Schiltz, Lee Sigelman, and Robert Neal "Perspectives of Managing Editors on Coverage of Foreign Policy News," *Journalism Quarterly* 50 (1973): 716–721.

[36] "Is Local TV News at Risk?," *Channels* (July/August, 1989): p. 20.

[37] William Adams, "Covering the World in Ten Minutes," in Adams 1982, *op. cit.*, pp. 114.

[38] Barry Rubin, *International News and the American Media* (Beverly Hills: Sage, 1977); Patrick Heffernan, "American Mass Media Coverage of International News," Unpublished Master's Thesis, University of California at Santa Barbara, June, 1978. See also William Adams, "Coverage of U.S. Evening Network News," in Adams 1982, *op. cit.*, pp. 15–44; Herbert Gans, *Deciding What's News* (New York: Pantheon Books, 1979); William Adams and Fay Schreibman (eds.), *Television Network News: Issues in Content Analysis*, (Washington DC: George Washington University Press, 1978); Newspapers vary widely in their use and placement of international stories; network news does not. See G. G. Stemple III, "Gatekeeping: The mix of topics and the selection of stories," *Journalism Quarterly* 62 (Winter 1985): 791–796.

[39] Wilber Schramm, *Mass Media and National Development* (Stanford, CA: Stanford University Press, 1964); Phillip Elliot and Peter Golden, "Mass Communication and Social Change: The Imagery of Development and the Development of Imagery," in Emanuel de Kadt and Gavin Williams (eds.), *Sociology and Development* (London: Tavistock, 1974); Adnan Almaney, "International and Foreign

Affairs on Network Television News," *Journal of Broadcasting* 14 (Fall 1970): 499–509; Others have found that U.S. coverage of the developing world, and indeed of most regions of the world, is often biased and slanted. In the case of the Middle East, see Ze'ev Chafets, *Double Vision: How the Press Distorts America's View of the Middle East* (New York: William Morrow, 1985); Robert Licter, "Media Support for Israel: A Survey of Leading Journalists." in William Adams (ed.), *Television Coverage of the Middle East* (Norwood, NJ: Ablex, 1981); Morad Asi, "Arabs and Israelis, and TV News: A Time-Series Content Analysis," in Adams 1981, *op. cit.*, pp. 67–75.

[40] James F. Larson, "International Affairs Coverage on U.S. Network Television," *Journal of Communication* 29 (Spring 1979): 136–147.

[41] *Gannet Center Journal* 3:4 (Fall 1989).

[42] I would argue that the media need the government far less than the government needs the media, since international news is a small part of the total news output, and news, while very profitable for ABC and NBC and CNN, is far less necessary to the bottom line than entertainment. And media have many other sources besides government for international news. Government, on the other hand, could not replace some of the functions of the news media, and would have a hard time paying to replace any functions.

[43] "Per Inquiry;" advertising involving an 800 or 900 telephone number and credit card donations or sales.

[44] The classic case is the global "Live Aid" concert on July 19, 1985, seen by 1.5 billion people in 160 nations. *Live Aid* raised $100 million dollars in one day, a new record for private international relief organizations. As a result of Live Aid, many other international telethons and rock concerts are now produced to raise money for causes ranging from farm relief to rainforst preservations. A small industry of independent producers, telephone solicitation and fulfillment companies, and media planners has emerged to produce international television fund-raising events. Hal Uplinger, *Live Aid* Executive Producer, personal conversation. See also Tony Vera, *Live TV* (Boston: Focal Press, 1987), pp. 119–129.

[45] Steven S. Wildman and Stephen E. Siwek, *International Trade in Films and Television Programming* (Cambridge, MA: Ballinger Books, 1988). See also "Hollywood Takes to the Global Stage," *New York Times* (April 16, 1989): 31.

[46] As was noted above, Kupperman et al. found in simulation exercises that the consideration of media response to various policy initiatives can eliminate them from considerations regardless of their intrinsic merit, giving media (or PIO's) a limited veto over policy options.

[47] In *Foreign Policy* (Spring 1989), 23–41, Dr. Norman Myers described six specific environmental situations which are now or would in the very near future become distinct security threats to U.S. interests. He noted that these situations indicate a problem in "the limited capacity of policymakers to think methodically about matters that have long lain outside their purview." The media now fulfill this function. See also Jessica Tuchman Mathews, "Redefining Security," *Foreign Affairs* (Spring 1989): 162–177.

[48] An example of this is Greenpeace which has 6 million members in over 50 countries and obtains national and international media exposure of its attempts to influence U.S. and international policy through direct action.

⁴⁹ *New York Times* (March 31, 1989).

⁵⁰ Personal interview, Brookings Inst., Summer 1988.

⁵¹ Graham T. Allison, *Essence of Decision: Explaining the Cuban Missile Crisis* (Boston: Little, Brown, 1971).

⁵² *Op. cit.*, pp. 9–11.

⁵³ Stanley Hoffman, "Restraints and Choices in American Foreign Policy," *Daedalus* (Fall 1962).

⁵⁴ Thomas Schelling, *Strategy of Conflict* (New York, 1962).

⁵⁵ Hans Morgenthau, *Politics Among Nations* (New York: Knob, 1978, 5th edition).

⁵⁶ Roger Hilsman, *To Move a Nation* (New York, 1967), pp. 13, 562.

⁵⁷ A descriptive analogy of the inside-outside capability is the virus, an entity which exists and operates outside the body, but which can and does penetrate the body and while in the body is used by certain entities within it and acts upon others.

⁵⁸ Allison, *op. cit.*, p. 80.

⁵⁹ Others have found that the informal communication with media representatives who work closely with certain officials may be more important in terms of policy influence than what is actually printed or broadcast. Both Linsky and Ebring found that the off-the record informal information exchanges between officials and reporters could have powerful effects on policy decisions. See Martin Linsky, *Impact* (New York: W. W. Norton, 1986), Chapters 6 & 7; and Lutz Ebring, Edie N. Goldenberg, and Arthur H. Miller, "Front-Page News and Real World Cues: A New Look at Agenda-Setting by the Media," *American Journal of Political Science* 24 (Feb. 1980): 41.

⁶⁰ Allison, *op. cit.*, p. 82.

⁶¹ For a detailed description of "global issues" and public and opinion leader attitudes toward them, see *Old Doctrines vs. New Threats: Citizens Look at Defense Spending and National Security* (Washington, DC: Roosevelt Center for American Policy Studies, 1989).

⁶² Quoted in Tran Van Dinh, *Communication and Diplomacy in a Changing World* (Norwood, NJ: Ablex, 1988), p. 52.

⁶³ This was reinforced during a simulation exercise held by Robert Kupperman involving senior policy makers and staff in a crisis. Robert Kupperman's team at CSIS found that the public relations aspects of the crises influenced and at times dominated the timing of decisions, the structure of the agenda, and the choice of options through the media and the congressional subteams, the control group was able to activate player presumptions about the domestic environment, which set clear boundaries to the range of policy alterntives. Robert Kupperman and Andrew Goldberg, (ed.), *Leaders and Crises: The CSIS Crisis Simulations* (Washington, DC: Center for Strategic and International Studies, 1987), p. 17. See ⁴⁶, above.

⁶⁴ Tran Van Dinh, *op. cit.*, p. 32; see also Chapter 2.

⁶⁵ Allison, *op. cit.*, p. 79.

⁶⁶ What is meant by "media techniques" in descriptions of output is that the sum total of government actions is designed to generate coverage and exposure in the mass media.

[67] Part of this environment was a positive public response to Sadat that would reduce opposition to the sale and give Congress the message that "here was an Arab we don't mind you doing business with." The Harris Poll on 1/22/77 showed that Sadat had turned around US opinion; he received very high positives during this period.

[68] In systems terms this may create a feedback link, with media informing the policy process and affecting the agenda, and the policy process utilizing media as an output, utilizing strategies designed to affect opinions and stimulate action to support policies. The existence of such a feedback system and its ramifications would be an interesting topic for further study.

[69] Michael David and Pat Aufderheide, "All the President's Media," *Channels*, (September, 1985): 20–24.

[70] Allison, *op. cit.*, pp. 162–163.

[71] *Ibid.*, p. 164.

[72] Allison, *op. cit.*, at p. 315, notes that including the NSA as a Chief is subject to debate because he has no statutory authority and supposedly does not command an action process, Oliver North notwithstanding. However, he appears to have almost equal standing to the Secretary of State or Defense in some issues areas. Allison supports his decision to include the NSA as a Chief on the role that McGeorge Bundy played and his observation that it has become institutionalized.

[73] Allison's term is "Indians," which I choose not to use due to its racial implications.

[74] *Ibid.*, p. 178.

[75] See Newton Minnow and John Martin, *Presidential Television* (New York: Basic Books, 1973).

[76] This is the same process used by CEOs and Presidents of very large multinational corporations to signal policy. See John Rydz, *Managing Innovation* (Cambridge: Ballinger, 1986), p. 136.

[77] Allision, *op. cit.*, p. 178.

[78] Allison notes that this proposition was first advanced by Ernest R. May. See also Roger Cobb and Charles Elder, *Participation in American Politics: The Dynamics of Agenda-Building* (Boston: Allyn and Bacon, 1972).

[79] For one of the more comprehensive arguments on this, see Stephen Hess, "The Golden Triangle: Press Relations at the White House, State Department and Department of Defence," In David Rubin and Ann Marie Cunningham (eds.), *In War, Peace, and the News Media*, a conference held at New York University, March 18–19, 1983, pp. 134–164. (New York: Center for War, Peace, and the News Media, 1987).

[80] Among the "outside" attributes of the mass media are their own internal incentive structures, professional guidelines, and hiring and training routines discussed earlier in the chapter. Television especially operates according to routines dictated by its economics and its technology. Television news structures its reporting in a story format, with a beginning, middle, and end, regardless of the reality of the issue at hand. Plus, the drive for TV ratings demands that news programming stresses conflict, violence, and surface reporting. The influence of sponsors who want to ensure that the programming is not uninter-

esting to U.S. audiences skews news programming toward issues and countries known to domestic audiences and away from countries, people, and issues that do not play well in the United States. While by no means exhausting the topic, the following provide a good range of the voluminous literature on the internal imperatives of the mass media: G. H. Stemple III, "Gatekeeping: The mix of topics and the selection of stories," *Journalism Quarterly* 62 (Winter 1985): 791–796; Edward J. Epstein, *News from Nowhere: Television and the News* (New York: Random House, 1973).

[81] Bernard Rubin, "Mass Media Stereotyping of Ethnic and Religious Groups," in Ungurait. *op. cit.*, pp 416–423; William Adams (ed.), *Television Coverage of the Middle East* (Norwood, NJ: Ablex, 1981).

[82] Ernest Lefever argues that television has made it impossible for the U.S. to fight another war. "The Prestige Press, Foreign Policy, and American Survival," *Orbis* 20 (1976): 207–225.

[83] Bernard Cohen, *The Press and Foreign Policy* (Princeton, NJ: Princeton University Press, 1963), p. 259. In some cases, the media actually stimulate the formation of organizations. The 1984 broadcast of *The Day After* on ABC stimulated the creation of *The Day Before Project*, a national organization set up to encourage viewing and to guide viewers to translate any emotions the program stimulated into political action. Some of the local chapters of this organization are still active. A similar, smaller organization was created in advance of the broadcast of *Threads* in the U.S. See also J. O'Neil, *Plato's Cave* (Norwood, NJ: Ablex, 1991).

APPENDIX 1: CASE STUDIES

The case studies are in the form of chronologies of stories in the print media and on the three network evening news programs of the time and policy events derived from news reports and other sources. These are "working case studies" in the form of nearly raw data from which the case study chapters were derived. They are included here for use by other analysts.

CONVENTIONS AND ABBREVIATIONS

Television

TOB—"top of broadcast hour;" indicates lead television story.
HEAVY COVERAGE—Television news coverage of 7 minutes or more in a single half-hour newscast.
MODERATE COVERAGE—Four to 7 minutes coverage in a single newscast.
LIGHT COVERAGE—up to four minutes coverage.
"w/film" or "film"—indicates a story with film or tape or (rarely) live image from the news scene.

Print media

Lead—lead story on the front page.
NA—"news analysis."
NYT—*New York Times* newspaper.
WP—*Washington Post* newspaper.
W/Photo (film, voice-over)—with photo or film or a voice-over.
IP—"inside pages" of newspaper.
SB—"sidebar stories" in newspaper.
Headlines or abstracted headlines appear in *italics*.

General

DOS—Department of State
DOD—Department of Defense
Bold type indicates an item directly related to the media's influence on foreign policy.

EXPLANATION OF DATA ENTRY FORMAT

Description of data entry	Example of data entry
Date and description of event.	**2/7/88: Continuing violence in occupied territories.**
Description of television reporting: *Top Of Broadcast* (lead story that night on at least one network). Overall level of coverage, average length of all network coverage of this event, indication of film, subjects shown, subjects reported but not shown; image shown.	*TV:* TOB. Light to moderate coverage. 2–3 minutes w/film. Involvement of American exchange student in Ramallah unrest shown. Stoning of W. Bank Israeli settler by Arabs reported; wife interviewed.
Description of print coverage: initials of publication, indication of *Front Page* story (headline in italics) and its continuation page (jump) and types of illustration. Indication of *Inside Page* stories, *Side Bar* stories. Indication of *Editorial* (with name of author, if available) title in italics, total number of articles and pages.	*Print:* NYT-FP-*In Jordan, anxiety and joy over Palestinian upheaval.*, jumped to page 5, w/photos, maps. IP- Israeli soldiers storm home of West bank clan. SB: homes blown up as punishment, w/photo. Ed.-(Shipler) *Turmoil could provide the seeds of peace.* 5 articles/6 pages.
Description of policy actions or events.	*Policy:* Reagan comment; Shultz talks continue; veto of UN vote.

CASE 1
A COMPARATIVE CHRONOLOGY OF EVENTS, MEDIA REPORTS, AND POLICY EVENTS DURING THE SADAT-BEGIN PEACE PROCESS AND CAMP DAVID, 1977–1978

Introduction

This chronology describes events, television reports, print reports, and policy actions by the U.S. government during the negotiations and events that led to the Camp David accords. It covers the period 11/9/77 to 4/12/79.

Television reports were compiled from abstracts of network news reports published by the Vanderbilt Television News Archive. Television summaries in this document blend abstracts from all three network reports. Noteworthy or unique reports by individual networks are indicated where appropriate.

Print reports are summaries of reports, features, graphics, and editorials printed in the *New York Times*, and in the *Washington Post* while the *Times* was on strike. Summaries reflect headlines and editorial content abbreviated for space reasons.

Policy events are drawn from print and television news reports. These events have been updated where possible through interviews.

Specialized reporting conventions and abbreviations were developed for use in this document to keep the summaries as brief as possible while providing necessary contextual and content information. Reporting conventions are listed at the beginning of the document.

I wish to express my appreciation to the staff of the Vanderbilt Television News Archive for their effort to provide this information in a timely manner.

CASE I: SADAT AND BEGIN

11/9/77: Israeli jets bomb Palestinian camps in South Lebanon, killing 100+ people. Sadat addresses Egyptian Parliament and urges efforts to reconvene peace talks in Geneva; Sadat says he will go to Israel to speak.

Television: 2–3 mins Reports of Israeli attack, then Sadat's comment re: gaining peace in the Mideast noted. Carter's remarks re: incident of Israeli attack and need for peace conference in Geneva

Print: NYT-IP—Israeli jets bomb Palestinian camps in S. Lebanon; President Carter meets with former Prime Minister Golda Meir, they disagree on Palestinian homeland issue. 2 articles/2 pages.

●11/10*—NYT-FP—with 2 pictures of relatives of victims mourning and FP map of Lebanon, Israeli jets strike Lebanon, 60 killed. **IP**—*Sadat urges drive to convene peace conference in Geneva*, with picture of Arafat being welcomed and hugged by Egyptian Foreign Minister; Israeli town where rockets hit, bury dead, get on with life; Lebanese village in rubble. 4 articles/5 pages.

Policy events: Carter meeting with Meir to send signal to Israel on U.S. disagreement with homeland issue.

11/15/77: Begin extends formal invitation to Sadat to address Knesset; also invites other Arab leaders informally to Israel for talks. Carter applauds Sadat; Soviets, other Arab nations criticize move.

Television: 3–7 mins TOB. All networks. Sadat/Begin remarks re: invitation from Begin when it will take place, no exact date. Knesset vote re: security/ceremonies to greet Sadat. Sadat's reported lack of concern re: security noted in meetings w/American Congressmen. Sadat's desire for agreement among all in area to live in peace. Reactions of Egyptian people. U.S. diplomats and Arabs. Sadat's efforts to change mind of American Congressmen and Israelis noted. Visit likened to Nixon in China. Interview with Kissinger evaluates signs of Sadat/Begin meetings.

Print: NYT-FP Lead—(magnified headline) *Sadat seeks Israeli invitation to address Parliament*, Begin agrees, wants U.S. help, with picture of each. IP—Transcript of Begin interview; transcript of Sadat interview; Arab league condemns Israeli attacks in Lebanon. 4 articles/5 pages.

●11/16—NYT-FP Lead—Begin formally asks Sadat to Jerusalem, Sadat ready to go: (1) Sadat says he attaches no conditions; (2) Parliament agrees to invitation. FPSB—U.S. endorses trip but still stresses talks in Geneva, with picture of Sadat and Congressman Wright in Cairo. IP—Contact in the past was indirect; Saudis let Israeli Arabs travel to Mecca ending 1948 ban. Ed.—(NYT) Momentum in ME; *Sadat again the master of decision.* 7 articles/10 pages.

Policy events: U.S. endorses Sadat trip but retains call for conference.

---

*Often complete print coverage of an event will appear the following day. In these cases, coverage from the day after the event is included with that of the day of the event.

11/17/77: Egyptian Foreign Minister resigns in disagreement with Sadat over Israel visit. Arab leaders sharply criticize Sadat, fearing separate agreement and abandonment of support for Palestinians.

Television: TOB. 9–15 mins all networks with film. Plans for Egyptian Pres. Sadat's visit to Israel on Saturday. Reaction/opposition from Assad. Reports on Sadat's visit to Syria. Sadat's wish to pray at Al Aksa cited. Discussion of Sadat's trip: will it advance peace efforts. Foreign Minister Famy resignation and departure of Foreign Minister Riad also noted. U.S. concerns noted that communist and Arab hardliners could create problems re: opposition to visit.

White House public optimism re: trip noted, also Begin's phone call to Carter and outlined significance of trip. Reaction of Arab delegates to the U.N. Syria's call for united Arab opposition. Presentation of formal invitation and Sadat's acceptance.

Print: NYT-FP—Sadat flies to Syria reportedly to talk about trip to Israel. IP—Israel planning visit, "feels breath of history;" Sadat sends message of greeting to Israeli organized symposium in Tel Aviv; Iraq, Libya and radical Palestinians condemn possible trip. NA—Sadat-Begin trip evokes high expectations and caution. 5 articles/6 pages.

•11/18—NYT-FP Lead—Sadat goes to Israel next day, his Foreign Minister resigns, Syria and Iraq condemn visit. FP SB—Carter asks Israel to bolster Sadat to insure results from his trip; Sadat to pray in old Jerusalem. IP—TV's role in ME, almost diplomacy; Al Fatah asks Sadat to cancel trip; U.S. Jewish leaders excited and hopeful; Arabs in U.S. stunned and puzzled by Sadat move; Trip criticized by Assad; Foreign Minister quits in Egypt, successor resigns hours later; Text of Egyptian, Israeli messages; Israel hunts for copy of Egyptian banner, printed Egyptian national anthem music.

Policy events: Carter asks Israel help in success of Sadat trip.

11/19/77: Sadat arrives in Israel, first Egyptian leader to do so.

Television: No coverage recorded in Abstracts.

Print: No coverage in NYT. See next day.

Policy events: No events reported.

11/20/77: Sadat addresses the Knesset, telling members that "we welcome you among us with all security and safety."

Television: TOB. Heavy coverage by all major networks 15–16 mins with film. Acceptance of Israel by Sadat. Quoted re: relations with Israel, relinquishing of lands and recognition of Palestinian state. Speeches by both Sadat/Begin recapped. Invites Syria to Israel to sign treaty. Pvt. Talks noted. Visit to memorial for Jews cited. Absence of state dinner at request of Sadat. Sadat speech tougher than expected, reaction of politicians in Israel noted.

Public response: Israel seen as peace key. Arab reaction/Egyptians call Sadat hero; others unfavorable. Religious holiday noted. American reaction favorable both publicly and privately. Carter/Mondale warn against expecting too much. Kissinger interviewed re: Sadat's motives. DOS reacts favorably.

Print: NYT-FP Lead—*Sadat arrives in Israel*, Begin says "we like each other," with 3 large pictures of the event. FP SB-*People of Cairo transfixed as they watch President on TV*. IP—U.S. rabbis voice hope for Sadat's trip; Israel flooded with journalists; Military Analysis—Egypt's forces reported weak in major areas; Israeli doves exult over visit; Kissinger sees trip as historic event; Protest and skepticism dominate Arabs' reactions; Egyptian Commander praises trip; Vast Israeli security force guard Sadat; Sadat gets warm Israeli welcome; Carter says all hopes are with two leaders; Query by Jerusalem Post Writer gave Sadat idea for journey; Sadat visiting old and new sites in Jerusalem today; Soviets condemn trip. 15 articles/17 pages.

Policy events: No events reported.

11/21/77: Sadat holds joint press conference with Begin and they express their desire for peace and hope that the Geneva peace conference will reconvene in the near future. Begin calls Sadat's visit a "great moral achievement."

Television: TOB. 7–9 mins all networks, with film. Conclusion of Sadat visit. Visit and gift exchange with Golda Meir noted. Begin speaks of no more war. PLO not discussed. Film of Sadat in Knesset shown. Tumultuous welcome of Sadat on his return. Sadat filmed riding in open car. Reactions to his visit cited. Other reactions: Oil nations staying silent; others believe Sadat enemy of the Arab world. Israelis' some doubts noted. Begin credits Carter with making meeting possible.

●*CBS Commentary:* 3 min. **Television's role in the Sadat visit considered. TVs' role as the 4th branch of the government noted. Discounted as prime factor in Begin/Sadat meetings. Called a moderator and described as the fastest modern communication process and a new actor in "public diplomacy."****

●*NBC Segment 3:* Interview with Begin/Sadat. Begin declares visit momentous. Sadat urges reconvening of Geneva Conf. Both agree in 1977. Carter's role noted. Sadat agrees that emphasis should be on security and peace. Begin hopes for peace beyond personalities.

Print: NYT-FP Lead (magnified)—with three pictures of them both, Sadat offers "peace with justice," but calls for return of occupied lands. Views by both Sadat and Begin restated; FPSB-NA-Political gap still separates but meeting marks major step for ME; Sadat in Jerusalem, day of challenges; Carter sees step toward peace but some officials voice doubt.

IP—(full page) Transcripts of Sadat and Begin addresses; Political profile of Sadat portrays him as shrewd, intuitive; Political profile of Begin portrays him as decisive, politically gifted; Sadat and Begin talk of further contact; Both Egyptians and Israelis stirred by Sadat trip, but some have doubts (no poll data cited). Points:

1. Egyptians' reactions,
2. Israelis' reactions;

One million Egyptians are expected to welcome Sadat; Herzog calls both speeches badly translated; (very small). Networks will cover Sadat's return; One full page of pictures of Sadat's visit; Reaction by world officials is guarded; Transcripts of Carter's remarks on ME: *Most New Yorkers feel buoyant after watching televised session*; PLO condemns speech by Sadat, calls for sanctions against him. 11 articles/23 pages.

Policy events: No significant policy events.

11/22/77: Syrian delegate to UN calls Sadat's act "a stab in the back," Egypt's delegate walks out. EEC adopts a resolution praising Sadat's visit.

Television: TOB. 6–8 mins all networks. Signs of rift among Arabs. Walkout by Egyptian Ambassador to UN noted after Sadat called enemy of Arab world. Look at the Egyptian economy: in poor shape especially with high expenditures on domestic problems needed as opposed to military described. Population problems, country's need for western investment cited to come only after peace.

*****Harris Poll Results:** American public reaction reported. Turn around seen re: real possibility of peace in Mideast. Sadat noted as Arab symbol for peace. Statistics show American belief in negotiations thru middleman like Sadat or Carter.

Print: NYT-FP Lead—with 3 pictures, Sadat and Begin vow "no more war" as Sadat departs—(1) *Sadat received in Egypt by crowds cheering "man of peace;"* (2) More talks pledged, visit by Begin indefinite; FPSB-NA-Sadat trip, psychology and substance. IP-Arabs at U.N. trying to close

---

****News commentary on the role of television in foreign policy or international events has been set in **boldface** for later analysis.

ranks; Transcripts of Sadat-Begin news conference; U.S. is glad Israel and Egypt still stress Geneva; Relics of Maccabee among gifts to Sadat; NY governor Carey hails Sadat trip; Some Arabs fear Sadat has provoked new rifts; Sadat's interaction in the Knesset, included is a picture of him and Golda Meir; **TV's function is highlighting symbolic event by "sheer drama of pictures," with picture of Israelis transfixed to the TV.** 11 articles/14 pages.

Policy events: No events reported.

11/26/77: Sadat invites all parties in the Middle East conflict to a pre-Geneva preparatory meeting in Cairo to resolve procedural differences. Israel announces it will accept a formal invitation to the Cairo conference. Syria, Lebanon, and Jordan reject the offer.

Television: 11/26. TOB. ABC—5–6 mins Invitations to USSR and others by Sadat to attend Cairo Conference. Begin says Israel will go even if Egypt and Israel are the only ones there. No negotiation with PLO.

Print: 11/27—NYT-FP Lead—*Sadat calls for a pre-Geneva meeting in Cairo of Arabs*, Israelis, U.S. and Soviets, Israel agrees, Syria refuses; FPSB-Response in Israel prompt; Syria says it will take part in a "refusal summit" in Libya. IP—*Excerpts from Sadat address to parliament*; U.S. views Sadat proposal cautiously; NA (but not labeled such)—*Analysts see Sadat proposal as a maneuver to force hard line countries to join talks with Israel*; Soviets silent on Sadat invitation. 7 articles/10 pages.

Policy events: US accepts invitation to Cairo.

11/29/77: Carter appoints Alfred Atherton to be US rep at Cairo talks. Soviets refuse to attend.

Television: 3–4 mins light to moderate coverage all networks. Reactions of Soviets: Gromyko's statement re: Soviet reps at Cairo. Refuse to attend.

Print: 11/30—NYT-FP—Soviets refuse to attend Cairo talks, U.S. accepts; FPSB-NA—U.S.Soviet relations upset by Sadat. IP—Waldheim accepts Sadat invitation, urges U.N. talks; List of ME conferences; Famous hotel near pyramids is site of parley; Foreign Minister Moshe Dayan visits Egyptian exhibition during trip to Bonn. 6 articles/8 pages.

Policy events: Cairo talks representative appointed.

12/2/77: Arab states declare a new resistance to thwart Egypt's peace process with Israel.

Television: 4–6 mins with film. Report on Begin's visit to Britain. Sadat's visit to town on Suez. Presence of first accredited Israeli reporter noted. Results of the NBCAP News Poll re: Sadat/Begin meetings. Ratings for

Carter/Sadat/Begin by general public. Report on Arab hardliners conference in Tripoli w/items discussed.

Print: 12/3—NYT-FP—*Arabs meet in Libya on opposing Sadat.* IP-NA—*Arab world in disarray, a lead by Saudi Arabia is awaited.* 2 articles/3 pages.

Policy events: No significant policy events.

12/5/77: Cairo severs diplomatic relations with Syria, Iraq, Libya, Algeria, and South Yemen, citing attempts to disrupt peace process. Egypt closes several Soviet consulates and offices.

Television: 46 mins. with film. Sec. of State Vance announces trip to Mideast. Egypts action in break of diplomatic relations with Syria, Iraq, Libya, Algeria, and S. Yemen. DOS position on Sadat's break with other Arab nations. Details of Vance's trip reported. Sadat's action surprised both government and populace. Sadat committed to position.

Print: 12/6—NYT-FP Lead—with picture of Sadat, Egypt cuts relations with Syria, Iraq, Libya, Algeria, and S. Yemen; FPSB-Vance set to visit ME for 6 days to support Sadat; NA—Sadat at home: national hero. IP—Sadat said to have allayed Saudi fears; Moscow is caustic to U.S. about ME; Israel limits scope of Cairo talks; Excerpts from Arab communique issued in Lybia; Hard-line Arab bloc formed in Tripoli, but at Syria's behest opposition to peace accord not declared. 9 articles/12 pages.

Policy events: Vance decides to tour ME capitals to support Sadat.

12/9/77: Vance visits ME states to persuade them to attend the Cairo conference.

Television: Heavy coverage of Vance's trip to Mideast. Most days TOB all three networks 2–5 mins with film. Reported change in U.S. role in Mideast peace talks. Begin cautions that negotiations should be done in Cairo, Geneva and Jerusalem but not in front of the T.V. Other Arab nations fear that Sadat will make separate peace. Sadat states he will negotiate if only he and Begin attend. Preliminary focus of Cairo conference reported. Announcement by White House that Begin will visit Carter on eve of conference reported. Sadat's approval noted.

●*Print:* 12/10—NYT-FP—*Vance flies to Cairo, stresses aim of U.S. is to support Sadat.* IP-*Assad urges Kuwait to join hardliners; Dayan tells Israelis U.S. is important role in ME talks.* 3 articles/4 pages.

●12/11—NYT-FP—*Vance gets pledge from Sadat to bar separate peace, Vance arrives in Israel.* IP—Carter says he expects Israel to show "courage" in response to Sadat; Saudi Arabia's king issues plea for Arab unity; Sadat warns PLO to alter its stand; Begin message to United Jewish Appeal tells of "real peacemaking process." 5 articles/6 pages.

●12/12—NYT-FP—*Vance in Jerusalem says U.S. is seeking end to Arab division, Begin pledges all out effort.* IP-NA—Split among Arabs over Sadat initiative puts PLO in precarious position; Brzezinski talks of new role for Geneva in ME peace; Syria rules out talks with Israel in Cairo or Geneva; Israeli gives lecture on Israeli politics and military to Egyptian Generals; Beirut fears an Israel-Egypt pact that omits issue of Palestinians. Editorial—*Sadat's visit has changed the whole nature of the ME conflict.* 7 articles/8 pages.

●12/13—NYT-FP—*Dayan says Israel may agree to partition occupied West Bank.* IP-King Hussein after conferring with Vance feels "a little more optimistic;" Cairo completes details of talks; Saudis affirm policy on Jerusalem. 4 articles/5 pages.

Policy events: Vance flies to Cairo, stresses aim of US is to support Sadat. Goes to Jerusalem for talks with Begin, Dayan, etc. Confers with King Hussein.

12/14/77: Cairo conference opens with U.S., Egypt, U.N., and Israeli representatives.

Television: TOB. All networks 6–8 mins with film. Report on opening of Cairo conference with U.S., Egypt and Israel in attendance. Remarks by Sadat re: Begin's trip and its effect on Cairo. Sadat thinks Begin's trip will give conf. new drive. Talks of more conf. issues. Announces invitation from Carter to come to DC at his convenience. Is open to joint meetings with Carter/Begin and himself. Opinions of American officials in Cairo noted. Asst. SOS Atherton sees Begin/Carter talks as reinforcement of primary talks.

Print: NYT-FP Lead—with picture of Egyptian delegation greeting Israeli delegation, *Begin says two sides will exchange treaty drafts in Cairo, delaying Palestinian and territory issues.* Points:

1. Begin coming to U.S. for talks with Carter
2. Excerpts from Begin interview.

FPSB—Conference opens today; Israelis in euphoric mood. IP—Vance in Damascus finds Assad adamant; Saudis hint favorable view on West Bank proposal; Excerpts of Begin's interview. 7 articles/11 pages.

●12/15—NYT-FP Lead—*Israel and Egypt meet,* with 2 pictures; FPSB—Begin visits Carter in U.S., praises Carter before leaving Israel. IP—Text of statements by Egypt, Israel, and U.S. at conference; Vance ends ME trip convinced an active U.S. role is needed; Morocco reportedly seeking Arab talks after Cairo. Ed.—*Begin should propose solution to Palestinian problem.* 6 articles/8 pages.

Policy events: Vance convinced active U.S. role needed in ME; Carter invites Sadat to U.S. U.S. talks with Begin.

12/25/77: Begin and Sadat hold a summit in Ismailia, Egypt, to draft guidelines for establishing peace in the ME. No substantive agreements on any major issues.

Television: TOB. One network 6 mins with film. Begin/Sadat meeting reported. Sadat's birthday on Dec. 25 noted. Foreign Ministers of both nations present. Talks reported going well. Sadat speaks of new talks.

Print: 12/26—NYT-FP Lead—2 pictures of Sadat, Begin. *Begin and Sadat meet in Egypt, agree to extend talks another day;* FPSB—Two leaders tour Suez canal city. IP—Carter feels Syria not essential to talks; Israeli Minister of Finance says Sadat set the term for peace; Palestinians rally in Beirut to denounce Sadat; Moscow rules out rubber stamp role in Geneva talks. 6 articles/8 pages.

12/27—NYT-FP Lead—with 2 pictures of leaders. Points:

1. Sadat and Begin end 2-day talks without accord on main issues but vow to press peace effort, Palestinian issue (West Bank) stalls meetings.
2. NA—*Ismailia talks test of stands.*

FPSB—Carter says U.S. will strive to keep up ME momentum. IP—Saudi TV shows Sadat and Begin, hinting support; (full page) with picture of both Defense Ministers, text of statements by Sadat and Begin and their joint news conference (3 articles); Begin minimizes inability to issue a joint declaration; PLO says Sadat has forsaken the Palestinians. 9 articles/10 pages.

Policy events: Carter states Syria not necessary for talks.

12/28/77: Begin submits his 26-point peace plan to the Knesset; they approve. Same plan was presented to Sadat.

Television: 2–5 mins Light to moderate coverage all networks. Begin presentation of peace plan to Knesset/opposition noted. Demonstrations outside reported. Sadat's rejection noted. Sadat's press conference re: talks w/Begin and future negotiations. Sadat hopes all can be resolved. Expectations from Egyptians that pressure from U.S. (public opinion) will make Israel change mind.

Print: 12/29—NYT-FP—Begin presents proposal insisting troops remain in West Bank; FPSB—Sadat urges Israel to reconsider stand; Carter in TV interview affirms opposition to Palestinian state. IP—*Saudis declare U.S. must press Israel;* Arab foes of Sadat plan to meet again before mid-January; Text of Begin's proposal; Soviets accuse Sadat of worsening ME situation. Ed.—(Tony Lewis) *Israel should give up West Bank.* 8 articles/11 pages.

Policy events: Carter affirms opposition to Palestinian state. DOS announces Vance will attend Jan. meeting of Israeli and Egyptian foreign ministers.

1/6/78: Carter unveils plan for joint Egypt-Israel administration of the West Bank and the Gaza.

Television: Light coverage. 1–3 mins all networks. Impression of Carter trip outlined. Effect on ME events noted, including meeting with Sadat.

Print: NYT-IP—U.S. to press Israel on peace principles; NA-PLO worried about losing peace role despite slogan. 2 articles/2 pages.

●1/7—NYT—Small news brief reporting Lebanese President's announcement that Palestinians must leave after peace.

Policy events: Carter plan for joint administration of West Bank and Gaza announced.

1/9/78: Shah of Iran meets with Sadat and endorses peace initiatives.

Television: TOB. All networks 3–4 mins with film. Report of Shah of Iran's endorsement of Sadat peace plan. Reports on preps for ME peace talks noted.

Print: NYT-FP—*Begin Cabinet bars further settlements in Sinai.* IP—Carter optimistic on Jerusalem talks; (very small story) First Egyptian tourist finds Israelis friendly; Saudis said to be boosting forces near Israel; (small) *Assad claims Sadat "destroyed" peace efforts;* (small) Sadat appears positive on suggestions by Carter. 6 articles/3 pages.

●1/10—NYT-IP—*Begin wins party backing of his peace plan.* 1 article/1 page.

Policy events: No significant policy events.

1/11/78: Egyptian-Israeli Political Committee meet in Jerusalem to discuss Israel's withdrawal from the Sinai as part of the agreement.

Television: All networks 4–6 mins with film. Continued discussion of Sinai issue between Israel/Egypt noted.

Print: NYT-FP—with picture of Israeli project in Sinai. Egyptian talks open in Cairo today. IP—Israeli settlers in Sinai uneasy on future. 2 articles/3 pages.

1/12—NYT-FP—Military talks begun by Israel and Egypt. IP-Israeli settlers urge annexation of Golan Heights to avert return to Arabs; ME peace drive a strain on Lebanese. Waldheim won't attend peace talks in Jerusalem. Ed.—(Lewis) Moderate Palestinians should be included in discussions. 5 articles/6 pages.

Policy events: No significantly policy events.

1/18/78: Jerusalem talks break down; Sadat recalls his delegation, charging Israel with submitting partial proposals and deadlocking meeting. Carter urges Sadat to continue the talks despite recall of delegation.

Television: Heavy coverage all networks. 6–12 mins. with film. Sadat recalls Foreign Minister Kamel and delegation. Apparent temporary end to own peace initiative. Apparent reaction to Begin's statements on Tues night re: unchanged position Sinai withdrawal and Palestinian question noted. Carter's phone call to Sadat and agreement to resume military talks in Cairo on Sat. reported. Surprise to delegates at Jerusalem Conference Agreed statement of principle on peace reported. Sadat's series of diplomatic surprises since peace initiative began in Nov. examined.

Print: NYT-FP—Israeli-Egyptian talks open in Jerusalem in uncertain mood, sharp words exchanged. IP—Israeli exuberance fades but hope persists (text of agenda is given); NA—cloudy outlook at peace talks. 3 articles/4 pages.

●1/19—NYT-FP Lead—Sadat recalls peace delegation, demands shift in Begin position. Points:

1. Israel dismayed;
2. Cairo talks still on.

IP—15 leading American Jews plan a dialogue in Egypt on religion; Carter calls Sadat, urges further talks; Decision by Sadat causes confusion; A Jerusalem hotel lobby breaks into bedlam as news arrives; Remarks by Begin at dinner for participants of talks; Transcript of Egyptian statement; Text of Israeli Cabinet statement. **Ed.—(NYT) Sadat's move is to get television attention, but he has accomplished a lot.** 10 articles/12 pages.

Policy events: Carter call to Sadat to urge further talks. DOS reaction: Sadat seeks to put international pressure on Begin re: Palestinian self-determination with responsibility in such an event going first to U.S. to organize.

2/3/78: Sadat arrives in the U.S. to press his plans for peace in the ME and to seek U.S. arms assistance.

Television: 2–5 mins. all networks with film. Sadat's arrival in U.S. for talks with Carter noted. Carter says that Sadat/Begin other interested leaders, and the American people have responsibility to rededicate toward peace. Sadat notes how fragile peace is and efforts toward it must be remedied. Details given of Egyptians concept of U.S. role in talks. Background on disagreements between the two nations re: Palestinian issue. Begin makes statement that no more settlements and no further expansion of existing ones would be allowed.

Print: NYT-FP-NA—Sadat's visit is an attempt to persuade U.S. to push Israel for concessions. IP—Sadat on way to U.S. sees King of Morocco on Arab rift; Leaders of the major American Jewish organizations decide not to meet Sadat in U.S. but some individual Jews will; *Behind Sadat's peace effort, Carter's concern.* Ed.—(Reston) *Decision by Israel to continue settlements on West Bank anathema to peace.* 5 articles/6 pages.

Policy events: Meeting with Sadat.

2/4/78: Sadat visit continues.

Television: Heavy news blackout on talks between Sadat/Carter.

Print: NYT-FP—with picture of Carter greeting Sadat, Sadat urges Carter to intensify ME peace role, IP-Hard line Arabs agree on strategy; NA—Sadat visit a policy quandary for U.S. 3 articles/4 pages.

Policy events: continuing talks.

2/5/78: Sadat visit continues.

Television: Light to moderate coverage. 2–3 mins. Carter/Sadat return from summit. News blackout on talks. Carter states agreement between self and Sadat on continued attempts to reach peace. Sadat's scheduled speech at National Press Club noted. Begin's position on Egyptian demands for Israeli withdrawal to pre-1967 borders and on Palestinian state reported. Stated in *Miami Herald* under Begin's name. Sadat article for same paper mentioned.

Print: NYT-FP—*Carter tells Sadat U.S. is trying to achieve fair ME peace plan;* IP—Sunday's Preview Section (FP)—with huge drawing of Begin and Israel, how much more "give" can Israel afford; Sadat may be on mission impossible. Ed.—*God, Sadat and Begin—an overview of the deadlock.* 4 articles/6 pages.

Policy events: continuing talks.

2/6/78: Sadat visit continues.

Television: Light to moderate coverage. 3–6 mins. Reports of Sadat's meetings with Jewish leaders and other Americans. Coverage of National Press Club speech. Sadat states that Israeli position is hardening instead of softening.

Sadat shows apparent dissatisfaction with weekend meetings. Statement that he has made all concessions he is going to make to Begin. Calls Begin's position on settlements a mistake. Request for arms to protect Egypt and not to fight against Israel noted. Lack of Israeli response to Sadat's remarks noted. U.S. decision to supply Egypt, Israel, and Saudis with arms reported.

Print: NYT-FP—New effort pledged by Carter and Sadat to revive peace bid. Ed.—**Reading Sadat's mind (satire on his manipulation of the media).** 2 articles/3 pages.

Policy events: Carter starts new effort for ME peace bid. Carter releases partial chronology of communications with Israel; Jody Powell denies any connection with Sadat's visit. Decision to sell arms to Egypt, Israel.

2/7/78: Sadat visit continues.

Television: Light to moderate coverage all networks. 2–6 mins. Sadat's talks to Congress members re: Mideast situation and Israel and also re: U.S. arms sales to Egypt reported. Details of Sadat's appearance on Capitol Hill. Sadat's request for arms to protect Egypt from its African neighbors noted. ABC news poll of members of House and Senate Foreign Affairs Committees on Egyptian arms sales, putting pressure on Israel and Palestinian homeland cited.

Print: NYT-FP—with picture of Sadat at Nat. Press Club, Sadat asserts *"I have given Israel everything"* to National Press Club (NPC) in an appeal for American support. IP—Excerpt from Sadat's address to NPC. 2 articles/3 pages.

Policy events: Continuing talks, arms sales move.

2/8/78: Sadat visit continues.

Television: 4–5 mins. Light to moderate coverage. Sadat's farewell visit to Carter noted. Carter calls Sadat foremost peacemaker. Sadat came here disheartened, but will return with more perseverance for peace efforts.

Lack of major policy changes in visit and re: arms sales to Egypt and no solid pledge to influence Israel noted.

Print: NYT-FP—U.S. again says it opposes Israel on settlements. IP—U.S. text on Israeli settlements; NA—with picture of Sadat and Sparkman laughing, Sadat makes an impression. 2 articles/3 pages.

Policy events: U.S. restatement of anti-settlement policy, continuing move for arms sales.

2/9/78: Sadat leaves the U.S. for Europe.

Television: Light coverage. 2–3 mins with film. Sadat's meetings with Europeans on oil rights in Sinai. Interview with Foreign Minister Dayan about the settlements. Carter quoted that settlements are obstacles to peace. Report of both Begin/Sadat lobbying Europe for support of their positions. Both critical of U.S.

Print: NYT-FP—*Carter and Sadat end talks, vow peace efforts.* IP-Begin in Geneva says new U.S. arms to Egypt would raise war peril; White House statement on Carter-Sadat talks; Dayan in NY gives Israeli side of settlement issue. 4 articles/5 pages.

Policy events: White House statement on talks.

2/11/78: U.S. announces $4.8 billion in jets to be sold to Egypt, Israel, and Saudi Arabia.

Television: No major coverage.

Print: NYT-FP—U.S. said to feel Israel must yield to Sinai settlements and West Bank. IP-Dayan blames Arab politics for halt in peace talks; Sadat meets Peres in Salzburg; Israel moves to reverse ban on controversial film about banishing Arabs. 4 articles/5 pages.

2/15—NYT-FP Lead—U.S. plans first jet sale to Egypt, reduces Israel order, Saudis get 60 F-15's. FPSB—Military Analysis—Israel's superiority is eroding. IP—First legal political opposition party since independence created in Egypt. Ed.—Lukewarm criticism to arms sale to ME. 4 articles/6 pages.

Policy events: White House statement on arms sale for Egypt; overall movement towards U.S. becoming source of new arms for Egypt.

2/18/78: Palestinian gunmen assassinate Youssef el-Sebai, Egyptian newspaper editor and close confidant of Sadat. Killers seize hostages at Larnaca airport.

Television: No coverage.

Print: 2/19—NYT-FP—2 gunmen in Cyprus kill top Cairo editor and take off with 17, victim is close friend of Sadat.

First of a series: Palestinian people in crisis are scattered and divided. IP—Egypt requests right to punish killers; Story on Palestinians in Kuwait who thrive in the economy but feel bias as aliens. Ed.—*U.S. spreads its arm around the ME,* (observation); The other Arabs divided, with cartoon of hard line countries throwing darts at Egypt. 6 articles/9 pages.

Policy events: No policy events reported.

2/19/78: Egyptian commandos attempt to free hostages; shoot-out with Cypriot national guard costs 15 lives. Palestinians free hostages and surrender.

Television: Light to moderate coverage. 3–4 mins. Egyptian commando raid on hostage plane at Larnaca. Terrorists holding plane are the same ones that killed Sadat's friend, editor Sebai. Sadat not at funeral for security reasons.

Print: 2/20—NYT-FP Lead—with picture of dead body, *up to 15 Egyptian commandos killed trying to rescue hostages when Cypriot National Guards open fire, Palestinians surrender, release hostages.* FPSB— Egypt says Cyprus was notified of rescue. *Part 2 of series*—Palestinians cling to vision of homeland.

IP—Arabs in Israel, identity crisis. 4 articles/7 pages.

Policy events: No significant policy events announced; inside talks, decision on packaging arms sales.

2/24/78: White House announces that ME arms sale must be a package deal; Congress cannot cut anything out of it.

Television: No significant coverage.

Print: 2/25—NYT-FP—*Vance asserts Arabs must get warplanes along with Israelis.* IP—(small story) *Atherton shuttles to Jerusalem with "helpful ideas" from Egypt.* 2 articles/3 pages.

Policy events: Arms sale official announcement.

3/14/78: Israel raids, invades Southern Lebanon in retaliation for attacks.

Television: TOB. Heavy coverage all networks. 6–8 mins. Expectation of Israeli retaliation for PLO raid in Israel. Sadat condemns raid prior to retaliation. Attempt to concentrate on domestic problems since return from DC. Outside interferences noted. Says vicious circle of retaliation will begin if peace settlement not reached soon. Calls for solution to Palestinian problem.

Print: 3/12—NYT-FP Lead—with 2 pictures of scene and injured. 20–30 Israeli civilians die in PLO attack in Tel Aviv. FP SB—Weizman summoned home, Begin puts off trip to U.S., Carter denounces act as outrageous. IP—Chronology of terrorist offensives in Israel. Ed.—Attack in Israel threatens ME peace; Begin losing popularity at home, with cartoon of Begin as Samson having his hair cut off by military, politicians; How Begin's loss of popularity effects his U.S. relations. 6 articles/10 pages.

●3/15—NYT-FP Lead—with map, (magnified headline) Big Israeli force invades southern Lebanon. (1) PLO reports jets, sea attacks on bases. (2) Israel says it is a limited action. FPSB—Sadat assails raid by PLO in Israel. IP—Chronology of earlier raids into Lebanon; Text of Sadat's remarks on PLO raid, with picture of him; Dayan tells Israelis that Egypt does not require that Jordan join in peace talks. 6 articles/9 pages.

Policy events: Carter denounces Israeli raid; Weizman returns to Israel.

3/15/78: Egyptian, Syrian, and Lebanese leaders denounce Israeli occupation of 6-mile deep stretch of Southern Lebanon and ask for world pressure Israel to withdraw. Israel withdraws 6 days later.*

Television: Heavy coverage all three networks. 6–12 mins. with film. Sadat and Foreign Minister Kamel greeting of Belgian for min. noted along with his reaction to Sadat's denouncement of PLO. Israeli raid reported. Kamel is most unhappy with situation; thinks problems can be solved in the process of peace only. Foreign Minister's statement condemning Israeli raid. Begin states that raid should not prevent peace if Egypt really wants it.

Print: 3/16—NYT-FP Lead—with picture and map. *Israel seizes 4-6 mile "security belt" in Lebanon and say troops will remain.* Points:

1. U.S. sympathetic to Israel's security needs, but sees it as impediment to peace.
2. major fighting ends.

FPSB—Guerillas join civilian retreat from attackers. IP—Moscow condemns invasion by Israel, cites role of U.S. Political profile of Weizman; (small story).

Saudis say if U.S. delays plans for jet deliveries, they will seek other vendors; (small story) PLO calls for Red Cross help; Lebanon and Syria urge world aid against Israel; Egypt denounces the raid as "organized

---

*Coverage of withdrawal not recorded by Archives.

genocide." Divided Lebanon again becomes a battlefield; Military Analysis—Invasion said to increase Israeli edge over Syria. Ed.—(NYT) Israel poses test to Arabs; Anti-PLO letter from Israeli; Pro-Israeli response. *14 articles/17 pages.*

Policy events: No significant policy events reported.

3/23/78: President Carter and Begin conclude two days of talks* in DC after failing to reach agreement on any of the major points blocking progress in the ME peace negotiations. Carter tells U.S. senators that the diplomatic process has "been brought to a halt."

Television: TOB. Light to moderate coverage. 4–5 mins. Begin appeals in National Press Club speech reported on network news. Makes direct appeal to American public for understanding of position. Film of send-off ceremonies at Washington Monument. Differences between two countries noted. Peace moves in ME noted. Special segment (ABC) on refugees in Lebanon.

Interview with Begin quoted: announced for later in news. Four min. segment of Barbara Walters interview broadcast at end of news. (ABC). Begin comes off very defiant.

Report on Begin/Sadat correspondence re: Israeli settlements on w. bank and in Sinai. DC talks repeatedly fruitless. Carter briefs Foreign Relations Committee. Carter said to be gloomy.

Print: 3/24—NYT-FP—with picture of Begin. Begin asks U.S. public to back Israeli policy after seeing Carter. FPSB-NA—Despite seriousness, U.S. aides say dispute with Israel not as bad as others. FPSB—with picture of refugees, Lebanon pleads for refugee aid to avoid catastrophe. IP—*Excerpts from Begin's news conference at National Press Club.*

More UN units enter Lebanon as Israelis to start pullout next week; Arabs fail in efforts to convene summit on Lebanese crisis. Small story on the issues of the ME debate; Weizman asks for new Israeli coalition. Ed.— (NYT) *Pro-Carter on Israeli issue.*

Policy events: Carter statement to senators, briefing for For. Rel. Committee.

3/30/78: Israeli defense minister goes to Cairo to meet with Sadat to try to revive talks.

Television: TOB. 4–5 mins light to moderate coverage, w/film from Egyptian T.V. of Weizman's visit, heavy security to protect him. Egyptians

---

*Opening coverage of talks not recorded by Archives.

attitude described to Weizman visit. Failure of Carter/Begin talks in DC. Israelis interest in separate peace with Egypt. Begin's letter to Sadat. Lack of new proposals from Israel, and Sadat's refusal to continue talks noted.

Print: 3/31—NYT-IP—*Battle lines forming on Carter's plan to sell jets to Arabs; Guns silent in Lebanon for first day since invasion; Weizman meets with Sadat in an effort to resume peace talks; Saudi Arabia retains a politically experienced public relations firm to lobby approval of foreign policy and to enhance image in the U.S. for the long term.* 4 articles/4 pages.

Policy events: Reports that U.S. wants Begin replaced. Carter denies reports. Pentagon notifies Congress of plans to sell Israel Hawk missiles and radars.

4/1/78: 25,000 Israelis rally in Jerusalem, calling on Begin to soften his position on giving up Israeli-occupied territory in the West Bank and Gaza.

Television: Light to moderate coverage. 3–4 mins. Sadat's comments: re: continued direct contact w/Israel, given in Cairo magazine reported. Report on Israeli cabinet meetings and probability of another meeting between Sadat and Weizman. Sources report on Egypt's call for breaks in Palestinian and occupied lands question. Begin's silence detailed. Sadat's statements on resumption of peace talks reported.

Print: 4/2—NYT-IP—Life in Beirut neither peace nor war; Lebanese Prime Minister says Arafat vows to honor truce; Israelis rally to urge return of land to Arabs. Ed.—*Sadat-Weizman meeting produces nothing, pessimistic; Chances of Lebanon pull-out are slim.* 5 articles/5 pages.

Policy events: Continued Congressional relations effort by Administration for arms sale.

5/15/78: Senate approves arms sale to Egypt, Israel, and Saudi Arabia.

Television: TOB. Light to moderate coverage. 5 mins with film (CBS). Activity noted in Senate as vote called on Carter's ME plane sales. Some think sale deals a blow to ME peace talks.

Print: 5/16—NYT-FP Lead—*Senate backs sale of jets, 54-44.* FPSB-NA—*Senate vote goes beyond sale to issue of ties to Israel and Arab moderates.* IP—Palestinians in Southern Lebanon agree to withdraw. Lobbyists on both sides of jet issue unrelenting—Senate roll-call given. Ed.—(Wicker) *Lukewarm support of jet sale.* 5 articles/7 pages.

Policy events: Congress votes arms sale.

6/6/78: In a speech to his troops, Sadat warns that if Israel continues not to understand what is behind his peace initiative, Egypt will have to go to war with Israel again.

Television: No significant coverage.

Print: 6/7—NYT-IP—with picture of civilian carrying automatic rifle on the street, Worst wave of violent crime since Civil War is keeping Lebanese in their homes at night; Israel asks UN to shield Christians in Lebanon after troop pullout. 2 articles/2 pages.

Policy events: No policy events reported.

7/5/78: Egypt formally announces plan for peace in the ME, which calls for Israeli withdrawal from occupied territories over 5 years and self-determination for Arabs in Gaza and West Bank.

Television: TOB all nets. Light coverage of Sadat's peace plan. Coverage of Israel's actions in West Bank. (4 min av. with film)

Print: 7/6—NYT-FP—evening edition—(announced on 7/6 as occurring on 7/6). *Egypt today makes details of peace plan public, calls for withdrawal from all occupied territories over 5 years and self-determination for Palestinians in Gaza and West Bank.* FPSB—Israelis disappointed by new plan but will go to talks. IP—Text of new peace plan; Another cease-fire collapsed in Lebanon. Ed.—(NYT) *More compromise is needed by both sides.* 5 articles/7 pages.

Policy events: No policy events reported.

7/9/78: Israeli Cabinet rejects Sadat's peace plan.

Television: Light to moderate coverage: Israeli opposition to Egyptian proposals reported along with vote to send rep. to meeting in London. Begin announces elections. Begin's cabinet discusses meetings in Vienna between Sadat and Peres.

Coverage of Sadat's remarks re: it would be easier to work with Peres than with Begin, but ready to meet with Begin when new ideas ready. (4 min av. with film)

●*Print:* 7/10—NYT-FP—Israeli Cabinet formally rejects peace plan. FPSB—Sadat and Peres meet in Vienna but no accord, with picture of both shaking hands. IP—Lebanese President insists he'll resign. Ed.—(Lewis) Support for jet sales is not anti-Israel. 3 articles/4 pages.

Policy events: Continued discussions on jet sales to Egypt, but no significant policy events found.

7/13/78: Sadat unexpectedly meets Israeli DOD Minister in Austria and gives him new peace plan.

Television: No policy coverage reported.

Print: 7/14—NYT-IP—*Sadat meets Weizman in Austria, Weizman calls talks "useful."* (with picture of Sadat and Weizman in front page). 1 article/1 page.

Policy events: No events reported.

7/22/78: Sadat calls Begin an obstacle to peace in the ME at a political rally.

Television: No significant coverage. Television covered Begin's rejection of Sadat's request for return of Mt. Sinai and El Arish as goodwill gesture on 7/23/78. Begin's letter to Sadat outlined: Ready to negotiate based on reciprocity. Begin responds to Sadat's speech in Cairo calling him an obstacle to peace. (4 min av. with film).

Print: 7/23—NYT-FP—with picture of Sadat, Sadat calls Begin "the only obstacle to Middle East accord," also calls to abolish major Arab party. Ed.—(NYT) Israel should give in on issue of West Bank; (Farrell) Israeli Cabinet gets nastier as divisions erupt. 3 articles/4 pages.

Policy events: No policy events reported.

8/8/78: U.S. announces Sadat and Begin will meet at Camp David in September to explore ways to resolve ME deadlock.

Television: Light to moderate coverage of upcoming ME conference with Carter/Sadat/Begin. Jody Powell announces that Sadat and Begin both accepted. Coverage of Begin, Sadat comments on summit. Vance states that U.S. is now a full participant in ME peace process, as Sadat requested in Alexandria meeting. (3–5 mins with film).

Print: 8/9—NYT-FP Lead—*Carter to meet Begin and Sadat in U.S. Sept. 5 to break stalemate.* FPSB-NA—Mediation offers by Carter holds political risks, but he is reportedly worried over military picture. IP—Sadat says he agreed to meeting when U.S. accepted a wider role; U.N. Lebanon chief appeals to Israelis to exert pressure on Christians to halt shelling. Ed.—(NYT) *The President's push for peace is a positive step.* 5 articles/7 pages.

Policy events: Major policy action to move peace process ahead.

8/14/78: Israel halts consideration of 5 new West Bank settlements pending outcome of Camp David.

Television: no significant coverage; see 8/13/78 coverage of Camp David,

Beirut bombing of Palestinian sector. Report on Carter interview with *US NEWS* in which he links his political future and success of Camp David.

Print: NOTE: PRINTING PRESSMAN ON STRIKE IN NYC. No NYT from 8/10/78–11/5/78. Stories taken from Washington Post until end of strike.

Washington Post

8/15—WP-FP Lead—With picture, Israel reassured aid, settlements held up—1) Vance says U.S. help not linked to summit results, 2) Cabinet shelves plan on five settlements until after U.S. meeting. IP—Israel and Egypt compete in aid to OAS nations. 3 articles/5 pages.

Policy events: Continuing movement on Camp David initiative, assurances of unconditioned air to Israel.

9/4–9/18/78: (events combined because news blackout required summary reporting. Day-to-day events not available during this period) Camp David talks in operation and two documents are signed: "A Framework for Peace in Middle East," and "A Framework for the Conclusion of Peace Between Israel and Egypt." Treaty signing Sunday Night at White House mentioned. Carter addresses Congress.

Television: (9/4) Heavy coverage all nets. Outcome of summit speculation. Begin arrives in NYC. Film of Begin stroll down Park Ave. but refuses interviews. Sadat stops off in Paris, meets Giscard d'Estaing. (9–12 min average, with film)

•(9/5) TOB heavy. Arrival of Sadat and full ceremony and welcome by VP Mondale, with film. Film of Sadat on plane. Film of Carter meeting Sadat at Camp David.

Film of Begin's Camp David arrival. Begin vows all possible efforts for peace. Powell press conference. Chance meeting of Begin and Sadat, anti-Sadat demonstrations in ME noted.

•(9/6/78—7 mins with film) Sadat tour of countryside reported. News Blackout at Camp David. Meetings between Carter and Sadat noted.

(9/7) Reports of meetings. Blackout continues, Powell statement, still photos released by White House.

(9/8) Light to moderate coverage on Camp David; news blackout continues.

(9/11) Light coverage of talks; blackout continues.

(9/12) Light coverage of talks; blackout continues.

(9/13) Light coverage of talks; blackout continues.

(9/14) Moderate coverage. TOB some nets: WH reports with photos; no progress, but no statement. Sadat call to Hussein mentioned. Phone interviews with Hussein (ABC) who commented on Sadat's hopes, later meeting in Morocco. Live report from Tel Aviv re: Sadat-Dayan meeting designed to keep Sadat and Begin apart.

(9/15) Light coverage. White House reports only, Powell comments on progress, meetings between Begin, Sadat, Carter, Vance, Mondale.

(9/16) No significant coverage.

(9/17) No significant coverage.

(9/18) TOB heavy coverage. Release by U.S., Egypt, Israel of text of agreements. Film and maps. Film of Sadat, Begin, Carter. Interviews, WH photos of negotiations. Much news analysis.

Sadat interview with network anchors, answers questions. Says would be happiest man in world for approval of agreement; is yearning to go to Mt. Sinai where God spoke to Moses, so he could pray. Said he almost walked out, but Carter talked him out of it.

Begin interviews on nets.

Reactions from Israel, Cairo, USSR, other locations.

Print: 9/6—WP-FP Lead—with 2 pictures, Carter welcomes Sadat and Begin to summit. IP—Terror bomb injures two in Jerusalem; Carter summit is compared to Theodore Roosevelt's summit which resulted in treaty ending Russian-Japanese War. 3 articles/4 pages.

9/7—WP-FP Lead—with picture, Carter, Sadat, and Begin hold first meeting. IP—Moscow labels talks trick to boost U.S. role. Ed.—(Kraft) Summit is PR triumph for Carter. 3 articles/4 pages.

9/8—WP-FP—with picture, Carter accelerates Summit pace. IP—Syria announces that if Israel signs a defense treaty with U.S., it will do so with Soviet Union; Journalists with very little to do wait for tidbits of information, with picture. Ed.—U.S. as ME overseer worth the risk. 4 articles/5 pages.

9/9—WP-FP-NA—Sadat needs clear cut outcome. IP—Carter meets Sadat and Begin separately. 2 articles/3 pages.

9/10—WP-FP—Summit progress seen but major hurdles remain. IP—Ed.—(WP) Summit should be kept private but not results. 2 articles/3 pages.

9/16—WP-FP—Carter seeks West Bank 3-way rule.

9/17—WP-FP—Summit to end today.

9/18—WP-FP Lead—with picture, Leaders concur on framework for settlement in ME. FPSB-NA—Sadat runs higher risk than Begin. FPSB—Main provisions of Summit accord. IP—Israel court blocks work on West Bank settlement; Excerpts of statements by all three; Israelis greet accord with joy and caution. 6 articles/9 pages.

Other: Special broadcasts on networks on treaty, summit.

Policy events: Talks.

9/19/78: Egyptian Cabinet approves Camp David agreements unanimously.

Television: Heavy coverage. 8–10 mins with film. Dissatisfaction with Camp David by Jordan and Saudi Arabia noted. Carter's farewell noted. Carter's concern re: Sadat/Begin's statements to press re: statements about agreements not released. Sadat/Begin's meetings with congressman noted. Aides play down Carter/Begin disagreement re: West Bank settlements.

Print: 9/20—WP-FP Lead—with 2 pictures. *Dispute on Israeli settlement snags accord.* FPSB—*Saudis, Jordan assail accords; The two intractable issues.* IP—Rightist Israeli faction attacks accord, with picture. Ed.—WP—*Critical of Begin's decision not to try to influence Knesset vote;* (Evans and Novack) Pro-Carter but success still depends on his efforts. 7 articles/10 pages.

Policy events: Continued talks.

9/24/78: Syria, Algeria, and other Arab countries break relations with Egypt. Knesset approves the Camp David accords; Vance in Damascus with King Assad.

Television: TOB Israeli cabinet agreement to abandon Sinai settlements. Statement from Begin in Jerusalem, Vance's return to U.S. after meeting with Assad. Report from Damascus: interview with Vance as leaving airport.

Other: Kissinger on *Meet the Press* comments that Arabs will join with Egypt when agreement concluded.

Print: 9/25—WP-FP Lead—Israeli Cabinet votes to support summit accords. FPSB—Vance-Assad talks called inconclusive. IP—Carter pledge for U.S. role called key to Sadat's agreement.

9/25/78 to 9/27/78.

Television: Light coverage of progress of agreements in ME, Israeli parliament debate, reactions of other Arab nations, no coverage of Sadat. Some interviews with Begin, reports of Sadat calls for removal of Sinai settlements. Details of communication links between Egypt and Israel.

Policy events: Carter briefed on Vance trip, ME events, comments on his confidence of peace accords success.

Print: Not available.

9/28/78: Knesset votes to approve the Camp David accords and dismantle settlements as required by the agreements. Carter press conference.

Television: TOB. Carter news conference with commendation of Knesset for approval of accords. Egyptian TV film shown, but no statement from Sadat; marching in Cairo streets in joy over accords. Sadat orders 2-wk pay bonus for govt. workers. Report from Israel on reactions, especially from settlers who have to move. Begin makes his remarks from Tel Aviv.

Print: WP-FP Lead—with picture, *Knesset votes 84-17 to approve accord.* FPSB—*Hussein faces difficult choice.* IP—*Egypt awaits peace talks calmly with no debate;* Assad presses hardline views on Kuwait; Carter disputes Begin on West Bank settlement. Ed.—(Kraft) *Profile on Begin,* pro-Begin. 6 articles/8 pages.

Policy events: Carter news conference.

10/12–21/78: Negotiations between Israeli and Egyptian delegations on a U.S. draft treaty between Egypt and Israel in Washington. Carter intervenes when talks break down and Sadat decides to recall his delegations. Carter obtains agreement on main elements of an agreement.

Television:

●10/12/78: Light to moderate coverage. 3–4 mins with film. Opening of peace talks to be held in Blair House. Carter pledges U.S. involvement. Dayan states peace possible. Issues under discussion, w. bank settlements, Sinai, and Gaza strip. Egyptian Defense Minister Ali hopes negotiations are successful.

●10/20/78: Light to moderate coverage. 4–5 mins with film. U.S. presentation of draft to negotiators reported. Israeli delegation said returning to Jerusalem. Cabinet of Israel charges Dayan with haste. Dayan suggests summit with Carter/Sadat/Begin.

Print:

●10/13—WP-FP—*Israeli-Egyptian talks begin.* IP—Text of opening remarks by Carter, Dayan, and Ali. 2 articles/3 pages.

•10/14—WP-FP—Egypt, Israel to work from U.S. treaty draft. IP—Israel may speed up West Bank plan; Sinai's exiles ready to go home. 3 articles/4 pages.

•10/18—WP-FP—Carter intervenes in Egypt-Israeli talks.

•10/19—WP-FP—Egyptians reportedly agree to sell Sinai oil to Israel. IP—Arabs charge Israelis defy court on West Bank project. 2 articles/3 pages.

•10/21—WP-FP Lead—Israelis go home to consult on U.S. plan—(1) Israeli anxiety evident (2) U.S. minimizes departure. 2 articles/4 pages.

Policy events: Carter intervention in talks.

10/25/78: Israeli Cabinet agrees to draft treaty in principle, but Begin adds amendments before submitting to Knesset.

Television: Light coverage. 2–4 mins all networks. Conditional approval by Israel and Egypt of peace draft reported. Approval by Israeli cabinet noted.

Print: 10/26—WP-FP—with picture, Israeli Cabinet gives approval in principle to compromise, will draft treaty. IP—After 30 years Israeli muslims to see Mecca; Egypt hints Saudi support of peace moves. 3 articles/4 pages.

Policy events: None reported.

10/26/78: Carter expresses concern to Begin regarding last minute amendments, new settlements. Egyptian threat to recall its negotiators in protest.

Television: Light to moderate coverage. 3–5 mins with film. Israelis recent decision (date of decision not noted) to enlarge of West Bank settlements. Reactions of Vance and Carter noted. Carter's complaint to Begin reported. Possible consequences outlined. Egyptian response reported, Sadat may recall negotiators.

Print: 10/27—WP-FP Lead—ME talks run into serious new problems:

1. U.S. and Israel at odds on West Bank settlements.
2. Israel stresses claim to occupied territories.

IP—Egypt may recall peace delegation to protest Israeli move; Syria and Iraq plan to join forces. Ed.—(WP) *Peace process still continuing, Saudi Arabia should support it.* 5 articles/7 pages.

Policy events: No public actions reported; behind the scenes attempt to hold the talks together, keep Sadat from pulling out.

10/27/78: Nobel Committee announces it will give Nobel Peace Prize to Sadat and Begin.

Television: Heavy coverage all networks. 8–10 mins with film. Awarding of Nobel Peace Prize to Begin/Sadat. Committee mentions Carter. Lack of comment by Begin/Sadat noted. Sadat frustrated by sharing prize with Begin noted re: Israeli decision to expand settlements in West Bank. Carter's message of objection to Begin noted. Events leading up to the first meetings of Sadat and Begin noted.

Print: 10/28—WP-FP Lead—*Sadat and Begin get Nobel prize as peace-makers.* FPSB—Egypt recalls 2 negotiators from talks. IP—with picture, Israelis "baffled" by U.S. reaction to settlements. 3 articles/5 pages.

Policy events: Negative response to settlements decision.

10/28/78: Sadat reverses decision to recall delegation from Washington talks after a personal plea from Carter.

Television: No significant coverage.

Print: 10/29—WP-FP—2 Egyptian negotiators to stay here after appeal by Carter. IP—Begin congratulates Sadat, Arabs assail Nobel choice. Ed.—(WP) *Nobel carries responsibilities, Begin should be aware of that.* 3 articles/4 pages.

Policy events: No public policy events reported.

11/4/78: Sadat refuses to meet with Arab delegation from Baghdad Summit.

Television: No significant coverage on 11/4; light coverage on 11/5 of Arab demands that Sadat give up accords.

Print: 11/5—WP-FP—Sadat snubs Arab envoy, article in inside page. Ed.—(Kraft) Observation of what he sees is a realignment in the ME. 2 articles/2 pages.

Policy events: No policy events reported.

11/10/78: Egypt asks Israel to agree to a timetable for relinquishing rule in the West Bank and the Gaza and transferring power to Palestinians.

Television: TOB: Light coverage, all nets. Continued differences between Sadat and Begin reported on issue of future settlement of Palestine problem. Sadat film: comments on potential for stalemate at DC talks, says he wants peace, not partial agreements or mere disengagements. Begin says may be an exaggeration.

Print: 11/11—NYT-FP—A new Sadat request to agree in advance to a detailed timetable for relinquishing military rule in West Bank and Gaza and transferring power to Palestinians delays treaty talks, U.S. aides concerned. IP—Peace talk tactics and aims bewilder West Bank Arabs, with picture of Israelis building homes on the West Bank. NA—*As talks lag, Sadat appears calm and sure of U.S. help,* with picture. 3 articles/4 pages.

Policy events: Reports of concern at White House and DOS over accords.

11/21/78: Israeli Cabinet accepts U.S. draft of treaty, but rejects Egypt's demands for linkage to a timetable for Palestinian autonomy. Egypt recalls chief negotiator from Washington.

Television: Light to moderate coverage. 3 mins with film. Carter calls Begin/Sadat in effort to speed up peace effort.

Print: 11/22—NYT-FP—with picture of Begin, *Israelis back pact as proposed by Israel, rejects a timetable.* IP—Arafat accepts U.N. peace force if Palestinian state is established; U.S. striving to keep ME peace talks alive; Sadat recalling chief negotiator from Washington in apparent show of displeasure. Ed.—(guest columnist) *Cairo and Egypt, separate and above the rest of the Arab states.* 5 articles/6 pages.

Policy events: Continued behind the scenes discussion of strategies to save accords during DC meeting. Vance to meet Begin.

12/1/78: Carter meets with Egyptian Prime Minister to receive Sadat's latest proposal. They agree to renew peace talks.

Television: Light to moderate coverage. 2–3 mins. Begin ready to resume peace talks after personal message from Sadat. Details of White House meetings between Carter/Vance/Egyptian PM Khalil reported. Sadat thought to be ready to accept American proposal in principle. Israelis lack of acceptance noted. Reaction of Khalil and Vance noted. Speculation about Sadat's possible decision to accept Nobel Prize with Begin noted.

Print: 12/2—NYT-FP—*Egypt and Israel will resume talks,* U.S. aides disclose. Carter gets Egyptian plan from Egyptian Prime Minister. IP—Begin and Sadat consulting with top aides on reopening talks with Egypt. 2 articles/3 pages.

Policy events: 11/12 Vance meeting with Begin. Continuing work on retaining Camp David agreements.

12/4/78: Begin tells Sadat he does not want to change the treaty but will discuss side letters.

Television: Light to moderate coverage. 3–4 mins. Letter from Begin to Sadat reported. U.S. reported to be waiting for reply to Sadat's proposal from Israel. Prospects for talks not good. Vances meeting with PM Khalil reported. Remaining issues of Palestinian autonomy and treaty precedence over Egypts other treaties mentioned.

Print: 12/5—NYT-FP—Begin tells Sadat he does not want to change treaty but offers more negotiations on occupied areas. IP—U.S. delays Egypt-Israel talks in effort to arrange compromises; Israel tears down West Bank houses. 3 articles/4 pages.

Policy events: Continuing work on retaining Camp David Accords framework.

12/7/78: Carter pressures Egypt and Israel to meet Dec. 17 deadline for treaty. Says new Jewish settlements on West Bank would violate Camp David accords.

Television: Light to moderate coverage. 3–4 mins. Carter's remarks on stalled talks noted. His remarks re: violation of deadline set for treaty reported. Sadat's view on deadlock including U.S. position. Contention of Sadat and other top Egyptians that summit involving Carter may be needed again.

Print: 12/8—NYT-FP—*Carter warns of delay in ME accord, stresses Dec. 17 deadline.* IP—*Young charges U.N. is slowing progress of ME peace talks;* Excerpts from Carter's meeting with reporters. 3 articles/4 pages.

Policy events: Carter warning speech; Andy Young charges.

12/10/78: Sadat and Begin receive Nobel Peace prize. Vance meets Sadat in Cairo in first session of expected shuttle diplomacy.

Television: No significant coverage recorded by Archives.

Print: 12/10—No print reports on Nobel prize (see 12/11).

•12/11—NYT-FP—(Only late NYT edition available) Vance starts talks with Sadat on pact; *Egypt and Israel air differences at Nobel ceremony.* IP—Police in Israel tighten security to prepare for Meir's funeral. 3 articles/5 pages.

Policy events: Vance meeting with Sadat.

12/12/78: Sadat accepts latest U.S. proposal which would resolve outstanding differences.

Television: Light to moderate coverage. 5–6 mins with film. Burial of former PM Meir noted. Carter restates importance of concluding Egyptian/Israeli peace treaty by 12/17/78. Believes Sadat has reaffirmed his intention to conclude treaty soon. Vances meetings in Cairo with Sadat noted. New proposals reportedly worked out.

Print: NYT-FP—*Vance wins Sadat backing on moves to break deadlock.* IP—Golda Meir is buried. 2 articles/3 pages.

Policy events: No events reported other than Vance meetings.

12/13/78: Vance gives Begin treaty proposals; Begin rejects side letters regarding Egypts legal responsibilities to other Arab nations and a target date for talks on Palestinian rule.

Television: TOB. Moderate coverage all three networks. 5–6 mins. Vance's arrival in Jerusalem from Cairo noted. Remaining peace talks outlined. Sadat's position on treaty status noted. Sadat will insist on Mt. Sinai as site of signing. Sadat's acceptance of Nobel Prize and check noted. Egyptians reaction to Sadat's sharing of prize with Begin described. Uncertainty about Sadat's reaction to latest Israeli rejections stated. Vance's plan to meet with Sadat/Begin again before returning home reiterated.

Print: 12/14—NYT-FP—*U.S.-Egyptian plans to resolve treaty rejected by Israel.* IP—Egyptians (in general) acclaim Carter peace role; Carter calls Cairo very generous; Sadat wants signing on Mt. Sinai. Ed.—Egypt-Israel peace initiative analyzed. 5 articles/6 pages.

Policy events: Carter remarks, no other events.

12/15/78: Israeli Cabinet rejects latest treaty draft.

Television: Light to moderate coverage. 5–6 mins with film. Israeli cabinet rejects peace treaty proposal. Begin says responsibility for lack of treaty is with the Egyptians. Comments on U.S. government attitude toward Egypt's proposals and outlook for peace. Sadat's refusal to comment on Israeli action noted.

Print: 12/16—NYT-FP—Israel rejects peace proposal, U.S. irritated, charges distortion. IP—Egypt denies seeking new terms. 2 articles/3 pages.

Policy events: No events reported.

12/17/78: Deadline for treaty signing passes. Vance says Egypt's proposals were reasonable and should be considered by Israel.

Television: No significant coverage.

Print: 12/18—NYT—No news articles on Israel or Egypt except for IP picture of Sadat kissing grandchild with note of treaty signing date passing. Ed.—(Safire) *Carter blames Jews for no treaty signing.* 1 article/1 page.

Policy events: Vance urges Israel to reconsider.

12/18/78: For. Min. Dayan says no new talks with Egypt until it drops its latest proposals.

Television: No significant coverage.

Print: 12/19—NYT-IP—Dyan rebuffs Vance, dismisses newest Cairo proposals; Outgoing Israeli Ambassador criticizes Carter's role. 2 articles/2 · pages.

Policy events: No significant coverage.

12/31/78: Begin willing to discuss Egypts proposal for exchange of letters on the status of West Bank and Gaza.

Television: Light coverage all networks. 2–3 mins with film. Begin's statements re: Israel ready to resume talks reported. Sets forth conditions and DC as likely meeting spot.

Print: 1/1—NYT-IP—with picture, Israelis decide to continue talks with Egypt on treaty; (small) New acts against Israel planned by Palestinians. 2 articles/2 pages.

Policy events: No significant coverage.

1/13/79: U.S. announces two-stage effort to revive ME peace talks. Sends Ambassador Atherton to Egypt and Israel.

Television: No significant coverage.

Print: 1/14—NYT-FP—U.S. reviving effort for ME treaty, Atherton going to Israel and Egypt. IP—3 Palestinian guerillas are killed in attempt to attack hotel in northern Israel. Ed.—(Kandell) Analysis of Israeli opposition of W. Bank issue. 3 articles/4 pages.

Policy events: Atherton to ME; major effort.

1/16–27/79: Atherton meets Egyptian and Israeli officials but no success.

Television: No significant coverage.

Print: 1/17—NYT-IP—U.S. envoy arrives in Israel; Lebanon worried about departure of some U.N. troops; Young asks for new look at PLO. 3 articles/3 pages.

1/19—IP—Rightists from Begin's party are loudly critical of Begin's attempts at peace; (small) Conference of Presidents of Major American Jewish Organizations criticize Young's PLO remarks. Ed.—NYT—Carter should aggressively push again for ME peace.

1/201/28—Nothing but infrequent and small IP articles on talks (emphasis on overthrow of Shah of Iran).

1/29—NYT-FP—U.S. envoy fails in attempts to revive talks. IP—2 dead and 34 hurt in Israeli bombing by PLO; White House disputes NYT magazine article saying it tried to undermine Begin. 3 articles/4 pages.

Policy events: Continuing attempts to revive talks.

2/12/79: Carter says he will favorably consider a summit meeting between himself, Begin, and Sadat if the treaty deadlock is not broken.

Television: No significant coverage.

Print: 2/12—NYT-FP—Israelis and Egyptians going to Camp David for talks this month. 1 article/2 pages.

Policy events: Carter statement on summit potential.

2/13—No significant events reported.

2/21/78: Egyptian, Israeli and U.S. officials arrive at Camp David to resume peace negotiations.

Television: Moderate coverage. 4–5 mins with film. Report on Camp David meetings among Foreign Ministers of Egypt & Israel with Vance. Major issue reported to be that of linking treaty to Palestinian autonomy on West Bank and Gaza. Sadat's attitude toward treaty noted. Concerns about peace and stability in ME outlined. Sadat's statement to DOD Sec. Brown that Egypt logical replacement for Iran as pro-Western force. Sadat's unwillingness to make more concessions noted.

Print: 2/22—NYT-IP—Egypt and Israel talks on accord resume. 1 article/1 page.

Policy events: No events reported, continuing efforts.

3/14/79: Begin arrives in Washington for talks with Carter. Carter gives Begin new proposals but still no success.

Television: 3/1/79: TOB. 3–4 mins with film. Begin arrives in DC for talks with Carter. Comments re: peace settlement with Egypt. Sadat mentioned. Position of U.S./Egypt cited as obstacle to talks by Begin. Reported invitation by China to Sadat for visit.

Segment 3: (NBC) 4 mins with film. Need of peace in Egypt noted. Sadat's action for peace said related to Egypts socioeconomic situation. High unemployment, air pollution and poverty problems cited. Corruption of government said dominated by Sadat also noted. Sadat needs more U.S. aid to provide help for Egypt.

Print: 3/1—NYT-FP—New U.S.-Israeli tensions develop on eve of Begin arrival for talks. IP—Egypt says ME peace accord possible if Begin reasonable; Begin says "grave issues" still block peace treaty. 3 articles/4 pages.

Television: 3/2/79—Light to moderate coverage. 3–4 mins with film. Report of meetings between Begin/Carter. American dissatisfaction with results noted. Begin's position remains unchanged.

Print: 3/2/79—NYT-FP—with picture, Begin lands in U.S. saying peace talks are in a "deep crisis," says U.S. plan would turn pact into a "sham document." IP—NA—As pressure grows, Israel acts to mold public opinion. 2 articles/3 pages.

3/3—NYT-FP—with picture, Carter confers with Begin on pact, no progress is seen. 1 article/2 pages.

3/4—NYT-FP—Carter and Begin apparently unable to agree on treaty. IP—Israelis cite basis for defense fears. Ed.—NYT—Pressure grows, and Israel feels it, for treaty; (NYT)—Issues between Egypt and Israel are minor, Egyptians should give in a little to save treaty. 4 articles/5 pages.

Policy events: Continuing efforts.

3/4/79: Carter announces he will fly to the ME to break the impasse blocking a peace treaty.

Television: 3/4/79: Light to moderate coverage. 2–5 mins with film. Sadat action re: Egyptian/Israeli peace treaty considered. Begin speaks of serious reflection and deliberations. Current state of talks noted. Carter reported in touch with Sadat re: talks.

Print: 3/5—NYT-FP—with picture, Carter gives Begin treaty suggestions to buoy talks. Ed.—(Safire) Pro Israel, critical of Carter. 2 articles/3 pages.

Policy events: New treaty suggestions to Begin.

3/5–7/79: Israeli Cabinet approves the latest proposals.

Television: 3/5/79: Moderate coverage. 5–6 mins with film. Carter's trip to Cairo then to Jerusalem this week announced. Attempt to keep possibility of peace alive in ME. Carter in touch with Sadat by phone. New Israeli/ Egyptian positions, outlined to Israeli cabinet. Acceptance of Carter's proposals reported. Egypt's lack of public acceptance noted.

Television: 3/6/79: Light to moderate coverage. 4–5 mins with film. Begin's pressure on Sadat to sign treaty noted. Sadat's popularity noted. Proposed U.S. takeover of Israeli air base reported. Administration denies.

Television: 3/7/79: TOB. Heavy coverage. 8–15 mins. Details of Carter's trip. Planned arrival at Cairo noted. Egyptian response to Carter's proposals noted. Dismissal of Mt. Sinai as treaty signing place noted. Isolation of Sadat by rest of Arab world noted.

Print: 3/6—NYT-FP Lead—Carter to go to ME this week hoping to complete final treaty, Israelis accept key U.S. change (1) Linkage is modified, (2) Egypt is first stop. FPSB-NA-President's mission seen as a great opportunity but risky. IP—Khalil sees chance for breakthrough, people on the streets (Egyptians) praise decision by Carter to visit; Israeli jets buzz Beirut. 5 articles/8 pages.

Policy events: Major effort: Carter decision to go to ME to complete final treaty.

3/8/79: Carter arrives in Cairo for talks with Sadat. Sadat says Egypt and Israel are on the verge of an agreement.

Television: 3/8/79–3/11/79: Moderate to Heavy coverage with film. 7–11 mins. Details of Carter's activities in Egypt and negotiations given. Carter address Parliament. Treaty issues listed, difficulties still remain. Anti-Carter demos noted. Palestinian issue said to be problem. Carter said to be leaving for Israel with Sadat counter-proposals.

Print: 3/9—NYT-FP Lead—with picture, *Carter and Sadat confer but some differences remained, crowd hails Carter.* FPSB—Sadat and Carter confer for 2-1/2 hours, intend to continue talks on unresolved issues. IP—Begin back home voices confidence; Syrians say U.S. arranged pact will not bring peace to ME; Carter's staying in royal palace. 5 articles/7 pages.

Policy events: Continuing Carter initiative.

3/10/79: Carter arrives in Jerusalem for talks with Begin to resolve outstanding issues.

Television: Moderate coverage w/film. Carter's arrival in Israel, details of his public activities and negotiations. Carter to address Egyptian parliament. Sadat says difficult issues remain-film. Comments on Vance mission, rejection of Carter offer to PLO to join talks.

Print: No coverage 3/10/78.

3/11—NYT-FP Lead—*Carter arrives in Jerusalem, says he sees hope peace pact is near.* Points:

1. Assures Egypt before leaving Cairo that he pledges to deal with Palestinian problem
2. Carter warns of some difficult issues ahead.

IP—with picture of Carter and Sadat, full text of addresses by Carter and Sadat; Carter gets a muted greeting in Israel. Article on Egyptian's fixation with Carter's visit. Ed.—*New gamble at treaty began at Camp David*, with large caricature of Carter as Moses parting a sea of tanks. 6 articles/9 pages.

Policy events: Continuing Carter ME initiative.

3/12/78: Carter fails to resolve outstanding issues, prepares to leave for Washington.

Television: 3/12/79: Moderate to heavy coverage. 8–9 mins with film. Carter leaves Israel and stops over in Egypt for meetings with Sadat. Mood in Cairo noted re: Carter's ME trip. Sadat's reaction to Carter's speech noted. Future of talks outlined.

Print: 3/13—NYT-FP—with picture, Carter nearing end of visit, to see Begin and Sadat again, obstacles still block peace, chides Begin and Sadat for refusing to "take chance" for peace. FPSB—Israeli parliament members listen silently to Carter, then heckle at Begin during his in protest of peace talks. FPSB—NA—Two ME sticking points—Israel's demand for guaranteed oil from Sinai, Egypt's demand for early self rule for Palestinians in Gaza; Text of Carter's address and Begin's reply, with picture; Carter will confer with Sadat at airport during Cairo stopover. 5 articles/8 pages.

Policy events: Carter address to Knessett.

3/13/78: Carter announces from Cairo that Sadat has agreed to the last striking points. Begin submits final points to Cabinet for compromise, threatens to bring down his administration if they don't approve.

Television: 3/13/79: Light to moderate coverage. 5–8 mins with film. Carter's meetings with Sadat detailed. Carter announces Sadat/Begin agreement. Cost of peace to U.S., possible economic sanctions against Egypt by other nations. Israel charges U.S. media pressure on Israel and coverage detailed, alleged manipulation by Carter aide, Rafshoon.

Print: 3/14—NYT-FP Lead—Sadat backs Carter terms, Begin agrees to Cabinet vote, then a test in Knesset. FPSB—with picture, Begin hails Egyptian acceptance, calls treaty possible within a week. IP—Statements by Carter and Begin on talks; Carter's return draws cheering crowd, with picture; For peacemakers (Carter and Vance) a hopeful turn; Cairo awaits Israeli treaty action. Ed.—NYT—Complimenting Carter; Reston—Kissinger's view of the ME conflict. 8 articles/10 pages.

Policy events: Agreement!

3/14/79: Israeli Cabinet approves the compromises.

Television: 3/14/79: TOB: Heavy to moderate coverage. 7–9 mins with film. Approval of compromise proposals by Israeli cabinet. **Sadat's reaction noted.** Weizman and Hassan Ali due in DC for military annex to treaty. Other Arabs call for economic sanctions.

Print: 3/15—NYT-FP Lead—with picture, Israeli Cabinet accepts changes, Knesset vote next week, easy passage is seen. FPSB—Carter is said to put new U.S. aid to Egypt and Israel at 4 billion; Weary Carter thanks legislature for their support; Many Arab nations assail Cairo pact. IP—Moves by Vance, Dayan, and Evron and Israeli fears of appearing intransigent are seen as key factors in success; Israel exchanges 66 Palestinians for soldiers captured in Lebanon; U.S. said to accept a direct role in talks on Palestinian home rule. Ed.—Lewis—How success happened. 8 articles/10 pages.

Policy events: Agreement.

3/15/79: Egyptian Cabinet approves treaty.

Television: 3/15/79–3/25/79: Light to moderate coverage. 5–7 mins with film. Egyptian cabinet approves treaty. U.S. defense pact with Israel noted, similar one with Egypt contingent upon Sadat. Sadat visits home town to celebrate treaty (film). Comments on effect of treaty on Arab world.

Print: No significant coverage.

Policy events: No events reported.

3/26/79: Begin and Sadat sign treaty.

Television: 3/26/79—TOB. Heavy coverage. 6–9 mins with film. Signing of treaty occurs 30 years after war. Sadat quoted, "It's Jimmy's show." Comments on treaty re: starting place for peace. Begin/Sadat tribute to Carter noted. Arab reaction noted.

3/27/79: Light to moderate coverage. 4–5 mins with film. Lobbying by Sadat/Begin on the hill re: financial support as stated in treaty. Sadat seeks U.S. pressure on Israel re: West Bank and Gaza strip. Begin asked U.S. not to doubt intentions re: Palestinian question. Sadat comments on price of peace. Negotiations in the future between Israel/Egypt re: West Bank and Gaza noted.

Print: 3/27—NYT-FP Lead—(magnified)—with 4 pictures, *Israel and Egypt sign peace treaty, ending state of war after 30 years, Sadat and Begin praise Carter's role.* FPSB—Mood of peace seems somber and uncertain; FPSB-NA—Treaty impact still unknown. FPSB—Palestinians, reacting to the pact, go on strike and denounce Egypt. IP—Officials at UN foresee grave political risks in role under pact.

Special Section devoted to treaty, 8 full pages—Excerpts of the transcript of Carter, Begin, and Sadat (3 articles), with huge map of effected areas; with picture, Arabs have little outlet for anger over treaty; Israelis remain somber after official revelry, with picture; W. Bank town is cut off in treaty; with picture, in Egypt peace is welcomed quietly with hope for a better life.

Profile of Sadat and Begin; Transcripts of statements by all three of them after signing treaty. *3 full pages*—*Text of treaty, with maps;* Treaty opens door to new power balance; U.S. faces major ME role in insuring peace commitment; 30 years of war, with pictures; White House staff celebrates, with pictures; NY celebrates; Begin's return will be greeted by doves not guns.

Policy events: Continuing agreement events.

4/1/79: Israeli Cabinet approves treaty.

Television: No significant coverage.

Print: 4/2—NY-IP—Israeli cabinet backs treaty; Egypt dismisses punitive damages by Arab states. 2 articles/2 pages.

4/1019/79: Egypt approves treaty.

Television: No significant coverage.

Print: 4/11—NYT-IP—Egyptian views of Israelis, old stereotypes of Jews cling; Treatment of Bedouins in Sinai by Israel stirs outcry; Egypt bars apology to Israel for private speculation on aid to Syria. 3 articles/3 pages.

4/12—NYT-IP—Sadat sets April 19th for national referendum on Peace Treaty.

CASE 2
A COMPARATIVE CHRONOLOGY OF EVENTS, MEDIA REPORTS, AND POLICY EVENTS DURING THE HIJACKING OF TWA FLIGHT 847, JUNE 14, 1985–JULY 3, 1985

Introduction

This chronology describes events, television reports, print reports, and policy actions by the U.S. government during the events and negotiations surrounding the hijacking of TWA Flight 847 and the subsequent release of the hostages take as part of the hijacking.

Television reports were complied from abstracts of network news reports published by the Vanderbilt Television News Archive. Television summaries in this document blend abstracts from all three network reports. Noteworthy or unique reports by individual networks are indicated where appropriate.

Print reports are summaries of reports, features, graphics, and editorials printed in the *Washington Post*.* Summaries reflect headlines and editorial content abbreviated for space reasons.

Policy events are drawn from print and television news reports. A second phase of this research updated events through interviews.

Specialized reporting conventions and abbreviations were developed for use in this document to keep the summaries as brief as possible while providing necessary contextual and content information. Reporting conventions are listed at the beginning of this document.

CASE 2: TWA 847 HIGHJACKING

6/14/85: TWA Flight 847 from Athens to Rome with 104 Americans and 39 others is hijacked and forced to land in Beirut, where 19 passengers are freed, mostly women and children. Plane flies on to**

---

*The *Washington Post* was selected for this case study, rather than the *New York Times*, which was used in the other two case studies, to gather information from the two print media most often cited by policy makers as their prime source of print information. Occasionally, when one of the two papers was not available on a particular day due to printers' strike or misfiling, the other one has been cited.

**Number of passengers reported vary depending on the date and the medium.

Algiers where 18 more passengers are released and gunmen threaten to kill remaining passengers unless Israel releases Moslem prisoners captured in Lebanon. Plane returns to Beirut and an American passenger is killed. Hijackers claim to be Islamic Jihad.

Television: TOB. Heavy coverage by all three nets (8–14 min) with film, pilot and tower voices, and voices of hijackers. Film of tearful interviews with families and religious groups connected to passengers; released passenger described the ordeal on camera.

Hijacker's demands listed. DOS handling of terrorism examined by all networks, expert interviews, U.S.-Israeli relationship examined in regard to terrorism. Controversy over Israel's release of 1200 prisoners of a few Israeli pilots discussed on-air quote from former Israeli negotiator saying it was a mistake that encouraged this hijacking.

Print: NONE.

Policy events: Reagan asks Algerian President to allow plane to land. Reagan vows no concessions but all possible being done. Delta Force moved to region.

6/15/85: TWA jet returns to Algiers for second time and 60 passengers are released, all non-American. It becomes known that two more hijackers boarded plane in Beirut.

Television: TOB. Heavy coverage by all nets with voices, film, standups; (up to 14 min of coverage per network news program). Update on plane in Algiers; voice of pilot describing murder of American passenger; hijackers' latest demands and warnings outlined and shown on screen. Examination of Greek government concessions to one of hijacker's demand, and of efforts of U.S. Ambassador. Mention of new releases of passengers. Examination of hurdles to rescue; terrorists' weapons and arsenal described. Film of interviews of relatives.

Print: WP, FP—(double) lead w/photo—TWA hijacked—(1) Captives include American, (2) Passenger is reported slain at Beirut airport. FPSB—Shi'ite militiamen take charge of Beirut airport. IP—Partial transcript of conversation between tower and plane. 4 articles.

6/16/85: Shi'ite Amal militia leader Nabih Berri, Lebanon's justice minister, assumes negotiations on behalf of hijackers. Eight Americans with Jewish sounding names are removed from jet.

Television: TOB. All nets give heavy coverage (14–15 min). Status of plane reported; latest demands listed; interviews with released passengers. Voice of pilot describing determination of terrorists to land in Beirut.

Nabih Berri introduced as intermediary and his role is highlighted as equivalent to U.S. Ambassador. Discussion of unstable U.S. position; U.S. options examined; negotiation problems examined. Impact on relations with Israel and internal Israeli politics examined. Prediction that U.S. will not use Delta Force because of problems in earlier rescue attempts in Grenada.

Report of death of kidnapped passenger's father, noted could be due to heart attack upon learning of son's fate. Letter from hostages to Reagan shown, discussed. Cancellation of strikes against Iran-controlled Shi'ites in Lebanon discussed as example of U.S. position, policy.

Print: WP, FP lead w/photo of plane. *Hijackers release 64 in Algeria, set new deadline.* FPSB—Hostages' families hold vigil. IP—Freed U.S. hostages recount ordeal; NA—U.S. turns again to Algeria to mediate, negotiate. Hijackings are a tool of terrorism especially for discontented in ME; Chronology of hijacking. No editorial. 6 articles/8 pages.

Policy events: DOD Secretary takes position on terrorism. Pres. returns early to White House of NSC meetings; warns terrorists; statements from Larry Speakes. McFarland phones Berri to discuss Israel's previous pledge to release hostages (presumed date of call).

6/17/85: Remaining 30 hostages removed from plane. It becomes known that hijacking was carried out by Amal splinter group called Akel Hamiyeh, also known as Hamzah.

Television: TOB. Film of Berri; Berri says he ordered passengers removed for security reasons and they are being held somewhere in Beirut. Berri and Syria's role in Lebanon profiled by networks. U.S. options examined; location of U.S. fleet in Med. sea shown. U.S. intelligence failures in Iran recalled.

Secret phone conversations between NSA McFarland and Berri detailed. Peres statement shown. Film of hostage families and released hostages shown. Reagan says won't ask Israel to release prisoners.

Print WP: FP lead w/photos and maps, heavy coverage, detailed lead stories on event details, "talks intensify." FP SB's: (1) *Hijackers get U.S. warning to release hostages.* (2) *Jet back in Beirut, one more released.* (3) *Ex-hostage describes airborne terror,* w/photo of him. (4) *Freed hostages pray for others.*

IP—Attendant describes "brutal" treatment, four marines reported on plane, one allegedly killed. NA—No viable military options available. Carrier Nimitz heads toward ME.; Passenger list, 15 unaccounted for. Israel says U.S. has yet to request freeing of Shi'ite prisoners. **How TV covered the story.** **

Editorial: *TV made pilot a hero.* 11 articles/16 pages.

Policy events: Reagan Administration declares that the U.S. will make no concessions to the hijackers and will not ask Israel to release 700 Shi'ite prisoners. Intense conversations with Israel ongoing. Says release of hostages would probably open way for Israel to free Shi'ites.

6/18/85: Crisis continues. Travel advisory on Athens airport announced by DOS.

Television: TOB. Heavy coverage of Nabih Berri. NBC film of Berri claiming to control hostages; NBC speculation he was behind hijacking. Film of his meeting with Algerian ambassador in 1980 in Teheran; film of his releasing 3 TWA hostages, threatening U.S. about intervention with Israel. Berri analysis of crisis shown. Pres. Gemayel absent from reports and noted that Berri seems to be functioning in his place. Film of hostage relatives, released hostages shown.

Examination of possible political implications of U.S.Greek relations. Film of pilots criticizing Athens airport. Reports of other breaches of security in European airports.

Israel's policy of mass arrests in Lebanon examined as precipitating hijacking, along with U.S. naval shelling of Beirut; (ABC slant that Israel is partly to blame.) Israeli reports claim U.S. pressuring Israel to negotiate with terrorists.

Examination of White House behind-the-scenes efforts to free hostages despite denials. Red Cross role examined; Red Cross refuses to pressure Israel. WH denies request to Red Cross. CBS reports U.S. agrees with Israel's position. ABC film of candidate Reagan calling for pre-emptive strikes against terrorists; other politicians' stands on terrorists recalled. Public opinion polls of what U.S. should do detailed on screen. NBC story on Jesse Jackson offer to intervene.

Print: WP FP lead w/photo—*Berri says he ordered hostages off plane.* FPSB—(1) Americans may be in Shi'ite suburbs in West Beirut. (2) U.S. officials pessimistic on swift release. (3) Hijack victim was Navy diver, family mourns.

IP—*TWA hijacking relives specter of Iran hostage ordeal.* w/chronology and map; Algeria underlines role in talks, balancing act between U.S. and

---

Stories on TV's influence on the situation are printed in **boldface.

radical Arabs; NA—Berri and his ties to both sides. Yellow ribbons greet freed hostages, vigil continued for others. TWA sees no collusion by Athens security staff. Hostages' identities guarded carefully; 16-year-old among Shi'ite prisoners demanded by hijackers, story of him; Captive Shi'ites role in drama.

Ed.—WP—*Everyone should stop telling government what to do, but terrorists must be dealt with firmly.* 13 articles/17 pages.

Policy events: Reagan vows at news conference that U.S. will never give in to terrorists or ask any other government to do so. U.S. asks Red Cross to find out the Israeli plan for Shi'ite prisoner release. Speakes criticizes Berri for release of small groups of hostages. DOS spokesperson Kalb criticizes Israel for taking Arab prisoners out of Lebanon in violation of Geneva convention. White House meeting with Tunisian President. Reagan's news conference dominated by crisis; he claims he never criticized Carter handling of Iran crisis (film to contrary shown later by NBC)

6/19/85: Crisis continues. Pan Am suspends flights to Athens.

Television: TOB. Interviews with TWA 847 pilot in Beirut; tells of possible retaliation if force is used to free hostages. Film of hostage families. Examination of Administration's attempts to appear unruffled by crisis. Red Cross actual role examined. Stories on safety of flying. Berri relatives in Dearborn, MI described along with Shi'ite population and problems hijacking causes them.

CBS speculation Berri lack of control over some hostages; possibility of Algeria working behind the scenes at U.S. request to free hostages. Film of Reagan, McFarland re: Red Cross. NBC speculates Reagan pressuring Assad to push Berri for release. Note Assad's unscheduled trip to Moscow 6/20/85.

NBC speculation Shultz and Reagan withholding criticism of Israel out of fear of weakening Peres gov't and opening way for Sharon. Film of Shultz saying no dealing with terrorist; hijacking delaying Israeli release of prisoners.

Print: WP: FP lead (double) w/photo on families' grief—Reagan vows to wait out hijackers. (1) 3 more hostages are released. (2) Generalized retaliation rejected by Reagan. FPSB—*Israel agrees to possible Red Cross meeting but won't talk to hijackers.*

IP—Transcripts of Reagan's press conference. NA—Reagan in Carter's shoes. Body of slain Navy diver returned w/photos of event and families waiting, crying; Beirut cease fire pact seen as retreat for Syria; Coverage of hijacking echoes of Iran hostage crisis; U.S. is forced to agonize over how to fight back at terrorism; Story on poll which found 58% would yield to demands (question is "Should U.S. negotiate if alternative is further injury to or murder of the hostages?"); U.S. warns Americans about Athens airport; Greece denies hijackers foiled airport security, were on plane before from Egypt; Doubt cast on reports that hostages removed for "Jewish names," Berri denies it; Spain awaits trial of two Shi'ites sought by hijackers, ignores their demands.

Ed.—Evans and Novack piece, Use Force—*Reagan Administration talks big, but has little clout.* 15 articles/18 pages.

Policy events: Reagan to meet with Red Cross. (ABC) McFarland says Reagan won't ask Red Cross to negotiate, denies such use, (CBS-NBC). **Reagan criticizes TV interviews with pilot of TWA 847.**

6/20/85: Hostages give news conference; Switzerland offers to be exchange point. Israeli goes public with anger over U.S. indecision on action re: hostages.

Television: TOB. Film of hostages news conference. Film of Berri describing hostage conditions, criteria for release. ABC speculates on Israel's responsibility for crisis. Film of Reagan questioning motives of hijackers re: press conference. Film of Rabin calling on Reagan to make up his mind on policy. Film of funeral for dead hostage. Reaction of families to press conference, Berri, Reagan attention to crisis.

Speculation Berri is not in control of TWA 847; some hostages may have been moved to Bekka valley.

Red Cross says it is ready to determine hostages' condition, will intervene if asked by all parties. NBC examines Reagan's refusal to negotiate, but willingness to talk. More discussion of opinion polls on Reagan.

News polls on Reagan handling of crisis shown, discussed, compared to Carter situation with Iran. Film: Carter says he will personally monitor crisis. Film: O'Neil criticizes Reagan for nonsupport of Carter while Democrats are now supporting him.

Print: WP: FP lead w/photo (taken off TV screen) of TWA capt. talking to reporters from cockpit, gunman next to him. Story on failed Red Cross plan, U.S. firm on stand against terrorists. FPSB—(1) *Amal may not hold all hostages, more militant group said to have some.* (2) *U.S. attempted swap during first 24 hours but failed.*

IP—Pan Am halts all trips to Athens; Reagan's plan to wait out the hijackers upsets some hostages' families: Israelis assert moving Shi'ites from Lebanon to Israel was not illegal under international law. Excerpt from TWA captain's interview; Freed passengers talk about missing Jews.

One of the Shi'ite prisoners in Israel defends his shooting of a Libyan diplomat.

Editorials—(1) *Journalism should not hype hijacking, Reagan's laid-back attitude better than Carter's personal involvement in Iran crisis-Kraft.* (2) *An eye for an eye,* pro-retaliation-Kilpatrick. (3) Pro-retaliation-Will. (4) *First negotiate, if fails, then take other measures*—WP.

Other: Nightline: Peres criticizes Reagan for indecision.

Policy events: Reagan orders VP Bush to head anti-terrorism task force, rather than taking any action. Peres apologizes for criticism of Administration indecision.

6/21/85: Crisis continues. Reagan schedules meeting with hostage relatives. Peres apologizes for criticism of Reagan.

Television: TOB. ABC, CBS examines Reagan's attempt to shift attention on hijacking away from his administration, and to put pressure on Israel. Film of anti-U.S./pro-hijacker demonstrations in Beirut. Compares TWA 847 to Iran crisis; shows films of both. **NBC interviews hostages on air.** Nabih Berry criticized on air by DOS Sec.

Released hostages interviewed; relatives of present hostages interviewed. Hostage families praise press.

Examination of Shi'ite movement; film shown of Shi'ites. Hizbullah leader Fadlalah introduced, denies holding hostages. **CBS examines role of media in terrorism.** Strong interviews with political leaders saying media should black out terrorists.

Print: WP: FP lead w/photo, *Hostages press conference, Reagan tough statements.* Hostage telecast, interview with relatives; plea from hostages not to try military rescue. Analysis of Israeli strain in this crisis. Inside commentaries. Hostage telecast messages to relatives. List of hostages; analysis of Shi'ite groups; analysis of Reagan political views.

Policy events: Peres, Shultz telephone call re: U.S.-Israeli agreement on crisis handling.

6/22/85: Crisis continues.

Television: TOB. CBS, NBC lead story. Berri shown threatening to stop negotiation due to U.S. overflights of Lebanon. Routine reports on Hostage location, condition. Film of crew; voice of hostages. Failure of Israeli overture to Berri examined. Shamir statements on delay of releasing Shi'ite prisoners due to crisis. Interviews, film. Pentagon denies overflights.

Media role in terrorism and hostage crisis examined. Carter-Iranian crisis compared to Reagan-TWA 847 crisis.

Contents of Peres-Shultz phone conversation reported, agreement between Israel and U.S. described.

Print: WP: FP leaddouble story: *U.S. attempts to downplay hope of hostages' early release and Peres offers release of Shi'ite prisoners if requested by U.S.* SB w/photo: *Anti-U.S. protest at Beirut airport.* IP stories: Jews separated, Israelis upset; Reagan meets with hostages' families; U.S. insists that any 3rd party mediation consist of unconditional release of the hostages.

Editorial: pro-negotiation. 10 pages/7 articles.

Policy events: U.S. demands release.

6/23/85: Israel announces plan to release 31 Shi'ite prisoners; release has no connection to TWA hostages; Amal says it has no plans to release Americans.

Television: Routine coverage. Israeli release of prisoners noted, Berri's voice used discounting release of hostages due to Israeli action. **Film of hostage asking Reagan to refrain from military intervention.** Berri claim of hostages playing on beach; hostage cuisine described.

Berri warning on Sixth fleet, military intervention called. Experts on camera commenting on best strategy.

Ceremonies for hostages in home towns shown. Film of relatives, hostages.

Print: WP: FP lead: *Berri warns U.S. not to "flex muscle,"* threatens to stop mediating. Sidebar: News analysis w/photo—Lebanese factions and their rise. Feature on the inside of Lebanese factions' map.

IP: Coverage of hijacking questioned, who's exploiting who? Full page layout of individual hostages w/high school yearbook brief; Life settles into routine at Beirut airport, Pravda says U.S. threatening Lebanon invasion; Reagan advisors differ in reaction to terrorism; Syria begins Lebanon withdrawal; Reagan says "marines' killers will not evade justice."

Editorials: (1) *Terrorism won't stop until U.S. accepts rapprochement with Iran;* Anti-force editorials (2 pgs.). (2) *Berri in on hostage taking, criticizes Reagan for simple attitude to complex terrorism problem.* (3) *Don't let hijacking sway us away from the more important issue of peace proposals in the ME.* 9 articles/11 pages.

Policy events: Reagan contacts Syrian Pres. Assad to ask for intervention for hostages. Bush goes to Europe to discuss cooperation against terrorism with leaders.

6/24/85: Berri sets new demands for hostage release: withdrawal of U.S. warships from Lebanese coast. Berri claims demand was made in defense of Lebanon and not in the name of the hijackers.

Television: TOB. Film of hitherto unseen hostages shown, messages sent to families. Film of relatives receiving hostage messages, world of loved ones. Examination of tension and effects on hostages discussed. Experts discuss film of hostages, claim they are free to speak. Former hostages recount trials. Possible hostage illness discussed; censorship by terrorists discussed.

Film of Israel release of prisoners; prisoners reported opposed to hostage release. Reports Reagan is depending on Syria and USSR to intervene for hostages.

Berri demands fleet move. Berri lack of control noted. Hostage warning to move 6th fleet discussed. DOD Sec. rejects demand to move fleet, discusses options, limits on U.S. power in area.

Print: WP: FP lead w/photo: *Israel to release 31 prisoners.* IP stories: Israel decided to release prisoners on Friday, 6/21; Berri says he controls about 30 hostages.

Editorial: Society's treatment of hostage crisis (general); *Analysis of Israeli political factions and their effects on Israeli's policy toward the hostage crisis.* 5 articles/6 pages.

Other: ABC special assignment broadcast on hijackings (3 min. during news)

Policy events: Reagan cancels vacation (reported at Nancy's request) to handle crisis. Reagan holds unscheduled WH meeting re: crisis.

6/25/85: Crisis continues. U.S. publicly discusses military options.

Television: TOB. Heavy. Larry Speakes says potential for blockade and other military action in Beirut mentioned under examination. Film, outline of options on screen, all nets. WH deadline implied by CBS. Bill Quant says PR gesture only. Haidar says AMAL may withdraw from negotiations if blockage imposed. Red Cross declines to describe visit to hostages. NBC explores psychological state of hostages; film shown on hostages.

Administration responses to Israel prisoner released. ABC poll compares Reagan and Carter in hostage situation.

Examination of blockade, military options; film, animation. CBS experts skeptical. DOS claims Assad offers help. Assad's role discussed.

Print: WP: 2 FP lead stories: *31 Arabs freed, public calls for massive release,* w/photo, and *Berri insists U.S. ships must withdraw from Leb. coast.* FP Sidebar: *U.S. believes some hostages may be held at Shi'ite base, prospects for release dim further.*

IP stories:

• Reagan cancels vacation to monitor crisis;
• Navy ships stay out of Lebanese territorial waters;
• Twelve hostages appear on videotape, angry, tired;
• Weinberger reserves right to military option, refuses Berri's request to pull out ships off Lebanese coast.

Editorial: *It's now Berri's move;* analysis pieces on Likud/Labor and their effect on hostage policy. 7 articles/10 pages.

Other: ABC special on U.S. Intelligence in Mid-East. Shows it's very weak.

Policy events: Negotiation with Israel, Syria, others.

6/26/85: Hostage Palmer released. Berri agrees to send remaining hostages to Western embassy or Damascus. Peres agrees to free prisoners as part of hostage deal.

Television: TOB. Heavy. Release of Palmer announced by Berri; movement on others described. Berri shown announcing new position, demands; acknowledges lack of control. Voice of Berri over film, words transcribed on film.

Interviews with Palmer. Film of Palmer wife after release. Film of pilot who says he hopes for quick release. Film of Shi'ite family describing their attitude toward hostages, war in Lebanon.

White House blacks out news on hostage movement. DOS explains, makes guarded statements. Sen. Lugar interviewed. Significance of Israeli Cabinet meeting discussed. Assad role discussed; USSR to be encouraging end of crisis to pressure U.S. to get 6th fleet out of area. (CBS) Discussion of role of France in breakthrough.

Special terrorism reports on ABC/CBS

Print: WP, FP double lead: *U.S. weighs blockading Lebanon* and *Boycotting the Beirut airport,* w/photo of terrorist shooting at camera from plane. Sidebars: *Crisis reflects Shi'ite rivalries, Baalbek harbors extremist groups, possible U.S. target.*

IP stories:

• U.S. concerned over status of military hostages;
• Syrian efforts to free hostages intensifies;

- Bush suggests Israel should free Arabs;
- Poll finds rising sentiment for distancing U.S. from Israel.

Editorials: Possible sanctions against hijackers may be futile and *Reagan shift risks forcing his hand if deadline passes.* 10 articles/14 pages.

Other: ABC Special on Terrorism (part II)

Policy events: Continuing negotiations with Israel, others. Agreement reached with Israel on terrorists demands. Decide to demand all U.S. hostages be released.

6/27/85: Negotiations for movement of hostages collapse due to problems with French, Swiss, and Austrian delegations. Hostages state sympathy for terrorists cause.

Television: TOB. Heavy on all nets. Film. Hostages interviewed on film, state support for terrorists' demands on Israel, deny brainwashing. Announcement (NBC) deal is off due to French, Swiss, Austrian conditions for interventions. Interviews with family of other U.S. hostages who resent being left out of negotiations.

WH links TWA hostages with all U.S. hostages; wants them all back. WH continues news blackout.

CBS claims terrorists were aiming for El Al flight; discusses clashes between Hizbollah and Amal groups over the hostages.

Examination of France role. NBC reports Israel and U.S. agree on terrorists demands.

Print: WP, 2FP leads on beginning of intensive U.S. diplomatic initiative. *Berri offers to shift hostages to Western embassy with French, Syrian roles possible,* and *Shi'ites release ailing American,* w/photo of Berri releasing him at news conf.

IP stories:

- Syria's Assad behind Berri offer, intensifies efforts to release hostages;
- Soviets offer help in crisis; U.S. pushes diplomacy again;
- Israeli "security zone" angers Shi'ites; Red Cross sees all hostages. 7 articles/9 pages.

Other: ABC Terrorism special, part II

Policy events: Continued communication with Syrian officials.

6/28/85: Unconfirmed reports that hostages are to be taken overland to Damascus. Berri meets with hostages; more live interviews.

Television: TOB. Heavy. ABC says new breakthrough possible. Hostages interviewed on camera again; voice support for terrorist causes, oppose inclusion of other 7 U.S. hostages in bargain, criticize U.S. handling of crisis, asks Reagan to bow to terrorist demands, send messages to families. Berri expresses sympathy to hostage wife. Film of sick hostage, Grossmeyer, saying Berri is waiting for doctors' report.

Berri holds lunch for hostage Conwell, TV press. Profile of Hizbullah shown.

Discussion of Assad's role in Lebanon and hostage crisis. Film of Assad. NBC discussion of Reagan attempt to pressure Israel without appearing to do.

CBS examination of media role; tape of hostage saying media will be accused of exploitation during hostage interviews. Ken Stein interviewed, accuses network correspondents of engaging in diplomacy instead of journalism. Network execs respond. Hostages say they are being used by networks to boost ratings.

Print: WP: FP lead: *Officials continue to express optimism for hostage deal.* FP 3 sidebars:

- Israel awaits U.S. call to free Arab prisoners,
- U.S. in turn expects Israel to take initiative
- Americans urge restraint in Beirut (which ones are unknown).

IP stories:

- India condemns hijacking, call for release of hostages;
- 3 ex-hostages left loved ones behind;
- NA-Syria tries to boost ME role with offers to help in hostage crisis.
- Chronology of U.S. reaction to crisis.

Editorials: *Do not cave into terrorist; Reagan may need to do something retaliation if crisis not solved diplomatically to avoid being "Carterized."* 10 articles/14 pages.

Other: Hostage interview on Good Morning America; ABC Terrorism Special, Part III.

Policy events: WH reconsiders asking media to curtail coverage. Continued communication with Assad, Syrian officials.

6/29/85: Berri blames delay in release of hostages on Reagan's speech calling hijackers thugs and murderers. Demands assurances that Lebanon will not suffer retaliation.

Television: Some TOB; not all nets heavy. Reporting of movement toward release, hitch due to Berri's new demands. Claims hitch partly due to

Reagan radio address calling for retaliation. Peres denies making deal for hostages with Americans. Larry Speakes statement hostages are leaving Beirut.

Film of preparation for hostages in Syria, Germany. Film of hostage families; other 7 U.S. hostage families critical, supportive of President. Interviews with separated hostages (those with Hizbullah). VP Bush flies to Germany to receive hostages.

Terrorists' farewell party for hostages described by ABC; Berri voice-over.

Print: WP FP lead w/photo of hostages having farewell dinner in Beirut restaurant, *Release of hostages reported near as captors begin preparing to take them to Syria, then W. Germany and then free,* FP SB stories: *Shi'ite spokesman backs Syrian role but asserts hijackers a "sole power center."* and *Reagan hints at retaliation.*

IP stories:

* Excerpts of interviews with hostages;
* Reagan administration disassociates from White House official's request to Jews to pressure Israel into releasing hostages;
* Freed hostage welcomed back to Little Rock w/photo of Palmer;
* Terrorist experts discuss Stockholm syndrome;
* Right critical of Reagan in hostage policy, some want Shultz to resign;
* U.S. and Israel reportedly agreed that prisoners should be released after hostages assured safe. 9 articles/12 pages.

Policy events: Shultz insists on all U.S. hostages being released. News blackout on other Navy divers in group to protect them from fate of other diver. No guarantees against retaliation given.

6/30/85: Hostages released.

Television: All nets devote entire newscast to release, review of kidnapping, Reagan response.

Print: WP double FP lead story on release of hostages hitting snag: *Berri demands U.S. disavow retaliation,* and *U.S. issues statement suggesting that it plans no retaliation.* FP SB: Bright prospects darken.

IP stories:

* Hostage release seen as step to freeing Shi'ites
* Peres denies deal
* Damascus embarrased by unexpected delay
* Networks turn eye at themselves—restraint viewed as important in crisis but impossible (Dan Rather justifies not going live with hostage interview; w/photo.

- Previously kidnapped not to be released now or soon.
- Chronology of events
- Reagan's statements

Editorials and editorial page features:

- Understand the terrorists,
- How we decided to use force in Iran crisis,
- Journalists should stop playing into terrorists hands,
- Press should not play censor,
- Media is just looking for ratings.
  16 articles/21 pages.

Policy events: No new events.

7/1/85: Hostages released and flow to Frankfurt, W. Germany after President Assad of Syria promises Israel will release prisoners.

Television: Story winding down, not TOB or even lead on all nets. Film of arrival in Germany, rehash of events, examination of roles of Assad, Israel, others, discussion of retaliation, polls on retaliation.

Print: WP FP lead (double) 39 hostages freed (1) President hails nation's joy but pledges to fight back at terrorism. (2) Intense diplomacy, Syrian weight ended crisis.

FPSB—"Turning points" (1) Sailor's shooting, act persuaded reluctant Amal militia "good Shi'ites" to get involved, others on board claim. (2) Berri changes his mind.

FPSB—House becomes more defense minded with hostage crisis and desire to shed anti-defense image. IP—NA—(1) Israel-U.S. tug of war ends in "understanding." (2) Assad boosted, opens new options in ME. (3) Syria boosted, showed its muscle in ME affairs. (4) Berri boosted, stronger within Amal and with Hizbullah. Reagan agenda may get lift with hostage success; Military retaliation unlikely option, Reagan settling for broad-based attack on terrorism's roots; Soviets assail U.S. actions in hostage release; Profile on Assad, "Syria skilled bargainer;" Profile on Berri, "voice of Amal;" Ex-hostage urges vigil for Shi'ite prisoners; Israel does not announce release of prisoners.

Editorials—(1) Defensive measures should be taken, pro-Reagan, No retaliation against Syria, WP. (2) Terrorism is state sponsored, pro-retaliation, Haig. (3) Shi'ite prisoners also hostages, Geyelin. 17 articles/25 pages.

Other: ABC Terrorism, Part IV.

Policy events: DOS reaffirms its belief that Syria is pro-terrorist, despite role in release. WH retaliation in various forms.

7/2/85: Released hostages arrive in U.S.

Television: TOB. Reagan meeting with released hostages, wreath-laying for dead hostage. Examination of sentiments towards captors; Conwell's endorsement of Berri, other captors punished. Psychological torture of one hostage explained.

Jihad's warning against retaliation reported. Polls on Reagan handling reported.

Stories of remaining U.S. hostages.

Print: WP FP lead (double) U.S. doctors call freed Americans healthy, upbeat (1) U.S. moves to close Beirut airport. (2) Israel sets release of 300 prisoners. FPSB—(1) Navy diver feared captors might kill him next, w/photo. (2) Hijackers taunted four held apart by Hizbullah, w/photo of one of them. (3) Reagan gets high rating in crisis, poll finds pessimism that terrorist would be deterred.

IP—Arrival ceremony brief, low key; Aides to Assad express displeasure with U.S.'s lack of gratitude; Happy reunion with families; At home, preparation for welcome, prayer of thanks, etc.; FBI curbed in fight against terrorism, Administration's limit on funding noted; Israel schedules release within 48 hours of 300 mostly Shi'ite prisoners.

ED—Pro-retaliation, Anti-Reagan, Anti-Syria, Will. (2) *We shouldn't have caved in,* Podhoretz. 13 articles/18 pages.

Other: ABC series on Terrorism Part V.

Policy events: Bush calls for boycott of Beirut airport.

7/3/85: Israel releases 300 of the 700 prisoners. Europe rejects boycott of Beirut airport called for by Bush.

Television: TOB reports of Jihad warning. Release is #2 story (ABC). Tape of DOS Sec. U.S. won't respond to threats; voice of Berri discussing Reagan's demand that hijackers be tried.

Interviews with released hostages, pilots, on mistreatment during captivity.

Film of Thatcher rejecting Beirut airport boycott.

Print: WP FP lead—*Reagan greets 30 ex-hostages.* FPSB—Assad's linkage idea broke hostage deadlock. IP—Whitmoyer from Severn, MD went through "rough times" as hostage; Transcripts of Reagan's remarks at Andrews AFB, relief, pride, and "promise to be kept;" Lebanese criticize American move to shut down airport, Islamic Jihad threatens attack if U.S. retaliates; Peres commends U.S. action.

ED—(1) Pro-retaliation, critical of Reagan, (Evans and Novack). (2) *Retaliation should only be taken if only to seek justice not for fear of possible weak image,* (Cohen). (3) Iranian link-analysis, professor. 9 articles/11 pages.

Other: **ABC Terrorism Part VI explores media and terrorism;** Nightline with Rabin defending Israel's conduct.

Policy events: U.S. military personnel told to travel abroad on tourist passports, not military id's. DOS Sec. offers reward for hijackers.

CASE 3
A COMPARATIVE CHRONOLOGY OF THE EVENTS, MEDIA REPORTS, AND POLICY EVENTS DURING THE *INTIFADA*, DECEMBER 11, 1987–MARCH 15, 1988

Introduction

This chronology describes events, television reports, print reports, and policy actions by the U.S. government during the period of unrest in the occupied territories in Israel, December 11, 1987, through March 15, 1988.

Television reports are compiled from unpublished abstracts of network news reports provided by the staff of the Vanderbilt Television News Archive. This information is scheduled for publication in the *Television News Index and Abstracts* with approximately a three-month time lag. Television summaries in this document blend abstracts from all three network reports. Noteworthy or unique reports by individual networks are indicated where appropriate.

Print reports are summaries of reports, features, graphics, and editorials printed in the *New York Times*. Summaries reflect headlines and editorial content abbreviated for space reasons.

Policy events are drawn from print and television news reports. A second phase of this research updated these events through interviews with policy makers.

CASE 3: THE INTIFADA

12/11/87: First reports of uprisings on the West Bank and Gaza strip (reports that it actually began Wed. 12/9/87 with truck running over a Palestinian). PLO commandos attack Israeli patrol boat.

TV: Light coverage with film. Issues discussed.

Print: NYT. Page 15. Israeli soldiers kill a Palestinian and wound 15 as violent unrest continues for the second day and demonstrations spread throughout the occupied territories. Palestinians threw rocks and burned tires, Israelis claim that they were forced to shoot themselves out of a dangerous situation.

Policy events: None reported.

12/12/87: Continuing violence in occupied territories.

TV: Light coverage, film. More violence. U.N. debate on PLO charge of massacre noted.

Print: NYT. Page 6. Three more Palestinians killed by Israeli troops. The army has been bolstered in anticipation of more unrest. An Israeli officer died and at least six more Palestinians within the last three days. Unrest set off by Israeli truck that hit four Palestinians.

Policy events: None reported.

12/13/87: Continuing violence in occupied territories.

TV: Light coverage, film. More violence. Israel blames PLO; statement from Shamir.

Print: NYT. Page 6. Five more Palestinians wounded in Gaza Strip. Shops closed due to violence, curfew imposed, further disturbances reported in other areas. Egypt condemns Israeli troop action.

Policy events: None reported.

12/14/87: Continuing violence in occupied territories. (ABC reports are that there has now been 6 days of violence, not 4 as earlier news has reported.)

TV: Light coverage, film. More violence. Israeli commentary that Palestinians teens are not afraid of Israel army; injured shown.

Print: NYT. Page 3 with photos of Palestinians throwing rocks at Israelis. Eleven more hurt in West Bank and Gaza. Israeli cabinet hears report on incidents. Gasoline bomb thrown at U.S. Consulate; no one hurt. Shamir states that terrorism by few is the most severe in several years. Arafat says Israelis planned violence, and that territories are on the edge of revolt. U.N. asked to intervene for Palestinians.

Policy events: None reported.

12/15/87: Continuing violence in occupied territories. Sharon moves into his Jerusalem apartment in Arab sector.

TV: Light to moderate coverage, film. Continued violence. Trouble in Jerusalem, as Sharon moves into apartment. Scenes of Israeli soldiers and Palestinian youths in confrontation; arrests of youths; brutality by soldiers; firebombs thrown by youths. Report of Israeli soldiers storming hospital in Gaza. History of occupied territories reviewed by NBC; note Israeli government report contradict events. Body count given; live ammunition in use pointed out.

Print: NYT. Page 3. Photos of Israelis dragging Palestinian youth from home after violent demonstrations. Arab killed in Gaza and another dies of wounds in the sixth straight day of unrest in occupied territories. Third day of general strike in the West bank. Map of areas affected by unrest. U.S. expressed concern.

Policy events: White House comments, expresses concern for problem, treatment of Palestinian youths.

12/16/87: Continuing violence in occupied territories. Israel calls upon military to assist with riot control; first use of live ammunition reported. (CBS report unclear on this, see 12/15/87.)

TV: Light coverage, film. More violence. Interviews with Israeli officers who are questioned about use of live ammunition. Scenes of Palestinian children making firebombs, confrontation.

Print: NYT. FP story jumps to page 10. *Kill us or get out. Arabs taunt as the toll in the Gaza turmoil rises.* Several hundred demonstrators appear at Shifa Hospital encouraged by a mosque loudspeaker. As women gathered stones patients watched from the hospital. Page 10 photo showing Palestinians throwing stones. Map included to show area of unrest. Army frustrated. Crowds turn on Western journalists. Most unrest occurring in the Bereij district. General strike still on. U.S. calls for restraint. Live ammo now being used.

Policy events: White House calls for Israeli restraint in riot control.

12/17/87: Continuing violence in occupied territories. Demonstrations retaliate against live ammo with fire bombs. Increased troop levels in Gaza.

TV: Light to moderate coverage, film. Scenes of violence. Interviews with Palestinians; scenes of Palestinian children chanting hatred of Jews (NBC).

Print: NYT. Page 15. Israeli army reinforced, trying to quell unrest. Map of Gaza strip detailed. Strike still continues, no deaths but some wounded. Unrest has shifted to the Arab quarters in the Old City.

Policy events: None reported.

12/18/87: Continuing violence in occupied territories. First Israeli obstruction of press reporting. Islamic Jihad threatens U.S. hostages if Israeli does not stop shootings.

TV: TOB (NBC) Light to moderate coverage, film. Continuing violence, scenes of Israeli soldiers telling press to leave. Interviews with Palestinians who have lost relatives. Islamic Jihad threatens U.S. hostages if Israel continues deadly force. Officers (on camera) tell soldiers not to overreact. More deaths reported. Call for general strike by Arab Parliament members.

Print: NYT. No stories.

Policy events: Fitzwater statement re: President's negative reaction to Israeli violence he has seen on television.

12/19/87: Continuing violence in occupied territories. Violence in E. Jerusalem; first demonstrations in Nazareth, Tel Aviv. Mubarak criticizes Israeli government.

TV: Moderate coverage, film. More violence, confrontations shown. Protest march by Arabs in Nazareth shown; demonstration by Israelis in Tel Aviv shown. Report of Mubarak, other nations, accusations of Israel. Divisive role of occupied territories in Israel noted.

Print: NYT. Page 3 with photo of Arab demo at Temple Mount. Three more Palestinians dead as violence continues. Prayers turn in to protests, 18 in the last 10 days. Map delineates area involved.

Policy events: None reported.

12/20/87: Continuing violence in occupied territories. Demonstrations in Sidon, Bethelehem.

TV: Moderate coverage, film. Scenes of confrontations between Israelis and Palestinians. Interview with Israeli Cabinet secretary re: support for military. Protest marches by Arabs in Sidon, Lebanon shown.

Print: NYT. FP with photo of Palestinian blockade. Fighting shifts from Gaza to Jerusalem. Organized gathering of high school students set up barricades. Demonstrations reported in Bethlehem, Hebron, and other areas. Jump to p. 19. Report on imposed curfew. Arabs angry at Sharon moving in to the Moslem quarter. 22 people detained. All quite in other quarters.

Policy events: None reported; Pope Paul calls for end to violence and injustice to Palestinians.

12/21/87: Continuing violence in occupied territories.

TV: Moderate coverage with film. Scenes of confrontations between Palestinians and Israeli citizens; fights with soldiers in territories, Jerusalem. Report of meeting between Ambassador Pickering and Shamir re: U.S.

position (details on screen @ ABC). DOS spokesperson Oakley explains U.S. continuing support for Israel.

Report of strong criticism of Israeli use of violence riot control by world leaders. CBS says embarrasses the U.S.; strains U.S.-Israel relationship. Upcoming U.N. vote on Israel noted; U.S. predicted to vote for resolution against Israel. Interviews, reports re: poor Christmas in Bethlehem.

Print: NYT. Front page with photo of rioting, cont. p. 14. Continuing violence. Highlights of typical Gaza life/attitudes. Unrest has caused strain on Israelis relationship with Egypt. Possible withdrawal from embassy.

Policy events: Complaint brought to Shamir by Ambassador; assurance of Israel's safety given by DOS.

12/22/87: Continuing violence in occupied territories. Reagan criticizes Israeli handling of situation.

TV: TOB. Moderate to heavy coverage, film. Film of Reagan criticism for Israeli handling of uprising in territories, warning to Israel to stop using military force. Calls it regrettable. Film of Rabin's visit to Gaza.

Report of new Israeli get tough policy. Interviews with Palestinians who say they are like slaves to Jews. Scenes of anti-terrorism classes in Jerusalem; interviews with children who are scared, but who have problem telling terrorists and other Arabs. Feature of school where Arab and Jewish kids meet.

Print: NYT. FP with picture of demonstrations. Detailed map of Israel. General strike by Arabs, at least 3 Palestinians killed. Total at least 20 in 13 days. Israeli Arabs join with territories. Jump to inside. Additional pictures of protestors. Arab zones shut down. U.S. DOS issues travel warning. Additional side stories. Arab Israelis demonstrate for "our brothers." U.N. breaks meeting over resolution on Israeli action. U.S. veto or abstention possible.

Policy events: None reported.

12/23/87: Continuing violence in occupied territories.

TV: Heavy; film. Scenes of arrest of Palestinians by Israeli soldiers; scenes of Palestinians in detention camps. Israeli brutality highlighted. Scenes of squalor in Gaza. General strike reported. Film of Shamir saying that more force would be used if needed. Worldwide criticism of Israeli tactics reported. History/context of occupied territories (ABC) U.N. resolution condemning Israel noted. Comments on sad Christmas in Holy Land.

Today Show: Israeli Foreign Minister, other Israeli reps. respond, appear angry. DOS Oakley urges Israel to change tactics, emulate S. Korean methods.

Print: NYT. Front page, cont. p. 6. Statement from White House-U.S. abstains from U.N. vote. Resolution passes 14 to 0. Twenty-two dead in two weeks. U.S. support in a precarious position. Photos of Rabin and a map of Israel accompany the following related stories. U.N. council deplores Israeli actions, calls for maximum restraint. PLO wants tougher position, criticism by U.S. softens position. Israeli officials defend actions. Arabs return to work.

Policy events: U.S. strong public criticism of Israeli riot control methods. Pressure on Israel to shift tactics. Abstains from U.N. vote.

12/24–25/87: Relative calm. Subdued celebrations in Bethlehem, Nazareth.

TV: Moderate coverage, film. Comparative calm reported; some scenes of confrontation. Scenes of security in Bethlehem in wake of recent violence. Celebrations in Bethlehem shown; comments tourists going to other locations to avoid violence. Interview with detained Palestinian family.

D.C. report: American Jewish groups challenge Reagan's criticism.

Print: NYT. Front page with picture of soldiers. Jump to p. 6. Army reinforces troops and arrests hundreds. More prisons opened/schools closed and newspapers shut down. P. 6 more photos of protestors and map of Israel. U.S. criticism is rejected. No political solutions seem possible. In two related stories: Israel rebuts the U.S. charges of excessive force; growing atmosphere of displeasure. Shamir and others comment on charges. DOS urges order be maintained without use of lethal force.

12/25/87: Continuing violence. Capture of PLO guerillas. Jewish protests re: their government's actions.

TV: Light coverage, film. Reports of further arrests by Israeli government. Scenes of protest by Jews of military handling of unrest. Capture of 3 PLO guerillas reported. Scenes shown of peace on West Bank.

Print: NYT. Front page jump to p. 6, with photo of Bethlehem. Conflict is regarded by Israel as a public relations problem vs. Palestinian view-Israel is Goliath and they are David. News analysis: no closer to solution, political issue obscured. Map of Israel delineates areas of unrest; photos of Palestinian protestors and Israeli soldiers shown. Side stories on the tension surrounding the Christmas celebrations, and U.S. Jewish officials argue Israeli case to DOS.

Policy events: Continuing criticism of Israeli tactics.

12/26/87: PLO guerillas captured trying to infiltrate. Demonstrations by Israeli's against govt.

TV: Light coverage, film. Reports of split in Israel over its role in occupied territories; protest march in Jerusalem against Israeli policy in territories.

Print: NYT. Front page cont. on p. 7. Israelis arrest nearly a thousand. Warrants issued by army, Israelis still maintain only a few are responsible for unrest. Hardline supported by most Israelis, some think tough stand is needed.

Policy events: None reported.

12/27/87: Relative calm; trials continue.

TV: TOB. Light coverage, film. Interviews with Palestinians in refugee camps about miserable life. Scene of opening of trials of Palestinians shown, prison abuses noted.

Print: NYT. Front page, cont. 12 w/photo of protestors. Israeli army a very heavy presence. Start of trials. Lawyer boycott in Gaza. Rumors of past torture, "mild physical pressure" reported. Also side story of Israeli capture of three guerillas from Jordan. Israeli crackdown frustrates Egypt. Position is one of being caught between other Arab nations and Israel. Pressure on Egypt from other nations. Egypt repeats demands to Israel. Additional story on possibility of PLO considering govt. in exile for the West Bank.

Policy events: None reported.

12/28/87: Relative calm; trials.

TV: Light coverage, film. Scenes of trials. Issue of torture-induced confessions. Deportation discussed. Comparative calm in camps noted. Scenes of W. Bank settlers; said they knew revolts would come sometime, now activists.

Print: NYT. Front page with photo of prisoners in Israel. Report of Palestinian rage that runs from father to son. Speculation that Israel may have missed chance for peace. P. 14 side story on West bank schools reopening. Trials cont. total approaching 600. Army thinks it is back in control. Photo of more Palestinian prisoners.

Policy events: Administration reported lobbying against deportation.

12/29/87: First reports of expulsion possibility for captured demonstrators.

TV: Light to moderate coverage. Scenes of prisoners, description of humiliating treatment. Reports of U.S. pressure on Israel not to deport detainees. Reports of more arrests.

Print: NYT. P. 3 w/two photos of Palestinian prisoners and parents. Israeli leaders said concerned with news coverage being negative. Side story re:

Arab News Service which tips journalists first about riots and shootings, etc.

Policy events: Continuing pressure on Israel not to deport.

12/30/87: Violence erupts again. Palestinians deported.

TV: Moderate coverage. Film from Gaza, tour of area by Rabin. Discussion of deportation issue. History of deportation described. Report of killing another teenager by Israeli troops, film of grieving family. Details given of escalating terrorism (NBC report).

Print: NYT. Page 3. Israeli troops receive riot training. Deportation is debated as solution to riots. New equipment is issued, photo of Palestinians awaiting trial. Side story on Egypt's only Palestinian refugee camp w/map and photo. Many refugees want to go to Gaza for jobs and schools.

Policy events: None reported.

12/31/87: Protests against trails. Criticism of Israeli tactics by Israeli military reservists.

TV: Light coverage—ABC only. Scenes of protest in Nablus. Statement by Israeli army reservists against Israeli actions, petition offered by reservists against tactics. Protests against Israeli actions reported.

Print: NYT. Front page with photo of Sharon's new apartment causes stir in Israel. Jump to p. 7. Map and history of area recounted. P. 6 Cont. reports of Arab lawyers boycotting trials. Israel insists deportation still viable alternative. Israeli soldiers kill man cutting barbed wire between Jordan and Israel; story w/photo. Side story on the issue of lack of leadership in both Israel and PLO. Both described as incapable of finding a solution, reluctant to take risks, unable to get over the same old problems with the same old methods.

Policy events: None reported.

1/1/88: Continuing violence in occupied territories.

TV: ABC pre-empted by football. Light coverage by CBS. Scenes of continuing violence, armored cars patrolling streets of Jerusalem. Interviews with Palestinians grieving, congratulating their sons on arrest.

Print: NYT. P. a-3 Uprising continues to fire Palestinian resistance. Report shows constant struggle between Israeli troops and Palestinians amid the latest army crackdown. At least 22 Palestinians have been shot. The refugee districts have been under siege since December, as Israel attempts to break the hold of the Shabiba, a youth group loyal to Al Fatah.

Policy events: None reported.

1/2/88: Relative quiet in occupied territories. Israeli rocket attack on south Lebanese villages. U.N. resolution deploring Israeli actions.

TV: Light coverage. Report of Israeli rocket attack on Lebanese villages, more unrest in territories. Recall of U.S. refusal to veto U.N. resolution deploring Israel's actions in territories. Interviews with Israeli spokespersons who say Palestinians don't want peace.

Print: NYT. Front page jump to p. 8. Israel puts army on street patrol to prevent riots. Photos of troops. Day of protest blocked by army to prevent commemoration of Yasir Arafat's first military operation against Israel. Troops mass to show Palestinians no demos allowed. Side story—In Egypt hundreds of anti-Israel protestors chanting Islamic fundamentalist slogans clash with police.

Policy events: U.N. resolution vetoed.

1/3/88: Violence erupts again.

TV: TOB. Light to moderate coverage. 3–5 mins w/film. Israel plans to deport Palestinians despite U.S. opposition. U.S. govt. policy hopes Israelis will not use deportation policy. Eruption of protest into violence reported in wake of deportation announcement. Freeing of some Palestinians by Israelis shown.

Special: On *This Week* Israeli Foreign Minister Peres defends deportation policy by Israelis. States that soldiers will carry live ammo. Palestinian National Council. Prof. Saide and Rabbi Schindler from American Hebrew Congregations call for U.S. role in peace process. Reasons for lack of action by Administration cited.

Print: NYT. IP: Continuing violence in occupied territories.

Policy events: Continuing pressure against deportation.

1/4/88: Violence erupts again. Palestinians deported.

TV: Light to moderate coverage. 3–5 mins w/film. Clash between Israeli and Palestinian youths on W. Bank reported. Deportees shown and rpts of no trial before deportation. Shamir states no other alternative. Palestinian lawyers and DOS noted as challenging Israeli deportation policy. Israeli patrol shown and interviewed about role in unrest.

Print: NYT. Front page w/photos. 21 dead as Israel launches attack against S. Lebanon in what is seen as retaliation for hang glider attack last year. Jump to page 10 w/maps showing area bombed. Cont. coverage of Israeli army's deporting 9 Arabs in the wake of more rioting. Israelis claim Arabs are chief instigators of riots. Arabs reported to have the right to appeal. Also reported death of Palestinian women shot by soldier pursuing stone throwing youths. Peres defends expulsion. U.S. withholds comment on raid, calls for restraint.

Policy events: None reported.

1/5/88: Violence erupts again. International complaints against Israel.

TV: Light to moderate coverage. 2–4 mins w/film. Violence continues in Gaza between Israeli army and Palestinians. Deportation policy spurred new unrest. Rabin shown touring town. Complaints of Egyptian Amb. to Shamir reported. Protest in Cairo reported against Israeli policy in occupied territory. Palestinians noted as needing riots to keep attention focused on problems.

Print: NYT. Cont. violence reported in occupied territories.

Policy events: None reported.

1/6/88: Continuing violence in occupied territories. U.S. complaints.

TV: Light to moderate coverage, one network TOB. 4–5 min w/film. Continued violence on W. Bank in the wake of Israel's decision to deport. Protest of deportation in Knesset reported. Reassurance by DOS that Israeli friendship will continue despite U.S. criticism of Israeli Policy. Admin representative noted asserting that U.S. not supporting violence but affirming human rights. Israeli troops shown using more riot control and less live ammunition in attempt to repair image.

Commentary: NBC. U.S. analogy to Israeli-Palestinian troubles. Situation noted as bomb ready to explode. Settlement necessary for state security.

Print: NYT. Front page, cont. p.10 w/photo of rioting Palestinians with caption. Story on p. 10 despite arrests and deaths youths appear unafraid. Latest riots began as demonstration against expulsion order. U.S. joins U.N. in vote against deportation plans of the Israeli army. Israeli officials claim PLO and extremists groups deliberately organized riots to subject Israel to international censure. Side story emergence of Egypt from ostracism in M.E. Mubarak starts M.E. tour.

Policy events: Comments on Israeli tactics.

1/7/88: Continuing violence in occupied territories, refugee camps. Shamir snubs U.S. envoy.

TV: Light to moderate coverage. One network TOB. 1–4 mins w/film. Continuation of violence at refugee camps reported. Israeli opposition to U.S. Sen. visit noted. Impact of U.S. vote against Israeli policy in U.N. on U.S.-Israeli rels. Response of Israeli Amb. to DOS re: U.S. vote in U.N.

Special Assignment: (THE PALESTINIANS Part I) Report on the historical roots of the Israeli-Palestinian conflict, and latest unrest shown. New attitude by younger Palestinians noted. Israeli poll results in public's support of policy during recent demos. Dilemma for Israel noted, lack of leadership of Palestinians and the possibility of more bloodshed noted.

Print: NYT. Page 3. Israelis unhappy with U.S. vote in U.N. w/photos. Despite vote Israelis uphold expulsion order noting right of appeal is available. More unrest reported.

Policy events: U.S. votes in U.N.

1/8/88: Continuing violence in occupied territories. U.N. envoy snubbed by Israeli government.

TV: Light to moderate coverage. 1–4 mins w/film. Cont. violence in Gaza refugee camps noted. Anti-Israel rally reported in Jerusalem. Shamir says Israel is fighting new kind of warfare but promises Palestinian terrorists will fall. Visiting U.N. official noted as being refused interview by Shamir. Jewish settlement among Gaza Strip featured. Risks of settling in area described. Settlement objectives discussed re: Palestinian resistance.

Nightline: Interview with Yasir Arafat.

Print: NYT. Page 6, w/maps and photos. Israeli troops wound seven in cont. unrest. Demonstrations broke out in Gaza a day before U.N. official arrived on a fact finding mission. In east Jerusalem stores observed a total commercial strike.

Policy events: None reported.

1/9/88: Continuing violence in occupied territories. Troops prevent TV coverage.

TV: Light to moderate coverage. 2–3 mins w/film. TOB one network. Cont. violence between Palestinians and Israeli forces in W. Bank and Gaza. Israeli prevention of press coverage noted. PLO Arafat calls for U.N. force to replace Israelis.

Print: NYT. Front page jump to p. 5. Israel jails Arabs without a trial. Officials report dozens of Palestinians have been held without trial for up to six months. Violence cont. At least 26 Palestinians have been killed and 200 wounded in the last month, and 2000 arrested. Photos and map of Israel and prison camps shown. Black bordered special story on the 9 Arabs set for deportation.

Policy events: None reported.

1/10/88: Continuing violence in occupied territories. More Israeli troops detailed to territories, E. Jerusalem.

TV: TOB. Light coverage. 2 mins w/film. Increases in military forces in Gaza reported. Continued violence and the use of hard-line military tactics by Israel in occupied territory reported. Protest march by Palestinian women in Jerusalem noted. Israeli govt. officials policy of not talking to Palestinians continues. Rabin states that Palestinians will cont. to suffer as long as disturbances continue.

Print: NYT. Front page. cont. on p.14. Israeli troops kill Gaza protestor in clashes during general strike. Troops clash with rioters after sealing off an area of 200 sq. miles to outside reporters. A general strike has been called in the Gaza area. Troops opened fire on rioters. Side story: PLO calls for U.N. force to protect Palestinians. Italy reports an increase in anti-Semitic vandalism in the wake of unrest in the occupied territories.

Policy events: None reported.

1/11/88: Continuing violence in occupied territories.

TV: Light to moderate coverage. TOB one network. 2–6 mins w/film. Continued violence in Israeli occupied territories. Report of Palestinian being shot by settler. Film of civilians being mistreated by troops. Palestinian students interviewed say they cannot take occupation any longer and will continue to fight.

Special Report: (*THE PALESTINIANS PT. II*) Report on Palestinians living in refugee camps on W. Bank near Bethlehem featured. Irony of Palestinians working for Israeli companies noted.

Print: NYT. Front page jump to page 8. Report on the support youths are getting from their Palestinian parents during unrest. W/map. P. 8 full page coverage of photos of troops in action. Reinforcements have failed to quell rioting.

Policy events: None reported.

1/12/88: Continuing violence in occupied territories. U.N. envoy barred from camps.

TV: Light to moderate coverage. 1–2 mins w/film. TOB one network. Refusal of Israelis to allow U.N. envoy Goulding to enter refugee camp. Israel rejects U.N. opposition to deportation of Palestinian ringleaders. Israeli riot control tactics noted. Shamir denounces Peres call for end to violence. Conservative supporters. Protest of Israeli justice system and deportations shown in Jerusalem.

Print: NYT. P. 8 w/map. Settlers in the West Bank kill a Palestinian. A Jewish settlement leader and his bodyguard opened fire on demonstrators in the West Bank. It was the first significant involvement by militant settlers in the unrest. Involvement of militant Jews could be volatile. SB w/photo of Arab deportees wife. Arab marked for exile. Report on Arab due to be deported and his fight to remain. Israeli friends call him man of peace.

Policy events: None reported.

1/13/88: Continuing violence in occupied territories. More Palestinians deported.

TV: Light to moderate coverage. TOB one network. 3–4 mins w/film. Deportation of four Palestinians from Israel to Lebanon reported. Accusations against them detailed. Deportees had no chance to talk to family. Report of U.N. Envoy Goulding's visit to refugee camp noted. Statement by Reagan Administration calling for stop to deportation and violation of human rights reported. Casualty figures reported. American Israeli leaders reported being silent re: deportation. DOS spokesman discusses Schultz's role in Israeli problem.

Print: NYT. FP w/photo of U.S. envoy rebuffed in Gaza Strip. Story on p. a-3 w/map. Israel moves to impose curfew on Palestinians. Envoy Goulding turned away from refugee district by Israeli troops and from another by Palestinians. The army imposed round-the-clock curfew in some areas to discourage the population from taking part in the unrest. Washington favors talks to end crisis. Spokesman repeats Washington's disapproval of Israeli methods against terrorists.

Policy events: Criticism of Israeli methods.

1/14/88: Curfew placed on some camps, crackdown on others. More confrontations.

TV: Moderate to heavy coverage. TOB two networks. 3–6 mins w/film. U.N. vote calling for Israelis to return deportees shown. U.S. reported abstaining from vote. Israel and U.S. reported as proceeding cautiously. Israeli troops reported using harsher tactics to control unrest.

Government curfew in refugee camps discussed. U.N. official quoted as to food supply and condition in camps. Israelis reported arresting journalists and lawyers. Report on loss of money by Jerusalem merchants during unrest. Reagan admin.'s reason for abstention discussed. U.S. reported resigned to lack of influence over Israel. Situation compared to S. Africa. White House statements quoted on U.S. actions toward Israel.

Print: NYT. FP jump to a-10 w/map. Four Palestinians are expelled to Lebanon. As deportations begin unrest continues. Israel flew 4 Palestinians out of Israeli territory in spite of international criticism. Expulsion orders are reported an attempt to quell unrest. Violence continued as 2 more Palestinians killed, bringing the total to 35. A special U.N. envoy visited the occupied territories to investigate the situation. U.S. critical of Israeli action. Dismay reported at U.N.

Policy events: Criticism of Israel, envoy talks in Israel.

1/15/88: Continuing violence. Reporters attacked.

TV: Light to moderate coverage. 1–2 mins w/film. Confrontation between Israeli troops and Palestinians reported outside mosque. Number of injured reported. Journalists shown being roughed up. Other demonstrations reported in Gaza and West Bank refugee camps relatively quiet.

Print: NYT. FP story jumps to p.a-8 w/map. As Arab workers stay home Israeli economy suffers. In the past month unrest has kept thousands of Palestinians away from jobs in Israel—a reminder that the country's economy is largely dependent on its political foes.

SB: *Israelis detain 10 key Palestinians.* Most regarded as moderates in a continued crackdown to quell scattered disturbances. SB: p.1-10 w/photo. U.S. opposed to deportations but would abstain from voting on second resolution, because repeatedly raising the issue will not restore order.

Policy events: Opposition to deportations.

1/16/88: Continuing violence.

TV: Light coverage one network. 1 min. Continuing violence in refugee camps reported. U.S. consul calls for easing of restrictions against Palestinians as unrest continues.

Print: NYT. FP jump to p. 5 w/photo. Jerusalem police fire tear gas at Palestinians in altercation at the Dome of the Rock. At least 70 Palestinians and several police reported injured. P. 5 additional photo and map. SB. PLO criticized for not strongly supporting protestors in occupied territories.

Policy events: Consul call for easing restrictions against Palestinians.

1/17/88: Commercial strike continues (no news reports on TV of strike's beginning). Continuing confrontations. Israeli court blocks further deportations.

TV: Light to moderate coverage. 1–2 mins w/film. Problems faced in refugee camps noted. Food lines reported. Issue of deportation detailed.

Israeli response to commercial strike noted. Continued protests and arrests noted. Israeli judge blocks deportation of 4 more Israelis.

Print: NYT. P.3 w/map and photo. A senior U.N. official in Jerusalem to investigate Palestinian refugee district was caught in a hail of rubber bullets and tear gas as Israeli troops chased protestors. Journalists are now being turned away from demonstrations and camps in attempt to quell the unrest. Israel acknowledges major propaganda defeat, especially on television. SB. Deportee vows suicide mission against Israel unless allowed to return home.

Policy events: None reported.

1/18/88: Continuing violence. First public comparisons with South Africa.

TV: Light to moderate coverage. 2–7 mins w/film. Lifting of curfew in camps reported. Public relations problem noted facing Israel due to reporting of violence in occupied territory noted. Israeli Foreign Minister's spokesman says he will explain context of Palestinian problem. His meeting with reporters and American. Jewish groups described. Israel's working paper rebutting comparison between S. Africa noted. Areas of comparison between the two countries detailed, incl. freedom of the press. Israeli response to comparisons reported.

Print: NYT. P.5. Israelis maintain wide Arab curfew. Pleas to counter protest seals 250,000 in refugee or occupied areas. Around the clock curfew continue as Israeli cabinet approves tough measures. Workers who reside in those areas are being replaced by Southern Lebanese, Europeans and high school students. Area relatively quiet.

Policy events: None reported.

1/19/88: Continuing violence.

TV: Light to moderate coverage. 2–5 mins w/film. Israeli govt. reported preventing food convoy to enter Gaza. Palestinians shown searching for food in Gaza, accuse Israel of using food as weapon. Rabin denies food shortages, blames lack of food on Arab merchants. Scenes of troops ordering shops to open, as PLO and Islamic fundamentalists call for closure. Egyptian support of Palestinians noted. Situation is noted as having no obvious solution.

Print: NYT. P. 3 w/map. Rabin vows to quell unrest. The disturbances of Palestinians on the west bank and Gaza strip are the most difficult ever faced by Israel. Rabin vows to bring unrest to "manageable level." SB. U.S. vetoes U.N. move to criticize Israel for its recent military attacks, saying it lacks balance and showed insufficient concern for Israel's security needs.

Policy events: U.S. veto of U.N., criticism of Israeli military attacks.

1/20/88: Continuing violence. Beatings policy initiated by Rabin. Curfew reimposed; food shortages reported.

TV: Light to moderate coverage. 2–3 mins w/film. Plus a 7 minute special segment on the Palestinian question which covered the Six-day War, Israelis' capture of the West Bank and the impact of the growing Arab population. Israeli forces reported to be attempting to break up strike by Palestinian merchants. New policy calling for military to beat up protesters reported. Cycle of conflict described. Rabin's new riot control policy discussed, Rabin quoted. Israeli strategy outlined.

Print: NYT. FP. w/photo jump to p.a-11. Israelis invoking Emergency power in East Jerusalem. Seeking to quell further unrest, Rabin acts to ban shipments of food to Palestinians in occupied territories unless Arab shopkeepers end strike. Map included to show areas affected. SB. P.a-11. Military analysis w/map. Israeli army playing unaccustomed role of policeman in putting down riots.

Policy events: None reported.

1/21/88: Continuing violence. Reports of fighting between Jewish settlers and Palestinians.

TV: Light to moderate coverage. 1–2 mins w/film. Plus a 4-minute special assignment on Israeli Arabs covering their situation and the conditions they face, beginnings of conflict with Israeli Jews also noted. State Dept. attack on Israeli policy of beating demonstrators reported. Warning by Rabin against demonstrations of support by Israeli Arabs for Palestinians. Commentary on Israel and Camp DAvid with discussion of Israeli's ignoring Camp David agreement.

Print: NYT. P.a-6. Discussion of mechanism set up between police and army in East Jerusalem in case of unrest.

Policy events: DOS criticism on beating policy.

1/22/88: Continuing violence. Demonstrations in U.S. in support of Palestinians.

TV: Light to moderate coverage. 2–3 mins w/film, plus 4-minute special segment on Arab-Americans covering protests by them in support of Palestinians, discussion of Arab-American lobby contrasted with Jewish lobby; Palestine Nat'l Council says pictures from Israel have made lasting impressions. U.N. reported asserting Israel used excessive force. Call by

Perez de Cuellar for Israel to respect Geneva Convention's protection of civilians in areas occupied by military reported. Palestinian unrest in E. Jerusalem reported. Shamir reported coming to U.S. to discuss Palestinian unrest with Reagan. Israeli officers shown beating Palestinians.

Print: NYT. P.a-10. w/photo of Israeli troops. Report of Israelis sending in psychologists to army units in the Gaza strip. Concern is being raised about the mental health of combat troops on riot duty.

Policy events: Plans for Shamir visit to Washington.

1/23/88: Continuing violence in occupied territories.

TV: TOB—Moderate. 3–4 mins w/film. Confrontations between Israeli forces and Palestinians in E. Jerusalem reported. Demonstrations by Israeli Arabs and Druse villagers in Golan Heights reported. Peaceful march in Nazareth shown. Protest in Tel Aviv by Israeli Jews against occupation policy shown. Israeli policy of beating protesters detailed. Rabin says aim of policy is to return to tranquility. Meeting of Arab league in Tunisia to call for further support of Palestinians reported.

Print: NYT-FP—w/photos of Palestinians demonstrating, and of severely beaten Palestinian-Arabs recount attacks by Israeli troops. IP—Israelis impose curfew on E. Jerusalem area; U.N. chief calls for urgent action by council on Arab-Israeli accord; PLO is said to delay on decision to set up a govt. in exile. 4 articles/5 pages.

Policy events: None reported.

1/24/88: Continuing violence in occupied territories. Confrontations in Jerusalem. Egyptian plan for peace proposed (unclear when announced).

TV: Moderate. 2–4 mins w/film. Confrontations between Israeli forces and Palestinians near Jerusalem and Gaza strip reported. Efforts of Israeli troops to break Palestinian commercial strike reported. Roughing up of ABC news camera crew by Israelis shown. Restrictions imposed on journalists detailed. Israeli Cabinet minister Bar-Lev says no beatings take place.

Criticism of Israeli policy in area by President of Union of American Hebrew Congress President, Alex Schindler. He opposes policy of beating civilians. Return of relative calm to Israeli-occupied territories reported. Diplomatic activities by USSR, Egypt, and U.N. noted. Meeting of Arab League in Tunisia to call for further support of Palestinians reported.

Print: NYT-FP—Israel says troops in Arab areas will be more closely supervised. IP—Wave of Palestinian unrest reaches once quiet villages. 4

Arab envoys ask U.S. aide for more pressure on Israel; Arafat sees support by Arab nations for protests staged by Palestinians; Israelis' views on the consequences of occupation. Ed.—NYT—Critical of Israeli response. 6 articles/7 pages.

Policy events: Arab request for pressure on Israel received.

1/25/88: Shamir rejects Egyptian plan. Continuing violence, beatings.

TV: Light to moderate coverage; 3 mins w/film. Shamir reported rejecting Egyptian plan to end Israeli occupied territories' violence. Shamir noted refusing Intl. peace conference proposal, Shamir quoted. Israeli govt's beating policy reported received with outrage. Palestinian lawyer reported filing complaint against Rabin. American Jews divided over beatings policy. American Jews' reactions to policy described.

Print: NYT-IP—Israel is rebuked on Arab beatings by a U.S. leader of Reform Judaism; Israelis worry about their image; 23 Palestinians seized by Jordan, plot to subvert regime is charged. 3 articles/3 pages.

Policy events: None reported.

1/26/87: Continuing violence in occupied territories, Nablus.

TV: Light to moderate. 1–3 mins w/film. More Palestinians reported injured by Israeli troops in occupied territories. Fighting in streets of Nablus. USSR and Egypt at U.N. reported proposing peace talks for Israeli-Palestinian question. Israeli policy iterated. Victims quoted regarding beatings. Shamir quoted from *Jerusalem Post* article regarding Palestinians in occupied Israeli territories.

Print: NYT-FP—Few Israelis dispute Army tactics in unrest. IP—U.S. Jews torn over Arab beatings. Ed.—(Rosenthal) Jews must not break bones. Ed.—(Garbus) Critical of Israel's military justice system. 4 articles/5 pages.

Policy events: None reported.

1/27/88: Continuing violence in occupied territories. Israeli troops attack CBS camera crew.

TV: Light to moderate. 1–3 mins w/film. Seeming appearance of leaders among Palestinians who keep protests going against Israeli policies in occupied territories reported. Israeli radio reported announcing number of injured Palestinians since beating policy instated. Scenes shown of arrested and beaten Palestinians.

Israeli soldiers shown attacking CBS camera crew, Israeli army officials reported apologizing for incident. Suggestion that Israel is seeking true representatives of Palestinians reported. Meeting of 2 Palestinian reps. with Schultz to call for Intl. peacekeeping force to replace Israeli presence in W. Bank and Gaza reported. Recent arrest of journalist Hanna Seniora recalled. Proposals for area by Mubarak detailed. Need for leadership by U.S. noted. Present situation between Israelis and Palestinians compared to British dominance over Jews during 1940s.

Print: NYT-FP—For Jews in Teaneck, NJ Israel is anguish and hope. IP— Israel asks U.S. critics 'what else can we do?' Shultz to meet 2 prominent Palestinians on unrest. 3 articles/4 pages.

Policy events: Shultz plans to meet Palestinians.

1/28/88: Mubarak visits Reagan in Washington, asks Reagan to take an active role in restraining Israel. Continuing violence in occupied territories; Coca Cola plant outside of Jerusalem attacked.

TV: TOB—Light to moderate. 1–5 mins w/film. Reagan's quandary regarding Israel's brutal (sic) policy toward Palestinians discussed. Mubarak's visit to Washington featured. Reagan noted being reluctant to criticize Israel. Reagan condemns violence in Gaza strip. Mubarak makes plea to Reagan to take active role in peace process.

Mubarak's plans illustrated. U.S. noted refusing to accept plan. U.S. officials quoted regarding lack of action due to election year. Israeli army reported claiming calm returning to occupied territories. Statements from Israeli that some soldiers punished for beating Palestinians reported.

Print: Not available for this date.

Policy events: Reagan criticism of Gaza strip violence; Mubarak talks in Washington.

1/29/88: Continuing violence in occupied territories. Israeli peace march in Jerusalem.

TV: Moderate. 2–6 mins w/film. Demonstrations by and beatings of Palestinians in refugee camps north of Jerusalem reported. Confrontational strategies of Palestinians against Israeli forces reported. Scenes shown of unrest in Nablus and Ramallah.

Rabin's position on policy and results of beatings detailed. Israelis' viewpoints on Palestinians featured, problems of Israel being both Jewish and democratic state reiterated. Israeli occupation army discussed. Psychologist comments on Israeli soldiers' anger.

Print: NYT-IP—U.S. and Egypt ask for 6 month Israel-Arab restraint; Israeli General describes charges of brutal beatings as just stories. 2 articles/2 pages.

Policy events: Joint request to Israel with Egypt.

1/30/88: Continuing violence in occupied territories.

TV: Light. 1–2 mins w/film. Renewal of outbreaks of violence in W. Bank and Gaza. Major outbreaks in Nablus and Ramallah shown. Counterattack by Israeli Arabs against police in Jerusalem reported. Israeli policy of beating protesters is mentioned.

Print: NYT-IP—Israel accused of more beatings. 1 article/1 page.

Policy events: None reported.

1/31/88: Continuing violence in occupied territories. Israeli soldiers try to break strike by forcing shops to open.

TV: Moderate. 2–3 mins w/film. Continuation of riots reported. Curfew in Nablus noted. Confrontation between Palestinians and Israeli forces following prayer interlude in E. Jerusalem reported, scenes show arrests and beatings of Palestinians. Ongoing general strike in Ramallah detailed. Scenes shown of cycle of Israelis reopening stores and Palestinians reclosing them.

Print: NYT-FP—10 Arabs wounded by Israeli gunfire. IP—(Front page of "Week in Review")—Tribal warfare, for Arabs and Israelis, maybe it never ends, w/photos of a Palestinian clutching stones, an Israeli soldier on patrol. 2 articles/3 pages.

Policy events: None reported.

2/1/88: Continuing violence in occupied territories.

TV: Light to moderate coverage. 1–2 mins w/film. Soldiers shown beating Palestinians. More Palestinians reported being shot and killed by Israeli soldiers in West Bank. Retired Israeli army general Matti Peled discusses soldiers' roles. Problem of restraint vs. forces by Israeli soldiers reported; soldiers comment on tactics.

Palestinian journalist Daoud Kuttab says policies have alienated many groups. Vetoeing by U.S. of U.N. resolution condemning Israeli handling of Palestinian situation reported. Israel's curfew discussed. Support reported strengthening for right-wing pressure to expel Palestinians.

Print: NYT-IP—On U.S. TV, Israelis find an inflattering mirror; 4 Palestinians and an Israeli wounded in clashes. 2 articles/2 pages.

Policy events: U.N. resolution veto.

2/2/88: Continuing violence in occupied territories. Schultz announces Reagan peace proposal.

TV: Zero to moderate coverage. 0–3 mins w/film. Role of Mubarak pushing U.S. role in area noted. U.S. proposals outlined on screen. Peres' call for a U.N.-sponsored peace conference noted. Shamir's position noted. U.S. raising issue of Palestinian self-rule reported. Israeli government reported reinstating curfews in W. Bank.

Print: NYT-FP—U.S. proposes new approach to ME peace. IP—U.S. vetoes U.N. resolution urging restraint by Israelis. U.S. plan is aimed to give Palestinians 'a stake in their future.' Ed.—(Hauser and Hertzberg) For local elections in the West Bank and Gaza. 4 articles/5 pages.

Policy events: U.S. proposals for ME peace/self-rule debated.

2/3/88: Continuing violence in occupied territories.

TV: Light to moderate coverage. 1–5 mins w/film. Plans for Asst. Sec. of State Richard Murphy to go to Syria and Saudi Arabia to seek support of peace plan. Death toll of uprising given. Israeli settlers reported being targets of Palestinian rioters. Soldiers shown firing at school children. Rabin comments on curfews. Shamir and Israeli settlers shown planting trees symbolizing permanence. Shamir tells settlers to be strong and Palestinians to be quiet. State Dept. spn. Redman comments on peace in ME. *Journal of Palestinian Studies* spn. Hisham Sharabi says Palestinians have new self-confidence.

Print: NYT-IP—Hussein weighing U.S. ME peace plan; Profile on Israeli settlement in West Bank (Tekoa); Many Arab schools are shut in Israeli bid to curb unrest; PLO plans to ferry Palestinian deportees to Israel. Ed.— NYT—Full-time envoy needed for ME peace process.

Policy events: Murphy trip to ME considered.

2/4/88: Continuing violence in occupied territories.

TV: Light coverage. 0–1 minute w/film. Shamir shown touring Gaza Strip refugee camp. Shamir's promise to improve living conditions in area noted.

Print: NYT-IP—Palestinian demonstrations continue. U.S. House members meet Israeli envoy Arad on shootings of Arabs. Ed.—(Lewis) Palestinians must make decision to compromise before solution can be found. 3 articles/3 pages.

Policy events: None reported (Members of Congress meet Arad)

2/5/88: Rock-throwing by Palestinians continuing in occupied territories.

TV: 0-moderate coverage. 0–3 mins w/film. Interviews with Palestinians from Ramallah now living here in U.S.; **one businessman says nature of issue changed by TV.**

Print: NYT-FP—U.S. State Dept.'s legal advisor pressing Meese to delay closing of PLO mission; Palestinian raid kills 2 soldiers, Israelis say. IP—Personality profile—Rabin; NA—ME tightrope-clashes stirring calls for talks. 4 articles/6 pages.

Policy events: Policy debated on PLO mission.

2/6/88: Violence between soldiers and Palestinians renewed.

TV: Light coverage. 1 min w/film. Anti-Israeli rally in W. Bank reported. Announcement by Israel of plans to build new settlements on W. Bank reported.

Print: NYT-FP Lead—From Palestinian rage, new leadership rises. FPSB-Israeli army also worried by Israeli settlers. 2 articles/4 pages.

Policy events: None reported.

2/7/88: Continuing violence in occupied territories.

TV: Light to moderate coverage. 2–3 mins w/film. Involvement of American exchange student in Ramallah unrest shown. Stoning of W. Bank Israeli settler by Arabs reported; wife interviewed. Statement by Jerusalem's mayor, Teddy Kollek, on collapse of Arab-Jew coexistence reported.

Print: NYT-FP—In Jordan, anxiety and joy over Palestinian upheaval. IP—Israeli soldiers storm home of West Bank clan. Ed.—(Shipler) Turmoil could provide the seeds of peace. Ed.—(Segal) Why Israel needs Arafat. Ed.—(Lewis) Time for Americans to face the truth of Palestinian oppression. 5 articles/6 pages.

Policy events: None reported.

2/8/88: Continuing violence in occupied territories.

TV: 0-moderate coverage. 0–2 mins w/film. Palestinians reported being shot by Israeli troops in W. Bank. U.N. officials quoted regarding Palestinian teenager being beaten to death. Palestinian mother shown mourning son's death. Army noted denying any beatings. U.N. spn. quoted on recent upsurge of violence. American fact-finding delegation member, Antonio Rodrigo condemns Israel's oppressive measures. Death toll given. Israeli army's stance outlined.

Print: NYT-FP—w/photo of mourners carrying bodies of 2 Palestinians killed in clashes, Five more dead in Arab protests. 1 article.

Policy events: None reported. (Congressional mission statements).

2/9/88: Continuing violence in occupied territories.

TV: 0-moderate coverage. 0–6 mins w/film. Arrest of Jewish settler for killing of Palestinian in occupied territories reported. Death of 2 other Palestinians noted. Reagan envoy Richard Murphy reported beginning talks with Shamir regarding Israeli-Arab peace prospects. Palestinians reported being killed in W. Bank and Gaza. Death toll given. Palestinian activists quoted regarding violence-induced progress. Palestinian journalist Maher Abu Khater comments on situation. Summary given of Arab-Jewish conflict.

Print: NYT-IP—Jewish settler kills an Arab amid continuing disorder; Israel's High Court urges government to create an appeals court in West Bank and Gaza. 2 articles/2 pages.

Other: CBS program *48 Hours* addresses Israeli troubles and Palestinian views.

Policy events: Murphy talks with Shamir.

2/10/88: Continuing violence in occupied territories. U.S. moves to close PLO observer mission at U.N.

TV: Light to moderate coverage. 1–4 mins w/film. U.S. Justice department's decision to uphold Congress' order to close PLO observer mission at U.N. despite State Dept. objection reported.

U.S. peace plan reported being introduced by envoy Richard Murphy to Israeli leaders. Peres noted endorsing plans but expressing reservations. PLO leaders noted objecting to plan. Special Assignment on American Jews and the Israeli-Palestinian conflict.

Print: NYT-IP—U.S. envoy Murphy arrives in Israel to meet Shamir on peace. 1 article.

Policy events: Murphy talks in Israel; DOS object to closing PLO mission.

2/11/88: UN Secretary General seeking legal action to bar U.S. from closing PLO's observer mission. No coverage of occupied territories given.

TV: 0-moderate coverage. 0–2 mins. PLO discussed. Congress reported ordering PLO office closed because of election year desire to assist Israel. NYC mayor Koch and State Dept. legal advisors quoted. Poor timing of action noted. Shultz reported refusing to sign legal advisors objections. Meese noted refusing to act. U.S. said shooting itself in foot.

Print: NYT-FP—Israel furious over Arab plan to ship Palestinian deportees back to Israel. IP—Peres welcomes a U.S. plan on Palestinian rule;

Meese postpones announcement on closing PLO's U.N. Mission; Israeli doves call for end of occupation. Ed.—NYT—Repeal the PLO shutdown law. 5 articles/6 pages.

Policy events: PLO mission debate continues.

2/12/88: Continuing violence in occupied territories.

TV: 0-moderate coverage. 0–3 mins w/film. Death toll given. State Dept. reported announcing Shultz visiting ME next month. Friday's religious services reported being followed by violence in W. Bank. Soldier quoted after being ordered not to shoot. Jerusalem reported no longer being "city of peace"; violence shown. Palestinians say they will close stores until freedom won. W. Jerusalem merchants mentioned enjoying strike. Jewish settlers comment on situation. Jerusalem Municipal Youth Orchestra comprised of both Arab and Jewish children featured.

Print: NYT-FP—Jerusalem becomes victim of unrest as Arab youths attack Jewish homes. IP—Shultz likely to undertake ME peace mission; After delay, PLO ship is set to sail to Israel; Troops kill Palestinian youth. 4 articles/5 pages.

Policy events: PLO mission debate continues; Shultz considers ME visit.

2/13/88: Unrest continues; no new events.

TV: **No coverage.**

Print: NYT-FP—New squabbling in Israel widens 2 leaders' split. IP—Unrest stiffens resolve of Jew and Arab alike. 2 articles/3 pages.

Policy events: None reported.

2/14/88: Violence spreads to Golan Heights.

TV: Light to moderate coverage. 1–2 mins w/film. Confrontation between Druze residents of Golan Heights and Israeli forces reported. Protests in W. Bank and Gaza shown. Denouncing of U.S. peace plan in Jerusalem by rightwing Knesset members reported; Knesset member Yuval Ne'eman opposes territorial concessions. Demonstration by Israelis in Jerusalem against Israeli policy in occupied territories shown. Shamir's opposition to concessions reported. Strained U.S.-Israeli relations noted.

Print: NYT-IP—Medical teams cite rising severity of beatings of Palestinians by Army; (Front page of "Weekend in Review") A Palestinian revolution without the PLO, w/photo of young Arabs waving Palestinian flag. Ed.—(Jimmy Carter) The U.S. need to lead in Israel. Ed.—(Lewis) Critical of closing of PLO mission. 4 articles/5 pages.

Policy events: None reported.

2/15/88: Israel arrests two Israeli soldiers for allegedly burying 4 Palestinians alive.

TV: Moderate coverage. 2–4 mins w/film. Israeli army reported investigating accusation that troops used bulldozers to bury Palestinian teenagers alive. Palestinians quoted regarding incident. Bomb reported exploding on ship in Cyprus that Palestinians planned to use for protest voyage to Israel. Israeli officials reported refusing to comment on PLO sabotage charges.

Print: NYT-IP—Profile of Palestinian returning to West Bank after years in U.S.; Villages in Golan Heights battle Israeli police. Ed.—(Safire) Analysis of Shultz mission. 2 articles/2 pages.

Policy events: None reported.

2/16/88: Continuing violence in the occupied territories.

TV: Light coverage. 0–1 min w/film. Modification of Israeli's use of force against Palestinians in occupied territories reported; role of Rabin in changing policy noted. Incident in which Palestinians were buried alive recalled. Arab Knesset member acuses Rabin of being responsible for policy of beating protesters. **Israeli soldier reported attacking NBC news cameraman; soldiers and reporter Martin Fletcher quoted.** Israeli officials quoted regarding disciplinary measures.

Print: NYT-FP—Israel detains 2 in burial alive of Palestinians; Blast disables PLO's "Exodus" ferry in port, w/photo of ferry. 2 articles/2 pages.

Policy events: None reported.

2/17/88: Continuing violence in occupied territories. U.S. appoints new ambassador to Israel, William Brown, to replace Pickering.

TV: Light to moderate coverage. 1–3 mins w/film. Death toll given. Farmers in village of Shuylh shown revolting against Israeli troops. Villagers noted viewing U.S. peace plan as irrelevant. Shamir reported opposing U.S. peace plan. Palestinians noted being opposed to any compromise. Israeli soldiers quoted regarding W. Bank patrol; says no one likes patrol. **Soldier shown attacking NBC camera crew; soldiers quoted.** Army reported consulting psychologists regarding solders' tensions. Israeli General Ze'ev comments on dangers of soldiers using so much force and on cases of stress. Ze'ev demonstrates use of homemade pistol. Note delay of PLO ship.

Print: NYT-FP—Arab nations reject bid to use Camp David as basis for peace, call for multinational talks. IP—PLO "Exodus" ferry faces a sea of trouble; For Arabs a quiet 'day of anger' on West Bank. 3 articles/4 pages.

Policy events: New Ambassador to Israel appointed.

2/18/88: PLO drops ship plans.

TV: **No coverage.**

Print: NYT-IP—a dozen Israeli playwrights, poets and other intellectuals addressing about 800 people in Tel Aviv make an appeal to the govt. to "talk peace with the Palestinians." PLO scuttles ship plans. 2 articles/2 pages.

Policy events: None reported.

2/19/88: Continuing violence in the occupied territories.

TV: 0 to moderate coverage. 0–3 mins w/film. Stepping up of Israeli patrols in E. Jerusalem reported. Psychological report on Israeli soldiers in area detailed. Call by Rabin for restraint recalled. Scenes shown of soldiers beating Palestinians. Israel reported having no clear idea about how to end unrest. Shultz visit discussed. Palestinians shown provoking troops and then being captured. Maj. Gen. Ehud Barak says youth provoked violence used against him. **CBS news cameraman shown being mishandled by Israeli troops in Jerusalem.** Plan to keep Jerusalem peaceful during Shultz visit discussed. Shultz noted visiting USSR prior to visit; USSR noted likely to endorse U.S. peace plan. Other countries that do are listed. Plan's ignoring of PLO discussed.

Print: NYT-IP—Arab nations seek U.N. debate on U.S. plan to close PLO office. Ed.—NYT—Israel needs to push for peace. 2 articles/2 pages.

Policy events: Shultz USSR-ME visit.

2/20/88: Continuing of violence in occupied territories.

TV: Moderate coverage. 2 mins w/film. Shultz reported bound to Israel after Moscow visit. Killing of two Palestinians by Israeli forces in W. Bank reported. Protest by Israeli army reservists shown. Shultz upcoming visit discussed. Peres reported agreeing with Shultz that Israel must give land back while Shamir disagrees. Shamir says Israel will decide what is in its best interest. Warning by PLO to Palestinians not to meet with Shultz reported. Call by Palestinians for increased resistance to show Shultz that talks without PLO will not work.

Print: NYT—No coverage.

Policy events: None reported.

2/21/88: Continuing violence in occupied territories.

TV: Moderate coverage. 2–4 mins w/film. Killing of two Palestinians reported. Rabin explains Israeli policy. Palestinian newsletter reported calling for week of protests during Shultz visit. Israelis' response to U.S. peace plan detailed. Shamir reported cool to U.S. ideas while Peres reported welcoming such ideas. Issue of U.S.-USSR role in ME peace hopes mentioned. Arrival of Shultz in Moscow to discuss ME with Shevardnadze. Shevardnadze says USSR wants greater role in peace efforts. PLO opposition to mtg. of Palestinian spokesperson with Shultz noted. Refusal by U.S. and Israel to speak to Arafat noted.

Print: NYT-IP—2 Arabs killed in clashes on West Bank. Ed.—(Kifner) West Bank enmity takes on the marks of permanence. 2 articles/2 pages.

Policy events: Shultz discusses ME policy in Moscow.

2/22/88: Two Palestinians killed in anti-Shultz protest.

TV: 0-Light coverage. 0–30 secs. Letter from Israeli Attorney General to Rabin stating that beating of Palestinians is illegal reported. No film.

Print: NYT-IP—PLO withdraws threat to revive attacks on Israelis outside of Israel and occupied territories; 2 more Palestinians killed in protest over Shultz visit. 2 articles/2 pages.

Policy events: Shultz trip continues.

2/23/88: Demonstrations against Shultz visit.

TV: Light to moderate coverage. 1–2 mins w/film. Israeli troops reported killing Palestinian teenagers in W. Bank. Death toll given. Protests reported designed to show Shultz the depth of opposition to Israeli rule.

Scenes shown of unrest and tour of Gaza strip by Australian Foreign Minister, who stated Israel needs to disengage from Gaza. Issue of whether Shultz and Palestinians will meet detailed. Palestinian journalist Hanna Seniora says Shultz has to meet with delegation of Palestinians from inside and outside territories. Shultz refusal to meet with PLO noted.

Print: NYT-IP—PLO withdraws threat to revive attacks on Israelis outside of Israel and occupied territories; 2 more Palestinians killed in protest over Shultz visit. 2 articles/2 pages.

Policy events: Plans for Shultz visit, attempt to move Shultz plan.

2/24/88: Continuing violence in the occupied territories. Shultz arriving in Israel tonight to present U.S. peace plan.

TV: Light to moderate coverage. 20 secs–3 mins w/film. Shultz noted also traveling to Jordan, Egypt, and Syria. Shultz quoted regarding Palestinians.

Palestinians reported killing another Palestinian accused of collaborating with Israelis. Israelis blame PLO for violence. Israeli boys shown being registered for military service in Tel Aviv. Palestinian and Israeli teenagers shown fighting; quoted regarding parents' failure to rectify problems. Palestinian father shown beating son for throwing rocks at Israeli troops. Israeli father reported tried to persuade daughter not to refuse to serve in military; daughter says she doesn't want to be exposed to violence. Schools noted closed in Ramallah.

Print: NYT-IP—As protests go on, more Palestinians are killed. Ed.— (Abba Aban) Israel's main goals and Mr. Shultz's. (Labor Party view). 2 articles/2 pages.

Policy events: Schultz talks.

2/25/88: Continuing violence in the occupied territories. Shultz in Israel presenting U.S. peace plan.

TV: Moderate coverage. 3–5 mins w/film. U.S. peace proposals for occupied territories outlined on screen. Upcoming negotiations with Jordan, Egypt and Israel noted. Scenes shown of Israeli security forces in Jerusalem. Shultz states visit's objectives. Shultz noted expecting Israel to compromise with Palestinians. Shultz reported not scheduled to meet with Palestinians during trip.

More Palestinian teens reported killed in W. Bank; scenes shown of unrest and funeral. Incident mentioned in which Palestinian fired into crowd of Palestinians and was then hanged. Israel's chief of staff quoted regarding troop's brutal beatings of Palestinians. **Soldier shown breaking Palestinian's arm by multiple beating with rock.**

Israeli government reported regarding situation. Peres urges Shultz to combat skepticism. Shamir noted refusing to compromise and criticizing Peres' position. Shamir and Peres reported not meeting together with Shultz for fear they'll argue. PLO noted calling for boycott of Shultz visit. Anti-Shultz demonstration shown. Palestinians shown tearing down walls to get rocks. Announcement by USSR that it would reestablish relations with Israel if there is a peace conference. Peres noted favoring proposition, Shamir opposing.

Print: NYT-FP—Reagan says outsiders foment Palestinian riots, declines to protest policy of Israeli forces. IP—Shultz to press eventual goal of an Israeli pullout; Boy killed and man lynched in a clash of Arabs. 3 articles/4 pages.

Policy events: Schultz talks to move mideast peace plan. Reagan statement re: outsiders causing riots.

2/26/88: Continuing violence in occupied territories.

TV: Moderate coverage. 2–3 mins w/film. Death of 4 Palestinians reported during violence by Israelis and Palestinians. Settler Rabbi Waldman says attack on family will not deter us. Statement from Shultz during his visit reported; says Palestinians' participation essential for peace plan. Impact of lack of Palestinian presence on mission detailed. Seniora says Shultz must talk to PLO reps. Reason for U.S. refusal to talk with PLO noted. Shultz reported encountering opposition to peace plan; Shamir quoted. Arab-Jewish coexistence noted becoming increasingly impossible.

Israeli Army officials reported stunned by CBS news video of four Israeli soldiers brutally beating two Palestinians for almost an hour. Maj. Gen. Mitzna quoted re: soldiers' punishment and what's he's doing to rectify matter. Mubarak noted attempting to attain PLO approval for Shultz to meet with Arabs Sunday.

Print: NYT-FP—w/photo of Shultz being greeted by Shamir, Shultz urges "historical" Israeli step to end impasse over Palestinians. FPSB—w/map, *New leaders in Arab unrest: Radical and loyal to PLO.* IP—Israeli troops kill 2 Arabs, Palestinian general strike protests Shultz visit; U.S. officials move to clarify Reagan remarks, Shultz says "fundamental origins" of the violence were "essentially indigenous." Ed.—NYT—ME, long shot worth taking. 5 articles/7 pages.

Policy events: Shultz peace talks, statements; attempts to set meeting with Palestinians.

2/27/88: Continuing violence in the occupied territories. Shultz travels to Jordan and Syria.

TV: Moderate coverage. 2–4 mins w/film. Two more Palestinians reported killed. Absence of King Hussein in peace talks in Jordan noted. Statement by Jordan For. Min. calls for intl. peace conf.; that PLO should be included in peace talks also noted; Shultz responds. Shultz reported traveling to Syria to meet with Pres. Assad. Belief of Shultz aides that a group of Palestinians will meet with Shultz before he leaves. March of Jewish settlers in Hebron shown; Palestinian unrest nearby shown. Demonstration by Israeli pacifists also noted.

Nature of Palestinian protest described, shown. Difficulty of task facing Shultz noted.

Print: NYT-FP—Shamir resists Shultz on parts of peace plan. IP—U.S. to order PLO mission closed; 4 more Palestinians killed in protests; For Israeli settlers, resolve to stay means "this is war." 4 articles/5 pages.

Policy events: Continuing Shultz talks; response to Hussein.

2/28/88: Continuing violence in the occupied territories. Shultz meets with Mubarak in Cairo after visiting Israel, Jordan, and Syria.

TV: Moderate coverage. 2–3 mins w/film. Details of Shultz's meeting with Mubarak given. Possibility of softening of positions of Shamir and Hussein on peace issues reported. Shultz says he has promising package; details of plan's points for Palestinian self-rule given.

Mubarak's trip to D.C. in Jan. recalled; scenes shown of Mubarak-Reagan meeting. Attempts to find Palestinians to meet with Shultz who are acceptable to PLO reported. PLO reported warning Palestinians not to talk to Shultz. U.S. law noted forbidding U.S.-PLO negotiations. Palestinian says nobody but PLO can make peace.

Peres comments on progress. Possibility that Shultz may return to region despite rejections by most Arab nations reported. Israeli army reported charging 3 soldiers in incident in which soldiers buried 4 Palestinians alive. Three more Arabs reported dying in occupied territories. Burial services of killed Palestinians shown.

Print: NYT-FP—Little gain seen as Shultz visits Jordan and Syria; (Small SB) Palestinian death toll exceeds 70 as 3 more are killed. IP—In the occupied West Bank another day of bloodshed; Arafat reported to name a delegation to meet Shultz; (Front page of "Week in Review" w/caricature), *Shultz tries to move the immovable in the ME.* 5 articles/7 pages.

Policy events: Continuing Schultz talks.

2/29/88: Continuing of violence in the occupied territories. Mubarak endorses U.S. peace plan.

TV: Light to moderate coverage. 20 secs–3 mins w/film. Shultz's peace mission discussed. Mubarak noted only leader to endorse U.S. peace plan. PLO noted not allowing Palestinians to meet with Shultz. Gaza lawyers assn. representative Fayes Rahme comments on PLO.

Shultz mentioned not able to speak to PLO leaders due to '75 agreement Kissinger signed. Hussein noted refusing to negotiate without PLO approval. Ex-Shamir aide Mosha Amirab says its time to recognize PLO. Amirab noted forced out of Conservative Party for beliefs. Speaking to Palestinians noted complicated by their refusal to cooperate without PLO approval. Shultz shown briefing both Peres and Shamir. Possibility of Israeli election referendum to determine how to deal with U.S. peace plan. More Palestinians reported shot.

Print: NYT-FP—w/photo of Shultz being greeted by Mubarak, Shultz said to get Mubarak support in talks in Cairo; **Israeli officers ordered to watch tape of 4 soldiers beating Arabs. IP—Profile of Kibbutz's reaction to** seeing one of their own, a soldier, on Israeli television beating Arab captives in West Bank. Ed.—(Ozick) a letter to Arafat, pleading for moderation to achieve peace. 4 articles/6 pages.

Policy events: Schultz talks continue.

3/1/88: Continuing of violence in the occupied territories. Shultz ending peace mission in ME.

TV: LIght to moderate coverage (ABC not reporting). 20 secs–5 mins w/film. Shultz noted mtg. with Hussein in London; Hussein quoted. Shultz mentioned briefing Reagan in Brussels and possibly returning to ME. Officials say Reagan may send Shultz back to ME after NATO meeting.

Kidnappers of Lt. Col. Higgins in S. Lebanon announce they will try Higgins on espionage charges in trial held on behalf of Palestinians. Kidnappers statement shown and quoted on screen. Analysts noted statement sign of kidnapper's weakness. Kidnapping noted angering many Islamic factions, especially Amal militia. *Mideast Mirror* editor says kidnappers not Palestinian but Shi'ite. Kidnappers reported citing Shultz's visit to the region and Israeli treatment of Palestinians as reason for action. Khomeini noted being true patron of kidnappers, not Palestinians.

Arabs in West Bank report that Israeli troops stormed into hospital, fired tear gas, and dragged Palestinian boys outside and beat them for several minutes. Americans returning from tour of West Bank reported stating that Israeli troops deliberately injuring protesters; scenes shown.

Physicians for Human Rights says hands and arms broken in most patients examined; photos shown of identical fracture. Doctors quoted re: injuries. Doctor demonstrates how one receives fractures. Palestinians noted telling doctors troops methodically breaking bones. Dr. explains how troops know which hand to break. Israeli Defense Ministry's response quoted. Drs. noted insisting med. evidence supports finding.

Print: NYT-FP—Israeli peace marchers struggle against occupation and apathy. IP—Jordan hints that Palestinians' role may be obstacle for Shultz peace plan; Syria calls Shultz plan a "fig leaf" for Israeli aims; Israel considers barring the press from Arab areas hit by turmoil; World Court ruling sought on PLO mission. 5 articles/6 pages.

Policy events: None reported.

3/2/88: Continuing of violence in the occupied territories. Announcement that Shultz will return to ME. Israeli Government threatening to prevent media from reporting events in West Bank.

TV: Light to moderate coverage. 20 secs–3 mins w/film. Israel noted refusing to negotiate with PLO; resulting boycott of Shultz talks by Palestinians noted. Shultz says sitting down with Palestinians is desirable: proposal is outlined on screen. Need for response to Shultz plan from Israel, Jordan and Palestinians reported.

Israeli troops reported firing tear gas into Arab hospital, seizing teen and beating him for several minutes. AP reported noted witnessing scene. CBS News video of similar incident recalled. **CBS News crew shown being prevented from taping scene in Jerusalem.** Knesset member Cohen says throw press out of country. **Israeli troops shown attacking camera crew.** Knesset member Ne'Eman comments on situation.

Majority of Israeli cabinet reported favoring media ban in occupied territories. CBS News video of soldiers brutally beating Palestinians recalled; scenes shown. **Rabin reported ordering soldiers to invoke emergency law that allows soldiers to close villages for unspecified periods of time.** Cohen says better for media to be distressed than govt. Media noted being stopped from covering stories even though official blackout nonexistent.

Print: NYT-IP—Shultz ends ME tour upbeat but empty-handed; Prominent U.S. Jews visiting Israel, voice unease. Ed.—NYT—Refuse to deal with PLO until it accepts peace with Israel, but keep trying to work with West Bank and Gaza Palestinians. 3 articles/3 pages.

Policy events: Continuing Schultz talks; no results, returns home.

3/3/88: UN vote against PLO mission closure order.

TV: No coverage.

Print: NYT-FP—w/photo of U.N. session, U.N. vote opposes U.S. on PLO mission closing; Palestinian fights Palestinian after rumor of collaboration. IP—Reagan backs return trip by Shultz to ME for peace mission; Israeli TV's editing brings harsh questions. 4 articles/6 pages.

Policy events: Administration plans to continue Schultz initiative.

3/4/88: Continuing of uprising in the occupied territories.

TV: Moderate coverage. 3 mins w/film. Two more Palestinians are killed in the West Bank. Death toll given. Closing of occupied territories to reporters by Israel reported; details given, scenes shown. **Likud member Berri says media is oxygen to terrorists.** Jewish settler shown blaming journalists for West Bank problems. Many Israelis calling for media blackout. Knesset member Cohen comments on situation. Military commanders reported authorized to seal off selected area indefinitely.

Military spokesperson Col. Efraim Lapid says media encourages the Palestinians. Soldiers shown critically beating Palestinians. Media blackout critics' assertion that govt. simply worried about image problems noted. Ex-govt. spokesperson Patir says press needs to do job without hindrance. Media blackout noted did not stop revolt. Destruction of freedom of press discussed. Attacking of reporters by Israeli soldiers noted. News cameraman Micheali says stone throwers do not act for camera. Scenes shown of villagers mourning near Bethlehem.

Shultz reported proposing another ME peace plan, Shultz quoted. Arafat reported complaining from Tunisia that U.S. excluding him from peace process. Shultz noted presenting plan to ME leaders and announcing deadline for answers; details given, scenes shown. Shamir says talk was friendly and useful. Shamir's negative response to other plan recalled. Shultz shown with Mubarak and with Assad.

Shultz noted never meeting with Palestinians. Shultz mentioned urging Hussein to represent Palestinians and refuses to meet Arafat. Shultz reported intended victim of car bombing in Jerusalem; details given, scenes shown. PLO noted claiming responsibility for attempt. Arafat reported claiming to reporter Doug Tunnell that PLO has met conditions for ME peace plan.

Print: NYT-IP—In Hebron, Jewish teenager stabbed, but Purim parade continues. IPNA—Shultz handicap: No meeting with Palestinians. Ed.— NYT—Critical of Congress' attempt at closing PLO mission. 3 articles/3 pages.

Policy events: Schultz talks in Egypt, Israel again.

3/5/88: Continuing of violence in the occupied territories.

TV: Moderate coverage. 2–4 mins w/film. Two more Palestinians reported killed in West Bank. Confrontations between Israeli army and Palestinians in Bethlehem, Gaza Strip, and near Jerusalem reported; scenes shown.

Army lifts media ban in West Bank but closes Nablus to press. West Bank Com. Gen. Mitzna says press restrictions is measure taken to calm down area, policy unchanged. Soldier says media heats things up. **Detention of ABC and NBC camera crews by officers reported. ABC News technician Schatz explains incident.** Kissinger reported denying *NY Times* story that he suggested Israelis restrict press and crush Palestinians in occupied territories.

Return of Shultz from peace mission reported; his meetings with Egypt, Israel, Jordan and Syria noted. Arafat condemning Shultz peace plan.

Scenes shown of Arafat in Tunis, says we can accept U.N. role for transitional period, says accepts all U.N. resolutions on ME. Shultz reported prevented by law devised by Kissinger from direct dealings with PLO. Arafat says Shultz has to deal with PLO or there will be no solution. Palestinian uprising reported giving Arafat and PLO new lease on life.

Print: NYT-IP—**Kissinger urged ban on TV reporting;** Israel curbs coverage of the West Bank; Shultz ending ME mission, gives leaders letter on U.S. plan. 3 articles/3 pages.

Policy events: Appears that Administration would like to deal with Palestinians or even PLO and looking for a way to do it.

3/6/88: Continuing of violence in the occupied territories.

TV: 0-moderate coverage. 0–4 mins w/film. Israeli soldiers reported killing two more Palestinians in West Bank. Meeting of Israeli cabinet to discuss U.S. peace plans for region reported; details given, scenes shown. Opposition by Shamir to concessions noted. Request by Shultz that Shamir respond to plan by next month reported. Shamir hopes that Israeli voters will also oppose Shultz plan noted.

Scenes shown of unrest. Letter from 30 senators to Shultz expressing dismay at Shamir's rejection of "land for peace" concept of Shultz plan reported; details given. Possible impact of pressure on Shamir detailed. Administration hope that letter will change Shamir's point of view reported. Administration hopes to keep peace process going without offending anyone noted.

Crackdown on media access to territories described; scenes shown of CBS broadcast from Feb. 25 in which soldiers beat Palestinians. Scenes shown of Palestinians' "flag day" demonstration.

Print: NYT-FP—Senator criticizes Sharmir's position on ME peace. IP— Palestinian radicals in Syria see return of power; Two Palestinians killed by Israeli troops; (very small) House Bill introduced to overturn order to close PLO mission; Shultz and aides return with hope for ME. Ed.— *Among Arabs, bitter views of the West.* 6 articles/7 pages.

Policy events: Senate letter; use by Administration to pressure Israel.

3/7/88: Continuing violence in the occupied territories. Palestinians hijack Israeli bus.

TV: Moderate coverage. 2–5 mins w/film. First incident in which Palestinian used hand grenade noted. Hijacking of Israeli bus near Beersheba by Palestinians who sneaked across Egyptian border reported; details given, scenes shown. Israeli authorities reported believing gunmen are PLO members. Photos shown of Israeli commando raid on vehicle. Possible link of Arafat to incident explained.

Shamir says episode focuses on real problem. Impact of episode on U.S. peace plan for Palestinian self-rule noted. Peres says you can't negotiate with weapons. Rabin says act another atrocity committed by Arafat's PLO. Shamir under pressure from cabinet to accept U.S. peace plan now refusing to embrace proposals.

Palestinian teens shown brandishing PLO flag. Israeli soldiers reported going to leaders' homes to arrest them for action but were injured from grenade attack. World sympathy for rock-throwing youths noted all but vanishing with grenade toss. Terrorist Specialist Yossi Melman says attack damaged chances for peaceful settlement. Israeli govt. media restrictions discussed, Kissinger mentioned.

Last month's video of troops beating Palestinian youths shown. **Israel noted claiming media's presence incited violence and should therefore be banned. Troops noted now possessing authority to declare any protest or event off limits to reporters.** Military analyst Col. Summers comments on situation. Kissinger's memo to Jewish leaders quoted on screen. Kissinger noted unavailable to comment on comparing Israel to South Africa. Jewish-American activist Morris Abrams defends Kissinger's comments. Israel's image noted being damaged by media restrictions. William Quandt comment on Kissinger's allusion to South Africa. Media's presence promoting violence noted unverifiable. Quandt says violence will continue.

Print: NYT-FP—Shamir foils vote on U.S. Peace Plan, two more Palestinians killed by Israeli troops. IP—Letter from 30 Senators on ME; Two Senators dispute criticism of Shamir. Ed.—(Benjamin Netanyahu) Oust the PLO mission at the U.N. 4 articles/5 pages.

Policy events: Behind scenes discussion reported.

3/8/88: Continuing of violence in the occupied territories.

TV: Moderate coverage. 3–5 mins w/film. Palestinian death in Nablus, confrontations between Israeli soldiers reported. Scenes shown of troops using motorized rocket-launcher against stone-throwing Palestinians. Another Palestinian reported killed by another Palestinian in West Bank. New Palestinian leaders featured; details given, scenes shown of hunt for collaborators.

Israeli army crackdown on refugee camp reported; scenes shown of Israeli search for Palestinian leaders. Masked Palestinian shown, says action is necessary. Scenes shown from refugee camp.

Walters reported meeting secretly with PLO leader in Tunis shortly after Shultz's distribution of peace plan and PLO hijacking of bus. PLO officials quoted. Ex-Ambassador Andrew Young fired for meeting with PLO member in 1979. **Arafat's interview with CBS News in Tunis recalled;** Arafat quoted, Arafat calls for independent Pal. delegation. Walters' agenda outlined.

Israeli settlers reported killing Palestinian busman. Several U.S. Senators reported writing letter to Shultz criticizing Israel's refusal to compromise for peace. Senate aides quoted re: letter from pro-Israel Senators showing support for Shultz.

Shamir reported unwilling to compromise for peace. Sen. DeConcini says simply making suggestion to Israeli govt. Letter shown. Jewish leaders reported dismissing Sens. criticisms. Sens. mentioned planning to personally express dissatisfaction with Shamir's inflexibility next week during his visit to DC.

Print: NYT-FP—6 killed as Arabs hijack Israeli bus. IP—For Israeli Arabs, a question of divided loyalties; (very small) Reagan "welcomes" Senators' Israeli note. Ed.—(Rosenthal) *Israel's actions against Palestinians wrong, but Israel did not create problem, Arab countries did.* 4 articles/5 pages.

Policy events: Vernon Walters meeting with PLO representative in Tunis.

3/9/88: Continuing of violence in the occupied territories.

TV: Light to moderate coverage. 10 secs–2 mins w/film. Three more Palestinians reported shot on West Bank. Violent scenes shown from West Bank. Jewish children shown being confronted by Palestinian youths. Settlers noted resisting U.S. peace plan which calls for land partition. Settler comments on plan, says wants all land in area. Settlers' determination noted. Shamir reported blocking cabinet vote on Shultz peace plan. Shamir quoted re: foreign pressure.

Walters reported denying reporter Tunnell's claim that he met secretly with PLO leaders in Tunis. State Dept. Spokesperson quoted. Walters quoted. CBS News President Stringer quoted.

Print: NYT-IP—Women lead Palestinian protest, two more Palestinians killed; Abram hails Israeli 'restraint.' Ed.—(Moshe Arens) Israel deserves better from its friends. Ed.—(Flora Lewis) Time to speak to Israel. 4 articles/4 pages.

Policy events: Denial of CBS report of Walters meeting with PLO.

3/10/88: Continuing of violence in the occupied territories.

TV: 0-Light coverage. 0–1 min w/film. Protest by Palestinian women in West Bank featured. Scenes shown of unrest between women and Israeli soldiers.

Print: NYT-FP—Shamir says note by Senators stirs doubts about U.S. IP—Two more Palestinians are killed in West Bank; Text of letter from Shamir on criticism from Senators; text of Shultz letter to Shamir. Ed.— (Lewis) *Israel must face the hard truth about the Palestinian issue.* 5 articles/6 pages.

Policy events: Release of Shultz letter to Shamir.

3/11/88: Continuing of violence in the occupied territories.

TV: 0-moderate coverage. 0–3 mins w/film. Tensions reported increased between Jewish settlers, violent scenes shown. Number of Jewish settlements mentioned increasing over past few years, scenes shown. Jewish settlers reported greatest obstacle to Shultz peace initiative.

Shamir reported denouncing Shultz peace plan. Shamir's upcoming meeting with Reagan to discuss peace plan previewed. Justice Dept. reported moving to shut down PLO mission in U.N. Controversy over shutdown featured. Protest of action by Perez de Cuellar reported Shultz attacks cong. legislation prohibiting U.S.-PLO relations. Impact of incident on U.S.-U.N. relations and on peace moves in ME reported.

Print: NYT-FP—Shultz seeing Arab "time bomb," urges Israel to rethink bombers. IP—NA—Arab and Jews in the winds of hate. 2 articles/3 pages.

Policy events: Shultz attack on law preventing talks with PLO. Move to shut down PLO office.

3/12/88: Continuing of violence in the occupied territories.

TV: TOB—Moderate coverage. 2–3 mins w/film. Bombing by Israel of alleged Al Fatah bases in Lebanon in retaliation for hijacking of bus in Israel reported. Syria reported rejecting peace proposal for Israeli occupied territories. Israeli response to Palestinian protest in West Bank reported; scenes shown. Resignation of hundreds of Palestinians employed as policemen in territories reported Israeli Min. of police Bar-Lev says resignation will affect law and order.

Issue of Palestinian collaboration further detailed, examples given. Murder of Palestinian policeman reported, photo shown. Abu Shani explains reasons for selling house to Ariel Sharon. Need to guard homes of Israeli-backed leaders in towns in area reported.

Shamir's upcoming visit to U.S. reported Rep. Obey says he gets letters asking what Congress is doing about problems in West Bank. Scenes shown of unrest. Brookings' Judith Kipper says there are differences of opinion between U.S. and Shamir. Shultz's plan for ME noted. Rep. Lee Hamilton says Congress supports Shultz. Sen. letter asking that Shultz's plan be given chance recalled. Shamir's rejection of letter noted. Jewish leader Abrams says Americans should not tell Israel what its negotiating stance should be. Hamilton says we should not back Shamir into corner.

Print: NYT-FP—Shamir rejects Shultz plan; Arafat rejects U.S. plan, stresses PLO role. IP-PLO told to shut mission in 10 days. 3 articles/5 pages.

Policy events: Support for Schultz, opposition to Israel in Congress; preparations for Shamir's visit.

3/13/88: Continuing of violence in the occupied territories.

TV: TOB—moderate coverage (No NBC), 2–5 mins w/film. Shamir reported headed for U.S. to discuss Shultz's plan for peace. Shamir's flexibility prior to his flight to U.S. reported. Shamir says there is need for concessions if you want to live in peace with neighbors.

Scenes shown of right-wing Israeli protest in Tel-Aviv and fighting in Bethlehem between Palestinian and Israeli forces. Resignation of more Palestinian policemen reported. Firebombed bus shown near Ramallah. Demonstration of Arab-Americans in DC reported; scenes shown.

Newspaper ad taken out by major Jewish org. in support of Shultz plan shown. Jewish leader Abrams says ultimate solution must come from face to face negotiations. Teach-in by supporters of Israeli peace movement reported; scenes shown. Pressure on Shamir from Senate noted. Shultz talks about peace plan. Shultz-Shamir talks previewed. Shamir's scheduled talks with Reagan announced. Protests in Beverly Hills, CA about Israeli govt. policy in occupied territories reported.

Print: Not available for this date.

Policy events: Shultz comments on peace plan prior to Sharmir visit.

3/14/88: Continuing of violence in the occupied territories. Shamir arrives in DC for meetings.

TV: Moderate coverage. 2–3 mins w/film. Shamir reported not compromising position by accepting Shultz's ME peace plan; Scenes shown. Shamir quoted. Redman comments on peace plan's aim. Shamir noted insisting Camp David Accord be used as guide to peace. U.S. officials mentioned asserting Camp David approach not appropriate in this instance.

American Jews shown demonstrating in support of Shamir in NYC. Letter from group of conservative sens. to Shultz quoted on screen; violent scenes shown from West Bank.

Israeli officials noted announcing implementation of curfew in Gaza. American Jewish representative Stone urges Shamir to talk to PLO. Shamir's problem in dealing with Israel's coalition govt. Israeli pol. scientist Sternhell says Shamir does not speak for all of Israel. Right-wing Knesset member Cohen comments on Shamir. Saturday's rally in support of U.S. peace plan and Sunday's rally in support of Shamir's strong stance shown. Cohen predicts Ahmir's impact on U.S. plan. Los Angeles Jewish group shown calling for peaceful compromise in solution. Carlucci shown conversing with Shamir. Upcoming Israeli elections mentioned deciding whether or not ME peace plan is accepted.

Print: Not available.

Policy events: Discussions, maneuvering with Shamir.

3/15/88: Continuing violence in the occupied territories.

TV: Moderate coverage. 2–3 minutes w/film. Two more Palestinians reported killed in Ramallah; scenes shown. Other incidents noted.

Israeli government noted banning travel between occupied territories. Curfew noted imposed on Gaza after police refused to patrol area. Rabin shown touring area. Meeting of Shamir and Shultz reported; details given, scenes shown. Begin's visit to U.S. to negotiate with Egypt in 1978 recalled. Shamir says Israel wants to negotiate directly and sees no role for Int. Conf. Shultz proposal outlined on screen. Shultz says that there are differences between Israel's views and that of U.S.

Shamir meeting with Members of Congress and Pat Robertson reported. Shamir's problems on eve of meeting with Reagan detailed. Speaking to United Jewish Appeal Reagan says U.S. would protect Israel's interests at Int. Conf. Hussein, Assad, and Arafat noted also rejecting peace plan.

Print: Not available for this date.

Policy events: Reagan speech at UJA; talks with Shamir.

APPENDIX 2:
INTERVIEW LIST

Note: All interviewee's answers were noted on an interview form. All but three were taped. Interviews conducted Summer, 1988.

Interviews recorded on tape

Robert Beckel, television commentator, Washington lobbyist
Former Assist. Secretary of State, former Special Assist. to Pres. Carter

Jimmy Carter, Carter Center
Former President

Hodding Carter
Former Spokesperson, Department of State

Arno duBorchgrave, *Washington Times*
Editor-in-Chief

Herman Eilts, Center for International Study, Boston University
Former Ambassador to Israel

Leon Furth, Senate Foreign Relations Committee
Minority Counsel

Dennis Harter, Department of State
Director of Press Operations

William Ingle, House Foreign Affairs Committee
Minority Counsel

Judith Kipper, Brookings Institute
Middle East Specialist, consultant to ABC, informal advisor on Middle East affairs to current and past administrations.

Dan Kurtzer, Department of State
Planning and Policy Division, Middle Eastern Affairs

Ellen Laipson, Congressional Research Service
Director of Middle East Division

Robert Lipshutz, attorney
Former White House Counsel, Carter Administration

Langhorne A. Motley III, LTM Corp.
Former Assist. Secretary of State for InterAmerican affairs.

Phyllis Oakley, Department of State
Deputy Spokesperson

Roman Papaduik, White House
Assistant Press Secretary for International Affairs

Robert Pastor, Carter Center
Former NSC, Latin American specialist

Jody Powell, Ogilvy & Mather
Former White House Press Secretary

William Quant, Brookings Institute
Former NSC, Middle East specialist

Dennis Ross, NBC
Staff specialist, Middle East

Harold Saunders, Brookings Institute
Former Assist. Secretary of State, NSC

Chris Van Hollen, Senate Foreign Relations Committee
Chief of Staff

Tony Verstandig, House Foreign Affairs Committee
Majority Consultant, Middle Eastern Affairs

Interviewed, but not taped

Charles Redman, Department of State
Spokesperson

Gardner Peckham, House Foreign Affairs Committee
Minority counsel

Robert Evans
Former CBS Middle East correspondent, former Moscow Bureau Chief

APPENDIX 3:
LINSKY INTERVIEW TRANSCRIPTS USED

**Transcripts used for personal interviews
by Martin Linsky's team**

Zbigniew Brzezinski
Cyrus Vance
Henry Kissinger
Betina Gregory
Robert Pierpoint
Sander Vanocur
Roger Mudd
Stewart Eizenstat

APPENDIX 4:
INTERVIEW QUESTIONNAIRE

MEDIA AND AMERICAN FOREIGN POLICY RESEARCH
INTERVIEW QUESTIONS

POLICY MAKER QUESTIONNAIRE   (ask questions as if the
interviewee were presently
making policy)

Name

Date

I. Interviewee's use of media in policy making

1. (a) In your daily routine, can you estimate how much time you spend getting information from the media, that is, reading newspapers, listening to radio news, or watching television? *(M2)**

   0-1 hour/day
   1-2 hours/day
   More than 2 hours/day

   (b) Can you estimate the percentage of this time that is spent watching television or reading summaries of television news programming? *(T5)*

   Can't estimate _____%

2. Which medium is most useful to you in your policy work?

   Print   Television   Other

---
*Codes for scoring purposes.

3. Some people say that television is a very useful medium to policy makers but its utility comes not from their watching it, but from what they read in the press that was carried first or more visibly on television, and from its impact on the electorate. Would you agree or disagree with this assertion? *(PL.3)*

    Agree   Disagree

4. *[hand list to interviewee]* Which of these television programs do you watch with some kind of regularity (once a week when possible)? *(M2 background)*

5. Which of those programs would you rate as most useful to you as source of information for policy making? *(T5)*

#4 #5	#4 #5
Network nightly news	*Nightline*
Network morning news	*CNN News*
CNN Headline News	*Crossfire*
Sunday intellectual/ news programs	*C-SPAN*
CNN World Report	*MacNeil-Lehrer News Hour*
60 Minutes	*None of the above*

II. Perceptions of the use of media as a policy-making tool

6. (a) Have you ever used the media to influence the behavior of another government? *(M1)*

    Yes   No   Refuse to answer

    (b) *[If yes]* Which medium did you use? *(T5)*

    Print   Television   Other

7. (a) Excluding disinformation campaigns, do you recall the media being used by foreign governments to influence the U.S. government? *(M1)*

    Yes   No

    (b) *[If yes]* What media was used? *(T5)*

    Print   Television   Other

8. One medium—television—enables national leaders to talk directly by satellite to the people of other nations. *(T2)*

   (a) In your opinion, is this a useful tool of diplomacy?

   Yes   *No*

9. The term "television diplomacy" is sometimes used to describe talks held on television between representatives of sovereign states or NGO's, for example, Ted Koppel's bringing together Palestinian and Israeli leaders during *Nightline.*

   Do you feel this use of television helps or hinders U.S. foreign policy? *(T2)*

   Helps   *Hinders*

   (b) Could you explain your answer?

   _____

   _____

III. Perceptions of the relative importance of TV and print media in American foreign policy

10. Which mass medium (print, radio, or television) do you feel would be most effective to: *(T5)*

    (a) influence the key decision makers in a foreign government?

    Print   *Television*   *Other*

    (b) influence the people of another nation?

    Print   *Television*   *Other*

III. Perceptions of the impact of media on international events

11. Some people say that the number of players in international relations has increased because the media, especially television, attracts people to critical situations, thus complicating attempts at diplomacy.

    Do you agree with this? *(PC3)*

    Yes   *No*

12. Some people say that the media elevate new personalities to the world stage by giving them global visibility, and this visibility gives them more power in international or regional affairs than they would have without the media visibility. Examples often cited include Abu Nidal, Yasser Arafat, Wallid Jumblat. Do you agree with this? *(PC3)*

    Yes   No

13. Some people maintain that the power of terrorists is magnified to large extent by the media, that is, that their actions would not evoke the same responses from governments if they did not receive press coverage. Do you agree or disagree with this statement? *(M4)*

    Agree   Disagree

14. Reporters and anchors have occasionally used their international status to serve as intermediaries or proxies for American diplomats. In other cases, television news reporters have—unknown to their government—tried to negotiate with terrorists holding hostages. *(M4)*

    (a) Do you think there is a place in diplomacy for this activity on the part of journalists?

       Yes   No

    (c) Do you know of other cases of journalists taking on a diplomatic role? (*Save stories for afterward if there is time.*)

       Yes   No

IV. Perceptions of the impact of media on the American process of foreign policy making.

15. (a) Have you or others you know of ever experienced a situation wherein television images contradicted official information or added an element of reality to official information so strong that it affected a policy decision? *(PC6)*

       Yes   No

    (b) [*If yes*] Could you describe the events? (*background*)

    _____

    _____

    _____

16. (a) Can you recall any other situations in which the mass media *provided information necessary* for foreign policy making *more accurately* than official sources [such as, cables and CIA or NSA reports if the interviewee needs prompting]? (*If yes*) what situations? *(CS2)*

Yes   No

(b) [*If yes*] can you describe the cases?

_____

_____

_____

17. (a) Can you recall a situation where the media was the only source of information to policy makers? *(CS3)*

Yes   No

(b) [*If yes*] Can you describe the cases?

_____

18. Some people say that the media are frequently the most rapid source of needed foreign policy information. Do you agree or disagree with this assertion? *(CS1)*

Agree   Disagree

19. (a) Some people claim that the media have accelerated the pace of foreign policy making thus reducing the time for policy formation. Do you agree or disagree with this? *(PC1, T4)*

Agree   Disagree

(b) [*If it has accelerated*] Does this lead to better or worse foreign policy? *(T4)*

Better   Worse
(why?, if time)

19. Some people say that television's propensity for focusing on personalities rather than substantive details subtly influences policy makers to respond to individuals rather than to problems. Do you agree or disagree with this assertion? *(PC7)*

Agree   Disagree

20. The media have the capability of "globalizing" a local or regional event by giving it world visibility. Examples include terrorist bombings in Lebanon, Iranian attacks on ships in the Gulf, or Shining Path rebels in Peru.

   (a) In your experience, has the media's "globalization" of regional events moved them or their regions higher on the U.S. foreign policy agenda? *(PC4)*

   Yes   No

   (b) In your experience, has the media's "globalization" of regional events created domestic pressures for foreign policy actions that would not have surfaced otherwise? *(T3)*

   Yes   No

   Can you give examples?

   _____

   _____

   _____

   (d) Does this globalization effect help or hinder the development and execution of sound policy? *(T3)*

   Help   Hinder

21. Some people say that the media, especially television, exert a subtle pressure on policy makers to simplify their responses to international events.

   Do you agree or disagree with this assertion? *(PC2)*

   Agree   Disagree

22. Some people argue that the media's focus on the White House for news about foreign policy shifts foreign policy decisions from State and Defense and puts them on the White House's agenda. Do you agree or disagree with this assertion? *(PL1)*

   Agree   Disagree

   (b) (*If yes*), which medium do you feel has this effect to the largest extent? *(PL2)*

   Print   Television   Other

23. Some people argue that heavy press coverage of an international situation or location that normally would not merit U.S. foreign policy attention often puts that item on the agenda of American policy makers? Do you agree or disagree with this statement?

    Agree   *Disagree*

EXTRA QUESTIONS IF TIME ALLOWS

24. (a) [*from question 6*] What were the instances in which you used the media to influence the policy of a foreign government? (*background*)

    _____

    _____

    _____

    _____

    (b) Was it effective, i.e., did it impact on U.S. policy or foreign relations? (*background*)

    _____

    _____

    _____

    _____

25. [*From question 8*] Use of television diplomacy to bring leaders together.

    In your opinion, are there dangers in this kind of television diplomacy? If so, what are they?

    _____

    _____

    _____

    _____

26. Some people hold that television's ability to provide visual information from around the world gives it a power to influence perceptions and beliefs far stronger than that of other media. *(TI)*

    Do you think this is true with regard to people who make and execute the nation's foreign policy, i.e., do you think the ability to show events and people in another country make television more powerful than other media in shaping the thinking of foreign policy makers?

_____

_____

_____

_____

27. [*Hand sheet to the interviewee*] In your experience, which of the four statements on the sheet best characterize television news (including CNN and Headline News) as: *(T5)*

faster than print news, but not as useful

faster than print news and equally useful

no faster than print news

not useful to your job regardless of how fast it is

If interviewee answers "not as useful," probe why not—is it due to accuracy? . . . completeness? . . . other reason?

_____

_____

_____

28. If you were to lose access to one of the mass media, which medium's loss would have the greatest negative effect on your work? *(CS4)*

Print   *Television*   *Other*

29. Some people say that television's impact on foreign policy making has increased significantly. Do you agree or disagree with this? Can you explain your answer . . . why/how?

_____

_____

_____

_____

APPENDIX 5
LINSKY QUESTIONNAIRE: ORIGINAL AS MAILED

ID   1-4   (A

Card 1

I. PRESS RELATIONS

DO NOT WRITE
IN THIS SPACE

1. On average, weekly, how many hours did you spend thinking about and dealing with press matters?

XXX.XX _____ hours

5-9   (5
5-

2. How would you describe the amount of time you spent thinking about and dealing with press matters in terms of accomplishing your policy goals? (CHECK ONLY ONE ANSWER)

10-10   (t

1 Too much time   ( )
2 The right amount of time   ( )
3 Too little time   ( )

3. Did you try to seek or influence news coverage regarding your office or agency?

11-11   (1)

1 Yes   ( )
0 No   ( ) —— PROCEED TO QUESTION 4.

IF YES:

a. Specifically, what did you do to try to seek or influence coverage?
  1. _____
  2. _____
  3. _____

b. Which of the above were most often successful?

  _____
  _____
  _____

c. Overall, how successful were you at getting or influencing coverage of your office or agency?

  (CIRCLE ONE NUMBER ON SCALE.)

1	2	3	4	5
Never Successful		Sometimes Successful		Always Successful

12-12   (.)

4. In general, what percentage of the stories which dealt with your office or agency were initiated by the news reporters themselves, what percentage were initated by you or your staff, and what percentage were initiated by a third party?

a. Initiated by reporters: XXX.X _____ percent   13-17   (5)
b. Initiated by you or your staff: XXX.X _____ percent   18-22   (5)
c. Initiated by a third party: XXX.X _____ percent   23-27   (5)

GO TO SECTION II, PAGE 3

Card I

II. EFFECTS OF THE PRESS ON POLICY AND PROCESS

1.   In your experience. which kinds of stories generally had the most impact on you and your job?

(RANK ORDER THE FOLLOWING STORY TYPES FROM 4 FOR THE GREATEST IMPACT TO 1 FOR THE LEAST IMPACT. IF YOU BELIEVE STORY TYPE HAD NO EFFECT. MARK NO DIFFERENCE.)

a.   Stories about personalities. reputations, hirings and/or firings   ____   28 - 28
b.   Stories about how your organization worked and how policy was made   ____   29 - 29
c.   Stories about immediate policy issues facing you   ____   30 - 30
d.   Stories about long-term problems in your area   ____   31 - 31
e.   No difference 5   ____   32 - 32

2.   In your experience. how significant was the impact of the press at each of the following stages of policy making?

(CHECK ONE ANSWER FOR EACH STAGE.)

Stages of Policy Making:	1 No Effect	2 Small Effect	3 Large Effect	4 Dominant Effect	
a. Identification of the problem	( )	( )	( )	( )	33 - 33
b. Formulation of solution	( )	( )	( )	( )	34 - 34
c. Adoption of policy	( )	( )	( )	( )	35 - 35
d. Implementation	( )	( )	( )	( )	36 - 36
e. Evaluation	( )	( )	( )	( )	37 - 37

3.a.   When an issue in your office or agency received what you saw as positive or negative coverage in the *mass media*. did that coverage:

(CHECK THOSE WHICH OCCURRED MOST FREQUENTLY IN EACH CATEGORY OF COVERAGE.)

1 = check
0 = no check

two question

	Positive Coverage	Negative Coverage		
Increase your chances for successfully attaining your policy goals regarding the issue	( )	( )	38 - 38	39 - 39
Decrease your chances for successfully attaining your policy goals regarding the issue	( )	( )	40 - 40	41
Increase the speed with which the issue is considered and acted upon	( )	( )	42	43
Decrease the speed with which the issue is considered and acted upon	( )	( )	44	45
Make action on the issue easier	( )	( )	46	47
Make action on the issue more difficult	( )	( )	48	49
Increase the number of policy options considered	( )	( )	50	51
Decrease the number of policy options considered	( )	( )	52	53
Reshape the policy options considered	( )	( )	54	55
Cause you to reassess your policy position on the issue	( )	( )	56	57
Galvanize outside support	( )	( )	58	59
Undermine outside support	( )	( )	60	61
Move responsibility for the issue to a more senior official or officials	( )	( )	62	63
Increase the importance of the issue within the bureaucracy	( )	( )	64	65
Cause the public and/or other officials to assume the information contained in the coverage is accurate	( )	( )	66	67
Have long term effects on your career	( )	( )	68	69
Affect your credibility on other issues	( )	( )	70	71
Have no effect	( )	( )	72	73

Card2
IO 1-4

3.b.   When an issue in your office or agency received what you saw as positive or negative coverage in the *trade press*, did that coverage:

(CHECK THOSE WHICH OCCURRED MOST FREQUENTLY IN EACH CATEGORY OF COVERAGE.)

1 = check
0 = no check

	Positive Coverage	Negative Coverage		
Increase your chances for successfully attaining your policy goals regarding the issue	( )	( )	5	6
Decrease your chances for successfully attaining your policy goals regarding the issue	( )	( )	7	8
Increase the speed with which the issue is considered and acted upon	( )	( )	9	10
Decrease the speed with which the issue is considered and acted upon	( )	( )	11	12
Make action on the issue easier	( )	( )	13	14
Make action on the issue more difficult	( )	( )	15	16
Increase the number of policy options considered	( )	( )	17	18
Decrease the number of policy options considered	( )	( )	19	20
Reshape the policy options considered	( )	( )	21	22
Cause you to reassess your policy position on the issue	( )	( )	23	24
Galvanize outside support	( )	( )	25	26
Undermine outside support	( )	( )	27	28
Move responsibility for the issue to a more senior official or officials	( )	( )	29	30
Increase the importance of the issue within the bureaucracy	( )	( )	31	32
Cause the public and/or other officials to assume the information contained in the coverage is accurate	( )	( )	33	34
Have long term effects on your career	( )	( )	35	36
Affect your credibility on other issues	( )	( )	37	38
Have no effect	( )	( )	39	40

4.   Approximately what percentage of all the issues you dealt with were reported by the press?

xxx.x _____ percent.

41-45

5.   To what degree did you rely on the following types of media organizations for information about your policy area?

	3 Very much	2 Somewhat	1 Very little	
a. The mass media	( )	( )	( )	46
b. The trade press	( )	( )	( )	47

6.   To what degree did you rely on the mass media for information about parts of government outside your policy area?

3 Very much   ( )
2 Somewhat   ( )
1 Very little   ( )

48

7.   a.   How useful were informal/unofficial communications from members of the media to you in performing your job?

(CIRCLE ONE NUMBER ON SCALE.)

49

```
    1        2        3        4        5
    |_____|_____|_____|_____|
   Not              Somewhat           Very
 Useful             Useful            Useful
```

b. Please describe the type(s) of informal/unofficial communications and how it was or they were useful to you.

DO NOT WRITE
IN THIS SPACE

_____

_____

_____

_____

8. While in office, were you concerned about leaks affecting policy you were working on or responsible for?

50

I Yes   ( )
0 No   ( ) —— PROCEED TO QUESTION 9.

IF YES: 1 = check   9 = skip
               0 = no check

a. Did that concern: (CHECK AS MANY AS APPLY.)

Cause you to limit the number of people involved in decision making	( )	51
Cause you to increase the number of people involved in decision making	( )	52
Expand the range of policy options that you considered	( )	53
Narrow the range of policy options that you considered	( )	54
Reshape the policy options that you considered	( )	55
Reduce the amount of information that you put in writing	( )	56
Increase the amount of information that you put in writing	( )	57
Other (please specify): _____	( )	58

9. Did you ever feel it appropriate to leak information to the press?

59

I Yes   ( )
0 No   ( ) —— PROCEED TO QUESTION 10.

IF YES: 1 = check   0 = no check   9 = skip

a. Why did you feel that it was appropriate? (CHECK AS MANY ANSWERS AS APPLY.)

To gain attention for an issue or policy option	( )	60
To force action on an issue	( )	61
To slow action on an issue	( )	62
To stop action on an issue	( )	63
To consolidate support from the public or a constituency outside government	( )	64
To inform other officials of a policy consideration or action	( )	65
To divert press or public attention from another issue	( )	66
To reveal your bargaining position on an issue	( )	67
To protect your position	( )	68
To undermine another's position	( )	69
To develop good relationships with members of the press	( )	70
To counter false or misleading information	( )	71
The reporter was enterprising in soliciting information	( )	72
To send a message to another branch of government	( )	73
Other (please specify): _____	( )	74

PLEASE GO TO PAGE 6 ON THE OTHER SIDE OF SHEET

10.   Overall, how great do you believe the effect of the media is on federal policy? (CIRCLE ONE NUMBER)

1	2	3	4	5
No Effect		Some Effect		Dominant Effect

75

11.   Imagine that the media did not exist. Describe how you think your job and the process of policy making in your area would have been different without the media.   (USE A SEPARATE SHEET OF PAPER IF YOU WISH)

_____

_____

_____

_____

_____

_____

_____

III. EVALUATION OF PRESS AND
OF PRESS-GOVERNMENT RELATIONS

1.   On balance, how would you characterize the relationship between you and the members of the press who were covering your office or agency? (CIRCLE ONE NUMBER ON SCALE.)

1	2	3	4	5
Hostile		Mixed		Friendly

76

2.   In your experience, to what degree did reporters use formal news channels (e.g., official press releases, on-the-record interviews, press conferences) as their source for news?   (CIRCLE ONE NUMBER ON SCALE.)

1	2	3	4	5
Never		Sometimes		Often

77

card 3
ID 1-4

3.   In your experience, did the ability of an individual or group outside of the government to gain attention in the media:

1= check   0= no check

(CHECK THOSE ANSWERS WHICH OCCURRED MOST FREQUENTLY)

Magnify the individual's or group's influence ( )   5

Gain attention from higher level officials for the individual's or group's views ( )   6

Have no effect ( )   7

Other (please specify): _____ ( )   8

4.   From your experience, describe a situation in which the press had a significant effect in advancing your policy goals.

_____

_____

_____

_____

PLEASE OPEN HERE

5. From your experience, describe a situation in which the press had a significant effect in undermining your policy goals.

_____

_____

_____

_____

6. Do you feel you have a good understanding of how the press operates and why they do the things they do?

1 Yes   ( )
0 No   ( )

9

IV. BACKGROUND INFORMATION

1. Are you serving and/or have you served in:

   1 The Executive Branch   ( )
   2 The Congress   ( )
   3 Both   ( )

10

2. Generally, do you consider yourself to be:
   1 A Liberal   ( )
   2 A Moderate   ( )
   3 A Conservative   ( )

11

3. What was your primary policy area or areas?

   Commerce/Agriculture   ( )
   Defense   ( )
   Trade/Economics   ( )
   Human Services   ( )
   Foreign Policy   ( )
   Environment/Scientific   ( )
   Legal/Law Enforcement   ( )
   Other, please specify:

                             ( )

1 = check
0 = no check

12
13
14
15
16
17
18
19

4. How many years have you served in federal office(s)?

   __XX.XX__ years

20-24

5. THIS QUESTION IS FOR THOSE NO LONGER SERVING IN THE FEDERAL GOVERNMENT. ALL OTHERS,
   PLEASE PROCEED TO QUESTION 6.

   How long have you been out of the government?
   1 0-5 years   ( )
   2 5-10 years   ( )
   3 10-15 years   ( )
   4 15-20 years   ( )
   9 skip

25

PLEASE OPEN HERE

6. Did the programs you administered serve a specific constituency rather than the general population?

    1 Yes ( )
    0 No ( )

    2 - Both

    26

7. Was your primary responsibility in the area of public affairs and/or media relations?

    1 Yes ( )
    0 No ( )

    27

8. How often, while in office, did you read, watch or hear the following types of media reporting?

    (CIRCLE ONE NUMBER ON EACH SCALE.)

	Never		Sometimes		Often	
a. Network News and Public Affairs	1	2	3	4	5	28
b. Newspapers	1	2	3	4	5	29 30
c. News magazines	1	2	3	4	5	31
d. Trade publications	1	2	3	4	5	

9. Please list the three specific news programs or publications that you relied on most for information.

    1. _____

    2. _____

    3. _____

    ..A · 2o
    42 - 4-?

10. ALL RESPONSES TO THIS QUESTIONNAIRE ARE STRICTLY ANONYMOUS. HOWEVER, IF YOU ARE WILLING TO BE CONTACTED SO THAT WE MAY ASK YOU FURTHER QUESTIONS ABOUT THE INTER-ACTION BETWEEN THE PRESS AND GOVERNMENT, PLEASE PROVIDE YOUR NAME AND AN AD-DRESS AND TELEPHONE NUMBER WHERE YOU CAN BE REACHED ON THE LINES BELOW. IF YOU DO NOT WISH TO BE CONTACTED, LEAVE THESE LINES BLANK.

    Name: _____

    Address: _____

    _____

    Telephone Number: _____

REVSON QUESTIONNAIRE

Code Sheet for Question IV.9

Newspapers		*Magazines*	
Newspapers	001	News Magazines	101
State Newspapers	002		
Washington Newspapers	003	Business International	110
Local Newspapers	004	Business Week	111
New York Newspapers	005	Congressional Quarterly	112
		Economist	113
Atlanta Constitution	010	Foreign Affairs	114
Baltimore Sun	011	National Journal	115
Chr. Sci. Monitor	012	National Reporter	116
Financial Times	013		
Int'l Herald-Tribune	014		
L.A. Times	015		
New York Times	016		
San Juan Star	017		
USA Today	018		
Wall Street Journal	019		
Washington Post	020		
Washington Star	021		
Washington Times	022		
San Francisco Chron.	023		
Arizona Republic	024		
London Times	025		
Chicago Tribune	026		
Denver Post	027		
New York Post	028		

Bibliography
and References

Abel, Eli. *What's News: The Media in American Society*. San Francisco: The Institute for Contemporary Studies, 1981.

Abelson, Robert, and Milton Rosenberg. "The Structure of Belief Systems." In *Computer Models of Thought and Language*, R. C. Shank and K. M. Colby (eds.). San Francisco: Freeman, 1973.

Adams, William C. "Nationwide Survey by G. W. Professor Finds No Fallout from *The Day After*." George Washington University Press Release, 21 Nov., 1983.

_____. *Television Coverage of International Affairs*. Norwood, NJ: Ablex, 1982.

_____, and Michael Joblove. "The Unnewsworthy Holocaust: TV News and Terror in Cambodia." In *Television Coverage of International Affairs*, William C. Adams (ed). Norwood NJ: Ablex, 1982, pp. 217–226.

_____. *Television Coverage of the Middle East*. Norwood, NJ, Ablex, 1981.

_____, and Phillip Heyl. "From Cairo to Kabul with the Networks, 1972-1980." In *Television Coverage of the Middle East*, William C. Adams (ed.). Norwood, NJ: Ablex, 1981, pp. 1–39.

_____, and Fay Schreibman (eds.). *Television Network News: Issues in Content Analysis*. Washington, DC: George Washington University Press, 1978.

Almaney, Adnan. "International and Foreign Affairs on Network Television News." *Journal of Broadcating* 14 (Fall 1970): 499–509.

Alexander, Yonah, David Carlton and Paul Wilkinson *Terrorism, Theory and Practice*. Boulder, CO: Westview Press, 1979.

Allison, G. T. *Essence of Decision: Explaining the Cuban Missile Crisis*. Boston: Little, Brown, 1971.

Almond, Gabriel. *The American People and Foreign Policy* (2nd ed.). Westport, CT: Greenwood Press, 1977.

_____, and G. B. Powell. *Comparative Politics: A Developmental Approach*. Boston: Little, Brown & Co, 1966.

Alon, Hanlon. *Countering Terrorism in Israel: Toward a Policy of Countermeasures*. Santa Monica, CA: Rand, 1980.

Altheide, David. *Creating Reality: How TV News Distorts Events*. Beverly Hills: Sage, 1976.

Altheide, David, and Robert Snow. *Media Logic*. Beverly Hills: Sage, 1979.

Altheide, David. "Iran vs. US TV News: The Hostage Story Out of Context." In *Television Coverage of the Middle East*, William Adams (ed.). Norwood, NJ: Ablex, 1981, pp. 128–157.

Atwan, Robert, Barry Orton, and William Vesterman (eds.). *American Mass Media: Industries and Issues*. New York: Random House, 1978.

American Institute for Political Communication. *Liberal Bias as A Factor in Network Television News Reporting*. Washington, DC: The American Institute for Political Communication, 1972.

Apter, David E. "The Nature of Belief Systems in Mass Publics." In *Ideology and Discontent*. New York: Free Press, 1964, pp. 206–61.

Associated Press. "United by Common Language of Film, U.S. Soviet Crews Work on Rock Video." *Atlanta Journal* (10/15/1988): A 20.

Association for Education in Journalism. *Role of the News Media in Shaping U.S. Foreign Policy*. Columbia, SC: AEJ, 1979

Axelrod, Robert, and John Brandsford (eds.). *The Structure of Decision: The Cognitive Maps of Political Elites*. Princeton, NJ: Princeton University Press, 1976.

Azar, E. E., Stanley H. Cohen, Thomas O. Jokam and James M. McCormick. "The Problem of Source Coverage in the Use of International Events Data." *International Studies Quarterly*, 16 (1972): 373–388.

Bachrach, Peter, and Morton Baratz. *Power and Poverty*. New York: Oxford University Press, 1970.

Bailar, Barbara A., and C. M. Lanphier. *Development of Survey Research Methods to Assess Survey Practices*. Washington DC: American Statistical Association, 1978.

Barnouw, Erik. *Tube of Plenty: The Evolution of Television*. London: Oxford University Press, 1975.

Batscha, Robert M. *Foreign Affairs News and the Broadcast Journalist*. New York: Praeger, 1975.

Becker, Lee B. "Foreign Policy and Press Performance." *Journalism Quarterly* 54 (1977): 364–368.

Benjamin, Burton. *Fair Play: CBS, General Westmoreland, and How a Television Documentary Went Wrong*. New York: Harper & Row, 1988.

Behr, Roy L. and Shanto Iyengar. "Television News, Real World Cues, and Changes in the Public Agenda." *Public Opinion Quarterly* 49:38–57.

Blanchard, R. O. *Congress and the News Media*. New York: Hastings House, 1978.

Bledsoe, Robert, Roger Handberg, William S. Maddox, David R. Lenox and Dennis A. Long. "Foreign Affairs Coverage in Mass and Elite Periodicals." *Journalism Quarterly* 59 (1982): 471–474.

Bloomfield, L. *The Foreign Policy Process*. Englewood Cliffs, NJ: Prentice-Hall, 1982.

―――――. *Public Opinion and U.S. Foreign Policy: Conventional Wisdom Revisited*. Cambridge, MA: Center for International Studies, 1978.

_____. *In Search of American Foreign Policy*. New York: Oxford Press, 1974.

Blumler, Jay G., and Dennis McQuaid. *Television in Politics: Its Uses and Influences*. Chicago: University of Chicago Press, 1969.

Bobrow, Davis B., Steve Chan, and John A. Krigen. *Understanding Foreign Policy Decisions: The Chinese Case*. New York: Free Press, 1979.

Bower, Robert. *Television and the Public*. New York: Holt, Rinehart and Winston, 1973.

Braley, R. *Bad News: The Foreign Policy in the New York Times*. New York: Regnery Gateway, 1984.

Bray, Charles W. "The Media and Foreign Policy." *Foreign Policy*, 16 (1974). 109–25.

Broadcasting. "The Uneasy Gestation of TV Marti." (July 4, 1988): 46–47.

_____. "AP, CONUS Form Satellite-fed News Service." (June 12, 1986): pp. 57–58.

_____. "No Newsmen in CIA's Future, But Past Still Haunts Some." (Feb. 16, 1976): 22–24.

_____. "Networks Deny Assertions That Their Newsmen Aided CIA, FBI." (Jan. 26, 1976): 21–22.

Broadcasting & Cablecasting Yearbook, 1986, 1987.

Brodin, K. "Belief Systems, Doctrines, and Foreign Policy." *Cooperation and Conflict*, 7 (1972): 97–112.

Buchanan, Patrick. "The Dangers of Television Diplomacy." *TV Guide* (1-28-1978): A5–A6.

Bullion, Stuart J. "Press Roles in Foreign Policy Reporting". *Gazette*, 32 (1983): 179–88.

Burgoon, M. (ed.). *Communication Yearbook 6*. Beverly Hills: Sage, 1982.

Carter, Jimmy. "Middle East Peace: New Opportunities." *Washington Quarterly*, (Summer 1987): p. 5–14.

_____. *The Blood of Abraham*. Boston: Houghton-Mifflin, 1985.

Caspary, William R. "The Mood Theory': A Study of Public Opinion and Foreign Policy." *American Political Science Review*, 64 (1970): 536–547.

Center for War, Peace, and the News Media. *War, Peace, and the News Media: Proceedings, March 18th and 19th, 1983*. New York: New York University, 1987.

_____. *American Press Coverage of U.S.-Soviet Relations, the Soviet Union, Nuclear Weapons, Arms Control, and National Security: A Bibliography*. New York: New York University, 1988.

Chafets, Ze'ev. *Double Vision: How the Press Distorts America's View of the Middle East*. New York: William Morrow, 1985.

Chaffee, Steven H., and Joan Schleuder. "Measurement and Effects of Attention to Media News." *Human Communication Research*, 3:1 (Fall 1986): 76–107

_____, and Miyo, Y. "Selective Exposure and the Reinforcement Hypothesis: An Intergenerational Panel Study of the 1980 Presidential Campaign." *Communication Research*, 10 (1983): 3–36.

_____, and Tims, A. "News Media use in Adolescence: Implications for Political Cognitions." In *Communication Yearbook 6*, M. Burgoon (ed.). Beverly Hills: Sage, 1982, pp. 287–326.

_____, and Chole, S. Y. *Communication Measurement in the March, 1979 NES Pilot Study*. Paper presented at the meeting of the American Political Science Association, Washington, DC, 1979.

_____, S. Ward, and L. Tipton. "Mass Communication and Political Socialization." *Journalism Quarterly*, 47 (1970): 647–659, 666.

Charney, Leon H. *Special Counsel*. New York: Philosophical Library, 1984.

Chira, Susan. "U.S. Olympic Reporting Hits a Raw Korean Nerve." *New York Times* (9/28/1988): p. 1.

Chittick, William O. *State Department, Press, and Pressure Groups: A Role Analysis*. New York: Wiley-Interscience, 1970.

_____. "State Department-Press Antagonism: Opinion Versus Policy-Making Needs?" *Journal of Politics*, 31 (1969): 756–771.

Clutterbuck, Richard L. *The Media and Political Violence*. New York: MacMillan, 1981.

Cobb, Roger, and Charles Elder. *Participation in American Politics: The Dynamics of Agenda-Building*. Boston: Allyn and Bacon, 1972.

Cockburn, Andrew. "Pictures from the Pentagon." *Channels* (June-July 1982): 15–16.

Cohen, Bernard C. *The Press and Foreign Policy*. Princeton, NJ: Princeton University Press, 1963.

_____. "Mass Communication and Foreign Policy." In *Domestic Sources of Foreign Policy*, James N. Rosenau (ed.). New York: Free Press, 1967, pp. 195–212.

_____. "The Influence of Special Interest Groups and Mass Media in American Security Policy," C. W. Kegley & E. R. Wittkopf (eds.). In *Perspectives on American Foreign Policy*. New York: St. Martin's Press, 1983.

Cohen, Michael D., James G. March, and Johan P. Olsen. "A Garbage Can Model of Organizational Choice." *Administrative Science Quarterly*, 17: 1–25.

Cohen, Raymond. *Theater of Power*. London & New York: Longman, 1987.

Collingwood, Charles. "Prestige. Glamour. Access to High Places. Now That the Role of TV's Foreign Correspondents has Changed, A Veteran Bids Goodby to All That." *TV Guide* (April 19, 1980): 6–10.

Comstock, George, and Steve Chaffee, Nathan Katzman, Maxwell McCombs, and Donald Roberts. *Television and Human Behavior*. New York: Columbia University Press, 1978.

Cook, Fay Lomax, Tom R. Tyler, Edward Geotz, Margaret Gorden, David Protess, Donald Leff, and Harvey Moltoch. "Media and Agenda Setting: Effects on the Public, Interest Group Leaders, Policy Makers, and Policy." *Public Opinion Quarterly*, 47 (Spring 1983): 16–35.

Cutler, Lloyd N. "Foreign Policy on Deadline." *Atlantic Community Quarterly*, 22 (1984): 223–232; (Reprinted from *Foreign Policy* 56 (Fall 1984).)

Czitrom, Daniel J. *Media and the American Mind*. Chapel Hill: University of North Carolina Press, 1982.

David, Michael, and Pat Aufderheide. "All the President's Media." *Channels*, (September, 1985): 20–24.

Davidson, W. Phillips. *The News From Abroad and the Foreign Policy Public* FPA Headline Series No. 250. New York: Foreign Policy Association, 1980.

————. "Diplomatic Reporting: The Rules of the Game." *Journal of Communication*, 25 (1975): 138–46.

————. *Mass Communication and Conflict Resolution: The Role of the Information Media in the Advancement of International Understanding.* New York: Praeger, 1974.

Deadline. "The Talk Shows and the Procurement Scandal." *Deadline* (Sept.-Oct. 1988): 11.

DeMaio, T. J. (ed.). *Approaches to Developing Questionnaires.* Statistical Policy Working Paper 10. Washington DC: U.S. Government Printing Office, 1983.

Deutsch, Karl W. *The Nerves of Government.* New York: The Free Press, 1966.

DeYoung, Karen. "Understanding U.S. Foreign Policy: The Role of the Press." *USA Today Magazine* (January 1985): 66–69.

Diamond, Edward. "Liberal Press, Lacky Press, (Choose One)." In *Sign Off: The Last Days of Television.* Cambridge, MA: MIT Press, 1982.

————. *Sign Off: The Last Days of Television.* Cambridge, MA: The MIT Press, 1982.

————, Stephen Bates, and John Boyer. "From Patriotism to Skepticism: The Turning of TV News." *TV Guide* (August 1982): 4–8.

————. *Good News, Bad News.* Cambridge, MA: MIT Press, 1978.

————. *The Tin Kazoo.* Cambridge, MA: MIT Press, 1975.

Dorfman, Ron. "Bringing the War Back Home." *The Quill* (January 1984): 14–16.

Dorman, William, Robert Karl Manoff, and Jennifer Weeks. *American Press Coverage of U.S.-Soviet Relations, the Soviet Union, Nuclear Weapons, Arms Control, and National Security: A Bibliography.* New York: Center for War, Peace, and the News Media, New York University, 1988.

Doweling, Ralph. "Terrorism and the Media: A Rhetorical Genre." *Journal of Communication*, 36 (1986): 12–24.

Downs, A. "Up and Down with Ecology: The Issue Attention Cycle." *Public Interest*, 28 (1972): 38–50.

Drew, D., and B. Reeves. "Learning from a Television News Story." *Communication Research*,7 (1980): 95–120.

Dull, James. *The Politics of American Foreign Policy.* Englewood Cliffs, NJ: Prentice-Hall, 1985.

Dye, Thomas R. & Harmon Zeigler, *American Politics in the Media Age.* Monterey, CA: Brooks/Cole Pub, 1983.

Easton, David (ed.). *A Framework for Political Analysis.* Englewood Cliffs, NJ: Prentice-Hall, 1965.

Easton, David. *Varieties of Political Theory.* Englewood Cliffs, NJ: Prentice-Hall, 1966.

Eban, Abba. *The New Diplomacy: International Affairs in the Modern Age.* New York: Random House, 1983.

Ebring, Lutz, Edie N. Goldenberg, and Arthur H. Miller. "Front-Page News and Real World Cues: A New Look at Agenda-Setting by the Media." *American Journal of Political Science*, 24 (Feb. 1980): 17–47.

Editor and Publisher. "Report Tells How CIA Used the News Media." *Editor and Publisher*, (Dec. 31, 1977): 9ff.

Efron, Edith. *The News Twisters*. Los Angeles: Nash Publishing Co., 1971.

Elder, Charles D., and Roger Cobb. *The Political Uses of Symbols*. New York: Longman, 1983.

Electronic Media. "NBC: Today America, Tomorrow the World." (January 30, 1989): 1ff.

————. "Q&A: Cable's top News Boss." (January 30, 1989): cover ff.

Elie, L. Eric. "Opportunity for TV Knocking in Europe," *Atlanta Constitution* (Nov. 22, 1988): C1.

Elliot, Phillip, and Peter Golden. "Mass Communication and Social Change: The Imagery of Development and the Development of Imagery." In *Sociology and Development*, Emanuelde Kadt and Gavin Williams (eds.). London: Tavistock, 1974.

Emery, Michael. "An Endangered Species: The International Newshole." *Gannet Center Journal*, 3:4 (Fall 1989): 151–164.

Epstein, Edward J. *News from Nowhere: Television and the News*. New York: Random House, 1973.

Feldman, Stanley, and Lee Sigelman. "The Political Impact of Prime-Time Television: "The Day After." *Journal of Politics*, 47 (1985): 557–578.

Feith, Douglas J. "Israel, the *Post*, and the Shaft." *Middle East Review*, 12 (Summer 1980): 62–66.

Fink, Arlene & J. Kosecocc. *How to Conduct Surveys*. Beverly Hills: Sage Publishing Company, 1985.

Fitzsimmons, Stephen H., and Hobart G. Osburn. "The Impact of Social Issues and Public Affairs Television Documentaries." *Public Opinion Quarterly*, 32 (1968): 379–97.

Ford, Gerald. "Making Foreign Policy: How TV Influences a President's Decisions." *TV Guide*, (Sept.-Oct. 1981): 5–8.

Foreign Service Journal. "The Press, and Foreign policy." (July-August 1982): 22-33ff (several articles).

Frank, Robert S. *Message Dimensions of Television News*. Lexington, MA: Lexington Books, 1973.

Fromm, Joseph. "The Media and the Making of Defense Policy: The U.S. Example." In *Defence and Consensus: The Domestic Aspects of Western Security, Part I*. Adelphi Paper No. 182. London: International Institute for Strategic Studies, pp. 29–35.

Galtung, Johan, and Mari Holmboe Ruge. "The Structure of Foreign News." *Journal of Peace Research*, 1 (1965): 64–91.

Gandy, Oscar H., Jr. *Beyond Agenda Setting: Information Subsidies and Public Policy*. Norwood, NJ: Ablex, 1982.

Ganley, Gladys, and Oswald Ganley. *Global Political Fallout: The VCR's First Decade.* Norwood, NJ: Ablex, 1988.

Gans, Herbert. *Deciding What's News.* New York: Pantheon Books, 1979.

George, Alexander L. *Presidential Decisionmaking in Foreign Policy: The Effective Use of Information and Advice.* Boulder, CO: Westview Press, 1980.

Gerbner, G., Gross, L., Morgan, M., and N. Signnorielli. "Political Correlates of Television Viewing." *Public Opinion Quarterly,* 48 (1980): 283–300.

———— and George Marvanyi. "The Many Worlds of the Press." *Journal of Communication,* 27 (Winter 1977): 52–66.

Gertner, Richard (ed.). *1986 International Television Almanac* 31st ed.). New York: Quigley Publishing Co., 1986.

Ghorpade, S. "Agenda-setting: A Test of Advertising's Neglected Function." *Journal of Advertising Research,* 26:4 (1986): 23–27.

Glasgow Media Study Group. *Bad News.* Glasgow, Scotland, 1988.

Gordon, Avishag. "The Middle East October 1973 War as Reported by the American Networks." *International Problems,* 14 (Fall 1975): 76–85.

Goren, Dina. "The News and Foreign Policy: An Examination of the Impact of the News Media on the Making of Foreign Policy." *Research in Social Movements, Conflicts and Change,* 3 (1980): 119–141.

Gordon, Raymond L. *Interviewing: Strategy, Techniques.* Homewood, IL: Dorsey Press, 1969.

Graber, Doris A. (ed.). *Media Power in Politics.* Washington DC: CQ Press, 1984.

————. *Processing the News: How People Tame the Information Tide.* New York: Longman, 1984.

————. *Mass Media and American Politics* (revised ed., 1984). Washington DC: CQ Press, 1980.

Greve, Frank. "Reporters, the CIA, and the Soviets." *Editor and Publisher* (Oct. 18, 1986): 76f.

Grossman, Michael, and Joyce Kumar. *Portraying the President: The White House and the News Media.* Baltimore: Johns Hopkins University Press, 1981.

———— and Francis E. Rouke. "The Media and the Presidency: An Exchange Anaysis." *Political Science Quarterly* 91 (1976): 455–70.

Gruson, Lindsey, "Salvador TV Dares to Tell the News." *New York Times* (9/27/1988): Y3.

Gutstadt, Lynn. "Television Impacts on Behavioral Development of South African Children: A Longitudinal Study." Unpublished Masters Thesis, Stanford University, 1986.

Haig, Alexander. "Can TV Derail Diplomacy." *TV Guide* (March, 1985): 4–8.

Halle, Louis. *American Foreign Policy.* London: G. Allen, 1960.

Hallin, Daniel C. "The Media Go to War—From Vietnam to Central America." *NACLA Report on the Americas* (July-August 1983): 2–35.

Halloran, Richard. "Calling for a Redesign of National Security." *New York Times* (April 2, 1989): p. E4.

Hanauer, Joan. "Ayatolla Uses Television the American Way." *Dallas Morning News* (Dec. 19, 1979).

Head, Sydney W. *World Broadcasting Systems*. Belmont CA: Wadsworth Publishing Co., 1985.

Heffernan, Patrick. "American Mass Media Coverage of International News." Unpublished Master's Thesis, University of California at Santa Barbara, June, 1978.

Henry, W. A., III. "Moyers and Mudd: Seers or Soreheads." *Channels* (April 1987): p. 57.

Hess, Stephen. *The Washington Reporters*. Washington DC: Brookings Institute, 1981.

————. "Structuring the Unseen Environment," *Journal of Communication*, 26 (Spring 1976).

————. *The Government-Press Connection*. Washington DC: Brookings, 1984.

————. "The Golden Triangle: Press Relations at the White House, State Department and Department of Defence." In *War, Peace, and the News Media*, a conference held at NYU, March 18-19, 1983, David Rubin and Ann Marie Cunningham (eds.). New York: Center for War, Peace, and the News Media, 1987, pp. 134–164.

Hickey, Neil. "Terrorism and Television." *TV Guide* (July 31, 1976).

————. "TV and Foreign Relations: Grading Presidents and Premiers." *TV Guide* (June 26, 1982): 4–8.

————. "Henry Kissinger and TV: 'Did I sometimes Use the Press? Yes.' " *TV Guide* (April 2, 1983): 2–9.

Hill, David B. "Viewer Characteristics and Agenda Setting by Television News." *Public Opinion Quarterly*, 49 (1985): 340–350.

Hill, William. "CIA Shouldn't Use Any Reporters: Editors." *Editor and Publisher* (Jan. 14, 1978): 14ff.

Hilsman, Roger. *To Move a Nation*. New York, 1967.

Hoffmann, Stanley. "Restraints and Choices in American Foreign Policy." *Daedalus* (Fall 1962).

Hofstetter, Richard C. and D. W. Morre. "Watching TV News and Supporting the Military." *Armed Forces and Society*, 5 (1979): 261–69.

————, Cliff Zufin, and Terry Buss. "Political Imagery and Information in an Age of Television," *Journalism Quarterly*, 55 (Autumn, 1978): 562–570.

————. *Bias in the News: Network Television Coverage of the 1972 Election Campaign*. Columbus, OH: Ohio State University Press, 1976

Holsti, O. R. "Foreign Policy Decisionmakers Viewed Psychologically: Cognitive Processes Approaches." In *Thought and Action in Foreign Policy*, G. M. Boham and M. J. Shapiro (eds.). Basek and Stutgart: Birhauser Verlag, 1977, pp. 10–74.

————. "The Operational Code Approach to the Study of Political Leaders: John Foster Dulles' Philosophical and Instrumental Beliefs." *Canadian Journal of Political Science*, 3 (1970: 123–157

Howell, Major Cass D. "War, Television and Public Opinion." *Military Review* (Feb. 1987): 71–79.

Interviews: "American Media and the Palestine Problem." *Journal of Palestine Studies*, 5 (Fall-Winter 1976): 127–149.

Iyengar, Shanto, and D. R. Kinder. "More Than Meets the Eyes: Television News and Public Evaluations of the President," in *Advances in Public Communications* (vol. 1.), G. Comstock (ed.). New York: Academic Press, 1984.

————. *News that Matters.* Chicago: University of Chicago Press, 1988.

————, M. Peters, and D. Kinder. "Experimental demonstrations of the 'not-so-minimal' consequences of television news programs." *American Political Science Review*, 76 (1982): 848–858.

————. "Television News and Issue Salience." *American Politics Quarterly*, 7:395–416.

Jenkins, Brian. "International Terrorism: A New Mode of Conflict," in *International Terrorism and World Security*. David Carlton and Carlo Schaerf (eds.). New York: John Wiley and Sons, 1975.

Jervis, Robert. *Perception and Misperception in International Politics.* Princeton, NJ: Princeton University Press, 1976.

Kalb, Bernard, and Marvin Kalb. "Along the Diplomatic Trail: Of Cannibals, Krushchev, and Kissinger." *TV Guide* (March 1984): 2–6.

Katz, E., Hanna Adona, and Pnina Parness. "Remembering the News: What the Picture Adds to Recall. *Journalism Quarterly*, 54 (Summer, 1977).

Katz, Elihu, and Paul Lazarsfield. *Personal Influence: The Part Played by the People in the Flow of Mass Communication.* Glencoe IL: The Free Press, 1955.

Keogh, J. *President Nixon and the Press.* New York: Funk and Wagnells, 1972.

Kern, Montague. *Television and Middle East Diplomacy: President Carter's Fall 1977 Peace Initiative.* Washington DC: Center for Contemporary Arab Studies, Georgetown University, 1983.

————, Patricia Levering, and Ralph B. Levering. *The Kennedy Crises: The Press, the Presidency and Foreign Policy.* Chapel Hill: University of North Carolina, 1983.

————. "The Press, the Presidency, and International Conflict: Lessons from Two Administrations." *Political Psychology*, 5 (1984): 53–68.

Keesing's Contemporary Archives, 1979-1987. London: Keesing's Ltd.

Kissinger, Henry. *American Foreign Policy.* New York: W. W. Norton, 1969.

Kollek, Teddy. "Israel and the Palestinian Uprising—Is TV Making It Worse?" *TV Guide* (October 4, 1988): 4–7.

Kondrake, Morton. "Eye on the Pentagon. Is TV Telling Us Enough?" *TV Guide* (August 25, 1979): 2–10.

Kraus, Sidney, and Dennis Davis. *The Effects of Mass Communication on Political Behavior.* University Park, PA: Pennsylvania State University Press, 1976.

Kupperman, Robert H., et al. *Leaders and Crises: The CSIS Crisis Simulations.* Washington, DC: Center for Strategic and International Studies, 1987.

Lambeth, E. "America's Window on the World: U.S. Network's Coverage of International-
al Affairs, 1972-1976." Unpublished Ph.D. Thesis, Stanford University, 1978.

Lambeth, E., "Perceived Influence of the Press on Energy Policy Making." Journalism
Quarterly, 55 (1978): 11–18, 82.

Larson, James F. Global Television and Foreign Policy. New York: Foreign Policy
Association, 1987.

——————. Television's Window on the World: International Affairs Coverage on the
U.S. Networks. Norwood, NJ: Ablex, 1984.

——————. "International Affairs Coverage on U.S. Network Television." Journal
of Communication, 29 (Spring 1979): 136–147.

Lazarsfeld, Paul, Berenice Berelson, and Hazel Gaudet. The Peoples' Choice. New
York: Columbia University Press, 1948.

Le Duc, Don R. "Television Coverage of NATO Affairs." Journal of Broadcasting,
24 (1980): 5–7.

Leahy, Michael. "It Was Get Out of the Philippines-or Else." TV Guide (Nov. 26,
1988): 12–18.

Lederman, Jim. "Interpreting the Intifada." Foreign Policy, 72 (1988): 230–246.

Lee, Raymond S. H. "Credibility of Newspaper and TV News." Journalism
Quarterly, 55 (1978): 282–294.

Leeden, Michael. "Public Opinion, Press Opinion, and Foreign Policy." Public
Opinion (August-September 1984): 5–7.

Lefever, Ernest. TV and the National Defense: An Analysis of CBS News, 1972-73.
Boston: Institute for American Strategy, 1974.

——————. "The Prestige Press, Foreign Policy, and American Survival." Orbis, 20
(1976): 207–225.

Leff, Donna R, David Protess, and Stephen C. Brooks. "Crusading Journalism:
Changing Public Attitudes and Policy Making Agendas." Public Opinion
Quarterly, 50 (1986): 300–315

——————, and Harvey L. Molltoch. "Media and Agenda Setting: Effects on the
Public, Interest Group Leaders, Policy Makers, and Policy." Public Opinion
Quarterly, 47 (1983): 16–35.

Lifton, Robert Jay. Revolutionary Immortality: Mao Tse-tung and the Chinese Cultural
Revolution. New York: Vintage Books, 1968.

Lindblom, Charles. "Policy Analysis." American Economic Review, 48 (June 1958):
306ff.

Nathan Leites. A Study of Bolshevism. Glencoe, IL: Free Press, 1953.

Lemert, J., W. Elliot, K. Nestvolk, and G. Rarick. "Effects of Viewing and
Primary Presidential Debate." Communication Research, 10 (1983): 155–174.

Lent, John. "Foreign News in American Media." Journal of Communication, 27
(Winter 1977): 46–51.

LeoGrande, William. Uneasy Allies: The Press and the Government During the Cuban
Missile Crisis. New York: Center for War, Peace and the News Media, 1987.

Lewis, Flora. "Little Brother Watches." New York Times (10/5/1988): Editorial.

Linsky, Martin. *Impact: How the Press Affects Federal Policy Making.* New York: W. W. Norton, 1986.

Lippman, Walter. *Public Opinion.* New York: Harcourt Brace, 1922.

MacKuen, M. J., and S. L. Coombs. *More than the News.* Beverly Hills: Sage, 1981.

MacNeil, Robert. *The People Machine: The Influence of Television on American Politics.* New York: Harper and Row, 1968.

Mandelbaum, Michael. "Ending the Cold War." *Foreign Affairs,* 68:2 (Spring, 1989): 16–36.

Madison, Christopher. "State Department Press Briefings Losing Value as Key Source of Diplomatic News." *National Journal* (Nov. 9, 1985): 2531–2534.

Manning, Robert. "Journalism and Foreign Affairs." In *Responsibility of the Press,* Gerald Gross, ed. New York: Simon & Schuster, 1966, pp. 184–198.

Manoff, Robert Karl, and Gerd Ruge (eds.). *Between the Summits: An International Conference on Media Coverage of Soviet-American Relations, Nuclear Issues, and Everyday Life.* New York: Center for War, Peace, and the News Media, NYU, 1988

Martin, L. J. "The Media's Role in International Terrorism." *Terrorism,* 8 (1985): 127–148.

McClure, Robert, and Thomas Patterson. "Setting the Political Agenda: Print vs. Network News. *Journal of Communications,* 26 (Spring 1976): 23–28.

McCombs, Maxwell E. "The Agenda-Setting Approach." In *Handbook of Political Communication,* Dan D. Nimmo and Keith Sands (eds.). Beverly Hills: Sage, 1981, 121–140.

_____. "Newspapers vs. Television: Mass Communications Effects Across Time." In *The Emergence of American Political Issues,* McCombs & D. Shaw (eds.). St. Paul, MN. West Publishing Co., 1977.

_____. "Structuring the Unseen Environment." *Journal of Communication* 26 (Spring 1976).

_____, and Donald L. Shaw. "The Agenda-setting Function of Mass Media." *Public Opinion Quarterly,* 36 (1972): 176–187.

McFadden, Robert D. "TV Atom War Spurs Vast Discussion." *New York Times* (Nov. 22, 1983): Y11.

McLeod, Jack M., and D. McDonald. "Beyond Simple Measure: Media Orientations and the Impacts on the Political Process." *Communications Research,* 10 (1985): 3–34.

McLeod, Jack M., Lee Becker, and James E. Byrnes. "Another Look at the Agenda-setting Function of the Press." *Communications Research,* 1 (April 1974): 131–166.

"Media Satellite Could Complicate Military, Foreign Policy Activities." *Aviation Week and Space Technology* (June 8, 1988): 22–23.

Merton, Robert K., M. O. Fisk, and Patricia L. Kendall. *The Focussed Interview.* New York: The Free Press, 1956

Michler, Elliot G. *Research Interviewing*. Cambridge, MA: Harvard University Press, 1986.

Miller, Mark Crispin. "How TV Covers War," In *Boxed In: The Culture of TV*. Evanston, IL: Northwestern University Press, 1988, pp. 151–169.

Minnow, Newton, and John Martin. *Presidential Television*. New York: Basic Books, 1973

Mishra, V. M. "News from the Middle East in Five U.S. Media." *Journalism Quarterly*, 56 (1979): 374–378.

Moltoch, Harvey, D. Protess, and M. T. Gordon. "The Media-policy Connection." *Working Papers Series*, Northwestern University Center for Urban Affairs and Policy Research, 1982.

————, and M. Lester. "News as Purposive Behavior: On the Strategic Use of Routine Events, Accidents, and Scandals." *American Sociological Review*, 39 (1974): 1–12.

Morgenthau, Hans. *Politics Among Nations* (5th ed.). New York: Knob, 1978.

Morris, Roger. "Foreign-Policy Coverage: Quarantined for the Campaign." *Columbia Journalism Review*, (Nov.-Dec. 1976): 19–22.

————. "Henry Kissinger and the Media: A Separate Peace." *Columbia Journalism Review* (May-June, 1974): 14–17.

Mosettig, Michael and Henry Griggs. "TV At the Front." *Foreign Policy* 38 (Spring 1980): 67–79.

Mueller, John E. "Editorials and Foreign Affairs in Recent Presidential Campaigns." *Journalism Quarterly*, 59 (1982): 541–547.

————. "Editorials and Foreign Affairs in the 1976 Presidential Campaign." *Journalism Quarterly*, 55 (1978): 92–99.

————. "Editorials and Foreign Affairs in the 1972 Presidential Campaign." *Journalism Quarterly*, 51 (1974): 251–255ff.

————. "Editorials and Foreign Affairs in the 1964 Presidential Campaign." *Journalism Quarterly*, 45 (1968): 211–18.

Neal, Fred Warner, and Mary K. Harvey (eds.). *The Requirements of Democratic Foreign Policy: Congress, the President, Partisanship, the Foreign Policy Establishment, and the Media*. Santa Barbara, CA: Fund for the Republic, 1974.

Neary, John. "Operation Red Flag: The Dogfights are Fake—the Fatalities Aren't." *TV Guide* (Oct. 3, 1981): 13–19.

Nessen, Ronald. *It Sure Looks Different From the Inside*. Chicago: The Playboy Press, 1978.

————. "Journalism vs. Patriotism: Should TV News *Always* Tell All?" *TV Guide* (June 27, 1981): 5–10.

Oberdorfer, Don. "Iran: Rare "Hinge Event." *Washington Post* (Nov. 25, 1979).

Oldendick, Robert, and Barbara A. Bardes. "Mass Media and Elite Foreign Policy Opinions." *Public Opinion Quarterly* 46 (1982): 368–382.

Paletz, David, and Robert Entman. *Media Power Politics*. New York: The Free Press, 1981.

Palmgreen Phillip, and Peter Clarke. "Agenda-setting with Local and National Issues." *Communications Research,* 4 (1977): 435–452.

Pappas, Ike. "My War and Peace with the Pentagon." *TV Guide* (Feb. 5, 1983): 14–18.

Paraschos, M. and B. Rutherford. "Network news coverage of the invasion of Lebanon by Israel in 1982." *Journalism Quarterly,* 62:3 (Oct. 1985): 457–464.

Patterson, Thomas, and Robert McClure. *The Unseeing Eye: The Myth of Television in National Politics.* New York: Putnam, 1976.

Perry, Jack. "Hacks are Destroying Professional Diplomacy." *The Washington Post Outlook* (Jan. 1, 1984).

Peterzell, Jay. "Can the CIA Spook the Press?" *Columbia Journalism Review,* (Sept.-Oct. 1986): 29–34.

Phillips, Bernard. *Social Research: Strategy, Tactics* (Second Ed.). New York: Macmillan, 1971.

Phillips, Kevin. "Media Elite's Influence on Foreign Policy." *TV Guide* (August 23, 1975): A3–A11.

Pollock, Hohn C. *The Politics of Crisis Reporting: Learning to be a Foreign Correspondent.* News York: Praeger, 1981.

Popper, Karl. *The Open Society and its Enemies.* New York: Harper and Row, 1963.

Powers, Ron. *The Newscasters: The News Business as Show Business.* New York: St. Martins Press, 1978.

Protess, David, Donna R. Leff, Stephen Brooks, and Margaret Gordon. "Uncovering Rape: The Watchdog Press and the Limits of Agenda-Setting." *Public Opinion Quarterly,* 49: 19–37.

Public Opinion Quarterly. "Face Off: A Conversation with the President's Pollster." (March 1981): 2–12.

Ranney, Austin. *The Impact of Television on American Politics.* New York: Basic Books, 1983.

Rather, Dan. *The Camera Never Blinks: Adventures of a TV Journalist.* New York: William Morrow, 1977.

Reeves, R. *American Journey.* New York: Simon & Schuster, 1982.

Reston, James. "The Press, the President, and Foreign Policy." In *Mass Media and Communication,* Charles S. Steinberg (ed.). New York: Harper & Row, 1972.

———. *The Artillery of the Press.* New York: Harper and Row, 1966.

Riffe, D., Brenda Ellis, Momo Rogers, Roger L. Van Ommeron, and Kierna A. Woodman. "Gatekeeping and the Network News Mix." *Journalism Quarterly,* 63 (1986): 315–321.

Roberts, D. F., and C. M. Bachen. "Mass Communication Effects." *Annual Review of Psychology,* 32 (1981): 307–56.

Robinson, Michael J., and Margaret Sheehan. *Over the Wire and On TV.* New York: The Russell Sage Foundation, 1983.

———. "The Media in 1980: Was the Message the Message?" In *American*

Elections of 1980, Austin Ranney (ed.). Washington, DC: American Enterprise Institute, 1981.

――――. "Public Affairs Television and the Growth of Political Malaise: The Case of 'The Selling of the Pentagon'." *American Political Science Review*, 70 (1976): 409–432.

――――. "American Political Legitimacy in an Era of Electronic Journalism," In *Television as a Social Force: New Approaches to TV Criticism*, Richard Adler (ed.). New York: Prager Publishing, 1975.

Roper, Burns W. *Public Perceptions of Television and Other Mass Media*. New York: Television Information Office, 1979.

Rosati, Jerel A. "The Impact of Beliefs on Behavior: The Foreign Policy of the Carter Administration." In *Foreign Policy Decision Making*, Donald A. Sylvan and Steven Chan (eds.). New York: Praeger, 1984.

Rosenau, James (ed.). *International Politics and Foreign Policy: A Reader in Research and Theory*. New York: Free Press, 1969.

Rubin, Barry. *International News and the American Media*. Beverly Hills: Sage, 1977.

Rubin, David. "Consider the Source: A Survey of National Security Reporters." *Deadline* (March-April 1986): 4–6.

Russett, Bruce, and Donald Deluca. "Don't Tred on Me: Public Opinion and Foreign Policy in the Eighties." *Political Science Quarterly*, 96 (1981): 381–399.

――――. "Pearl Harbor: Deterrence Theory and Decision Theory." *Journal of Peace Research*, 2 (1967): 89–106.

Rydz, John. *Managing Innovation*. Cambridge, MA: Ballinger, 1986.

Sahin, Hauk, Dennis K. Davis, and John P. Robinson. "Television as a Source of International News: What Gets Across and What Doesn't." In *Television Coverage of International Affairs* William Adams (ed.). Norwood, NJ: Ablex, 1982, pp. 229–244.

Said, Edward W. "Iran." *Columbia Journalism Review*, 18 (March/April 1980): 23–33.

Sanderson, Arlene. "The CIA-Media Connection." FOE Report No. 432. Columbia, MO: Freedom of Information Center, University of Missouri School of Journalism, 1981.

Savage, Robert L. "The Diffusion of Information Theory." In *Handbook of Political Communication*, Dan D. Nimmo and Keith R. Sanders (eds.). Beverly Hills: Sage, 1981.

Schiltz, Timothy; Lee Sigelman, and Robert Neal. "Perspectives of Managing Editors on Coverage of Foreign Policy News." *Journalism Quarterly*, 50 (1973): 716–21.

Schlesinger, Arthur M. *The Coming of the New Deal*. Boston: Houghton Mifflin, 1959.

Schmid, Alex, and Jenny de Graf. *Violence as Communication: Insurgent Terrorism and Western News Media*. London: Sage Publications, 1982.

Schmidt, Dana Adams. *Armageddon in the Middle East*. New York: John Day, 1974.

Schneider, William. "Television's Gift to the Policymaker." *Chronicle of International Communication* (May 1982) 6–7.

Schorr, Daniel. "The CIA at CBS: Cloak-and-Camera at Black Rock." *New York* (Sept. 26, 1977): 40–47.

Schramm, Wilber. *Mass Media and National Development*. Stanford, CA: Stanford University Press, 1964.

Schultz, John H. "Liberalism and Conservatism: A Study of Mass-Media Foreign Policy Attitudes." Ph.D. dissertation, University of Southern California, 1968.

Schilling, Warner. "The H-Bomb Decision: How to Decide without Actually Choosing." *Political Science Quarterly*, 76 (1961): 24–46

Sears, D. and S. H. Chaffee. "Uses and Effects of the Debates: An Overview of Empirical Studies." In *The Great Debates, 1976: Ford vs. Carter*, S. Kraus (ed.). Bloomington: Indiana University Press, 1979, pp. 223–261.

Seymore-Ure, Colin. *The Political Impact of Media*. Beverly Hills: Sage, 1974.

Shaheen, Jack. *The TV Arab*. Bowling Green, OH: Bowling Green University Popular Press, 1984.

————. "Images of Saudis and Palestinians: A Review of Major Documentaries." In *Television Coverage of the Middle East*, William C. Adams (ed). Norwood, NJ: Ablex, 1981.

Shales, Tom. "Terrorism." *Washington Post* (Dec. 11, 1979).

Sigal, Leon V. *Reporters and Officials: The Organization and Politics of Newsmaking*. Lexington, MA: D.C. Heath, 1973.

Simon, Herbert. *Administrative Behavior*. Cambridge, MA: MIT Press, 1982.

Snyder, Richard C., H. W. Bruck, and Burton Sapin. *Foreign Policy Decision-Making: An Approach to the Study of International politics*. Glencoe Il: Free Press, 1962.

Spragens, William C. "Camp David and the Networks: Reflections on Coverage of the 1979 Summit." In *Television Coverage of Interntiaonal Affairs*, William Adams (ed.). Norwood NJ: Ablex, 1982, pp. 117–128.

Sprout, Harold, and Margaret Sprout. *Ecological Perspectives on Human Affairs*. Princeton, NJ: Princeton University Press, 1965.

Sreebny, Daniel. "American Correspondents in the Middle East: Perceptions and Problems." *Journalism Quarterly*, 56 (Summer 1979): 386–388.

Stemple, G. H. III. "Gatekeeping: The mix of topics and the selection of stories." *Journalism Quarterly*, 62 (Winter 1985): 791–796.

Steel, Ronald. "NATO'S Last Mission." *Foreign Policy*, 76 (Fall 1989): 83–95.

Story, Douglas J. "Television Network News Coverage of the International Affairs Content of Presidential News Conferences." Unpublished Master's Thesis, The University of Texas at Austin, August, 1983.

Strauch, Ralph E. "A Critical Look at Quantitative Methodology." *Policy Analysis*, 2 (Winter 1976): 121–144.

Strouse, James. *Mass Media, Public Opinion and Public Policy Analysis: Linkage Explorations*. Columbus, OH: Charles E. Merrill Co., 1985.

Surlin, Stuart H. " 'Roots' Research: A Summary of Findings." *Journal of Broadcasting*, 22 (1978): 309–20.

Sussman, Barry. "Freeze Support Grows Slightly after War Show." *Washington Post*, 23 (Nov., 1983): A1,A8.

Swanson, Charles E. "Predicting Who Learns Factual Information from the Mass Media." In *Groups, Leadership, and Men*, Harold Guetzkow (ed.). Pittsburgh: Carnegie Press, 1951.

Sylvan, Donald A. and Steve Chan. *Foreign Policy Decision Making: Perception, Cognition, and Artificial Intelligence*. New York: Praeger, 1951.

Tebble, J., and J. M. Watts. *The Press and the Presidency*. New York: Oxford University Press, 1985.

Television/Radio Age. "Use of 'alternative' TV news services keep on growing." (October 28, 1985): 31ff.

The Guardian. "CIA's Global Rent-A-Reporter Program." (Jan. 4, 1978): 19.

Thomas, Marlo. "Soviet and American Kids: They Share a Common Language— Rock'n'Roll." *TV Guide* (Dec. 12, 1988): 9–10.

Thorson, Stuart J., and Donald A. Sylvan. "Counterfactuals and the Cuban Missile Crisis." *International Studies Quarterly*, 26 (1982): 539–71.

Townley, Rod. "Local News Goes Overseas—And Sometimes Overboard." *TV Guide* (April 24, 1982): 10–16.

Ungurait, Donald, Thomas W. Bohn, and Ray Eldon Hiebert. *Media Now*. New York: Longman, 1985.

U.S. Advisory Commission on Public Diplomacy. *Report—1983*. Washington, DC, 1983.

U.S. Congress, House. Permanent Select Committee on Intelligence. Subcommittee on Oversight. *The CIA and the Media*. Hearings, 95th Congress, 1st and 2nd sessions, Dec. 27–29, 1977; Jan. 4–5, April 20, 1978.

US News and World Report. "The Long Arm of Local News." (Mar. 16, 1987).

Van Dinh, Tran. *Communication and Diplomacy in a Changing World*. Norwood, NJ: Ablex, 1988.

Vanderbilt Television News Archive. *Television News Index and Abstracts*. Nashville: Vanderbilt University, January 1976–1980.

Varis, Tapil. "The International Flow of Television Programs." *Journal of Communications*, 34 (Winter 1984): 143.

———— and Karl Nordenstreng. *Television Traffic, A One-Way Street* Paris: Boudin/UNESCO, 1974.

————. *The International Flow of Television Programs*. Paris: Boudin/UNESCO, 1984.

Vera, Tony *Live TV: An Inside Look at Directing and Producing*. Boston: Focal Press, 1987.

Walker, Stephen G. "The Interface Between Beliefs and Behavior: Henry Kissinger's Operational Code and the Vietnam War." *Journal of Conflict Resolution*, 21 (1977): 129–68.

Washington Quarterly. "Media Watch: The Networks and Foreign News Coverage [interview with Kalb, Kopple, and Scali]." (Spring, 1982): 39–52.

Wall, James E. "TV Hostage Coverage Cooled Hot Heads," (discussion of July 3-10, 1985 article "Terrorism temps TV rto waive noble right), *The Christian Century*, 102(1985): 773.

Wallach, John P. " 'I'll Give It To You on Background': State Breakfasts." *Washington Quarterly*, 5 (Spring, 1982) 53–66.

Waters, Harry F. "Fallout over 'The Day After'." *Newsweek (Oct. 24, 1983): 126.*

Weaver, David H., Doris A. Graber, Maxwell E. McCombs, and Chaim H. Eyal, *Media Agenda-Setting in a Presidential Election.* Boston: Praeger Publishing Co, 1981.

Weaver, Paul. "Newspaper News and Television News." In *Television as a Social Force: New Approaches to TV Criticism,* Richard Adler (ed.). New York: Prager Publishing, 1975.

Weimann, Gabriel. "The Theater of Terror: Effects of Press Coverage." *Journal of Communications* 33 (Winter 1983).

Weisman, John. "Covering International News: The Hazards of Inexperience." *TV Guide* (May 28, 1983): 2–8.

Westin, Av. *Newswatch: How TV Decides the News.* New York: Simon and Schuster, 1982.

White, Theodore H. *America in Search of Itself.* New York: Harper and Row, 1982.

––––––––. *The Making of the President 1972.* New York: Bantam, 1973

Wildman, Steven S., and Stephen E. Siwek. *International Trade in Films and Television Programming.* Cambridge, MA: Ballinger Books, 1988.

Wohlstetter, Roberta. *Pearl Harbor: Warning and Decision.* Stanford: Stanford University Press, 1962.

Wolzien, Tom. "Watch Your Loved One Brave Bombs and Bullets." *TV Guide* (Jan. 26, 1980): 5–6.

Zaremba, Alan J. *Mass Communication and International Politics.* Salem, WI.: Sheffield, 1988.

Author Index

Subject Index